# IMAGINING VESALIUS

An Ekphrastic, Scholarly and Literary Celebration
of the 1543 *De Humani Corporis Fabrica*
of Andreas Vesalius

Editor

# RICHARD M. RATZAN

First published in 2020

by the University of California Medical Humanities Press

UCMedicalHumanitiesPress.com

© 2020 Richard M. Ratzan and authors

University of California Medical Humanities Consortium

Department of Humanities and Social Sciences UCSF

490 Illinois Street, Floor 7

San Francisco, CA 94143-0850

Designed by Virtuoso Press

Cover photo: Koblenz: Courtesy of Bibliothek des Staatlichen Görres-Gymnasiums

ISBN: 978-0-9963242-9-8

Library of Congress Control Number: 2020943584

Printed in USA

DEDICATION:

ὅν οἱ θεοί φιλοῦσιν ἀποθνήσκει νέος


Kenneth Dale Beernink (1938-1969)
Michelle Boisseau (1955-2017)
Rita Iovino (1956-2000)
J. D. McClatchy (1945-2018)
Lawrence J. Schneiderman (1932-2018)

# ACKNOWLEDGEMENTS/PERMISSIONS

We wish to acknowledge with gratitude the permission to reproduce the following works that have appeared in earlier publications:

"Eye Contact" by Richard M. Berlin: This poem has previously been published in Psychiatric Times and the 2019 Hippocrates Award Anthology where it received a "Commended" poem award.

"The Anatomy Theater of Padua" by Michelle Boisseau: This poem appeared in *Understory*, published by Northeastern University Press in 1996.

"Human Atlas" by Boruch, Marianne: This poem appeared in *Cadaver, Speak*, published by Copper Canyon Press in 2014.

"The Last Words of Saint Anthony of Padua" by Margaret Lloyd: This poem appeared in *The Ekphrastic Review* on January 22, 2020.

"The Fabric: A Poet's Vesalius" by Heather McHugh. This essay appeared in *Poetry* magazine in December 2007.

"Anatomy at the Dinner Table" by Leslie Adrienne Miller: This poem appeared in *The Resurrection Trade: Poems*, published by the Graywolf Press in 2007. Copyright © 2007 by Leslie Adrienne Miller. Reprinted with the permission of The Permissions Company, LLC on behalf of Graywolf Press, Minneapolis, Minnesota, graywolfpress.org

"Vesalius at the Gibbet of Montfaucon" by Clare Rossini: This poem appeared in the 25th Anniversary Poetry Retrospective, *Green Mountains Review* (Vol. XXV, No. 1), Summer 2012.

"Vesalius in Zante (1564)" by Edith Wharton. This poem appeared in *The North American Review* 1902; 174:625-631.

We also wish to thank the following for permission to reprint images in this book:

Google
Himetop - The History of Medicine Topographical Database: himetop.net
Library Company, Philadelphia
Metropolitan Museum of Art
National Library of Medicine
Universitätsbibliothek Basel: https://www.e-rara.ch/
University Library of Pecs
Wikipedia

# TABLE OF CONTENTS

* Number within parentheses refers to *Fabrica* page number
  (published # [corrected #]) - see Foreword

## Translations

# FOREWORD

I have been interested in ekphrasis since high school when, in Gil Feldman's Latin class at Poly Prep in Brooklyn, I first read the ekphrastic description of the shield of Aeneas in Virgil's book 8. When I next encountered it, reading about the shield of Achilles in James Notopoulos's Homer class as a Classics major in Trinity College here in Hartford, I was hooked on the marriage of art and words. Using the word vínculo ("bond" or "chain" or "link") rather than "marriage," Canseco and Antolín sum up my ideas on ekphrasis neatly:

> El vínculo entre imagen y literatura entendida, ésta en su sentido humanístico, favoreció no sólo una concepción del arte, sino también la consideración del pintor como humanista y la importancia cada vez mayor de la erudición en la pintura. (Canseco page 16)

> The bond between image and a literature understood in its humanistic sense favors not only a conception of art but also the consideration of the painter as humanist and the increasing importance of erudition in painting. (translation by RMR)

It was therefore not surprising when, in late 2017, at the tail end of a career in the medical humanities, I had an interesting idea: why not put together an ekphrastic collection of poetry, art and short prose to celebrate the inimitably conceived and executed anatomical woodcuts of Vesalius's *De Humani Corporis Fabrica*? As I soon discovered, this idea was as enticing to the poets and writers and artists to whom I proposed it as it was to me. In no time at all I had enlisted dozens of talented writers and artists who wished to contribute to this volume, creating their own imaginative constructs linking images from 500 years ago to thoughts that Vesalius himself may have entertained while looking at his dissections, at times bonding these images to more modern and, sometimes painfully so, semi-autobiographical flights. None fails to instruct and all give the reader/viewer the joy of a synthetic appreciation of image *cum* word, or in the works by Driscoll and Feder, image *cum* image. Vesalius, and, one hopes, Melanchthon, would have welcomed this celebration of the world of deeper anatomical thoughts.

But the idea and its completion represent the extent of my contribution. It is the wonderful creative work of all the artists, writers, poets and translators in this book that makes it such a special addition to the medical humanities, medieval scholarship, and the genre of ekphrasis. A special joy in the invitation phase of this volume was realizing that, like the Book of Genesis, there were lineages of "begats". Thus, Jack Coulehan "begat" Chuck Joy. Dennis Barone "begat" Jim Finnegan. In some instances the "begats" traversed three generations of invited ekphrastic contributors: Kelley White "begat" Jenna Le who "begat" Amit Majmudar and Stacy Nigliazzo. In short order this volume became a truly communal effort. As with the medical humanities conference organizing I did 30 years ago, the greatest personal joy and enduring benefit of this book has been to meet so many creative, industrious and kind new friends, including RH, the one who got away. And to rediscover how generous one's colleagues in the medical humanities are, like Dániel Margócsy, in the Department of History and Philosophy of Science, the University of Cambridge, who promptly, unselfishly and repeatedly lent me his knowledge and assistance, from the correct pagination of the *Fabrica* to answering numerous questions to invaluable advice about sources and permissions.

Without the in-house counsel of Jack Coulehan, Cortney Davis, Jessica Greenbaum, Danielle Ofri and Larry Schneiderman, this book would have been a much lesser work of excellent collegial art than it is. I owe them a great deal of thanks for their wise and judicious advice. And it is with much sadness in my heart that I cannot express that gratitude personally to Larry who died in the summer of 2019, ending over 30 years of friendship and mutual admiration despite his being a far better medical humanist and writer than I.

I would like to acknowledge the generous support I have received from the following institutions and individuals: the University of Connecticut School of Medicine; Yale University's Harvey Cushing/John Hay Whitney Medical Library; the Watkinson Library at Trinity College and the invaluable help of its Henry Arneth; and the resources and staff of the Hartford Hospital Medical Library, especially Lori Hayes and Grace Kucharzyk. Shawn London's support has been crucial to the success of this book. I am very grateful to John Harley Warner for introducing me to Katharine Park's essential book, *Secrets of Women*, which truly was, as John rightly called it, "transformative." Dániel Margócsy has most generously afforded me the breadth and depth of his amazing experience with all things Vesalius and his and his colleagues' *The Fabrica of Andreas Vesalius: A Worldwide Descriptive Census, Ownership, and Annotations of the 1543 and 1555 Editions.* (See bibliography.) A special round of applause to the numerous institutions and their representatives who promptly and graciously afforded me permission to reproduce images from their copies of the *Fabrica*. I would be equally remiss not to acknowledge what so many researchers use but do not always acknowledge: the infinitely useful help from Wikipedia and Google, from initiating a search to clues where next to look. Without Google, especially Google Scholar and the unbelievable resources of Google Docs and Google Books (from Jakob Balde and Philip Melanchthon's original texts to text word searching in modern day books), this volume would still be in the planning stages, had I had to rely, as I so often had to do early in my career, on the glacially slow – compared to today's internet speed – interlibrary loan or trips to distant research libraries, as much fun as those were.

A nod of grateful thanks as well to the following individuals, communities and software programs that made this book much easier to complete: First and foremost to Brian Dolan, my talented and very patient editor at University of California Medical Humanities Press for making this book happen; James Hoover and his versatile and free word processing program, Bean (especially 2.4.5), my workhorse the past 30 years; Eric Böhnisch-Volkmann and his incomparably versatile DEVONthink Pro and its filing, organizational, tagging and word processing resources (everything in this book is in that program's database!); Aquamacs for much of the heavy lifting when it came to plain old writing; and the endlessly helpful, generous and patient communities of emacs, Apple and Stack Exchange; ImageMagick for its indispensable image manipulation; and tesseract-ocr for optical character recognition on Apple's terminal program.

Finally, you would not be holding *Imagining Vesalius* in your hands or reading this introduction were it not for the UConn Humanities Institute, chaired by Professor Alexis Boylan, that graciously awarded me a publication subvention grant to help underwrite the expenses of this book, and the unimaginable patience and enthusiastic (well, most of the time) encouragement (ok, endurance) of my dear wife of "51 long, lonely years," Susan Kovage Ratzan, MD.

A few words about the organization of this book. After the cogent and pellucid introductions by Professors Kusukawa and Heffernan, the ekphrastic works will accompany the images in the order in which the latter appear in the *Fabrica*. The woodcut inspiring the work will be on the left and the ekphrastic work on the right. When several works have used the same woodcut, the image will appear only once on the left followed by the several creative works.

Following the ekphrastic works, which are mainly poetry with some prose-poems and several pieces of graphic art and sculpture, a section of translations of poems involving Vesalius will demonstrate the almost instantaneous acknowledgment of his achievement and the thoughts of the intellectual community about the relationship of human anatomy to God's working, a natural consequence of Vesalius's working in an intensely Christian environment, indeed, a most fervent time – the Reformation – for Christianity and Europe. Notes – historical and literary – to the ekphrastic works and a bibliography with online resources and biographies of the contributors end the book. In-text references to works listed in the book's bibliography will simply list the author's name and page number.

Since hundreds of the pages, but not all, in the *Fabrica* were misnumbered and printed as such, the pagination for the images from the *Fabrica* in the Table of Contents follows the convention of Margócsy, et al., in their *The Fabrica of Andreas Vesalius*, i.e., the first number is the one printed in the 1543 edition, followed by a second, correct number in brackets if the first number is incorrect. For example, the page in the *Fabrica* for the Vesalian woodcut for Jack Coulehan's quiet, *kinderszenen* poem, "Behind the Curtain," is identified as "Page 262 [362]," meaning that this image occurs on (the incorrectly numbered) page 262 in the original 1543 book, a page that is actually, due to misnumbering by the printer, page 362. An exception is the last poem, Edith Wharton's "Vesalius in Zante (1564)," which has "(1564)" in its title and appears with the gracious permission of the *North American Review*. Although Ms Wharton apparently regretted having written this poem during her dramatic monologue phase (see *Selected Letters*, Lewis and Lewis, page 75, in bibliography), we are most glad she did.

An excellent site for viewing the *Fabrica* is the Universitätsbibliothek Basel in Switzerland, for which the homepage is: https://www.e-rara.ch/bau_1/ content/titleinfo/6299027. One can see individual pages there and thumbnails or download the entire *Fabrica* as a pdf and peruse it at one's leisure. The pagination is the original, often incorrect, one of publication. This is the site whence all the *Fabrica* images used ekphrastically in this book derive. Although the original woodcuts, and the *Fabrica*, were in black and white, many owners, as did the owner of the text used by Universitätsbibliothek Basel in Switzerland, paid for hand-coloring and embellishment of the plates. For such matters, see the indispensable census of Margócsy, et al.

A final note: on pages that otherwise would have been blank, e.g., between sections of the book or between ekphrastic works, we have placed woodcuts from Vesalius's *Fabrica* not used elsewhere in this volume. The pages are entitled "Invitation to Ekphrasis." Please consider these pages an invitation to create your own Vesalian ekphrastic poems or prose poems or even to transcribe a favorite poem or passage you think will enhance this image – to "make it new," in Pound's words. This has been a tradition for readers of the *Fabrica* going back to the 16th and 17th century owners of this revolutionary book. (The census by Margócsy et al. documents numerous instances of this tradition.) See, for example, page 230. You can thank Susan, my wife, for this invitation. It was her idea and I thank her for that.

# INTRODUCTORY ESSAYS

## VIVITUR INGENIO: ANDREAS VESALIUS'S *FABRICA*
Sachiko Kusukawa

A ndreas Vesalius was not yet twenty-eight years old when he penned his dedication to Emperor Charles V of his book, *De humani corporis fabrica* (*On the Fabric of the Human Body*), published in 1543. The dedication was couched in the language and style of the Renaissance, a time when revival of the achievements of Greece and Rome was deemed a significant way of contributing to contemporary knowledge and scholarship. In the dedication, Vesalius thus described how the ancient practice of healing based on diet, medicines and surgery, all of which required hands-on engagement, had been lost after the incursion of the Goths. Since then, European physicians had come to see these areas as beneath their dignity, particularly as they involved the use of their hands, and thus relegated them to carers, druggists or barbers who had no idea or appreciation of the work of the Ancients. Thanks to the support of the Emperor, Vesalius wrote, knowledge of the Ancients was now being recovered in various fields, and Vesalius too hoped to do his bit, by bringing anatomy back from the dead. Praising the great and the good as supporters of learning was another move common at the time among those who sought patronage. Vesalius's family had a tradition of imperial medical service, and his father was an apothecary to the Emperor. Now the apothecary's son was hoping to impress the Emperor with the dedication of *Fabrica*. Its companion piece called *Epitome*, a short summary of *Fabrica*, was dedicated to the Emperor's son, the future King Philip II. Soon after the dedication, Vesalius was appointed one of the physicians to the Emperor Charles V.[1]

Vesalius's *Fabrica* and *Epitome* were printed in Basel in 1543. Compared to the other famous book published in the same year in Nuremberg, Nicolaus Copernicus's *De revolutionibus orbium coelestium* (*On the Revolutions of the Heavenly spheres*), *Fabrica* was larger and longer, and the *Epitome*, though much shorter, larger still. The pages of Copernicus's book were about 27.5 cm high, those in Vesalius's *Fabrica* about 43 cm, and the *Epitome* about 56 cm.[2] Difference in the amount of paper used was partially reflected in the price: Copernicus' book was sold at 1 florin in 1545 and in 1543, *Fabrica* and *Epitome* were offered together at just under 5 florins. There were further differences between *Fabrica* and *De revolutionibus*. Copernicus was seventy by the time his book was going through the press, and the supervision of the printing was left to others: Georg Joachim Rheticus first, and then to the local Lutheran minister, Andreas Osiander. However, the proof-reading was far from thorough. One of the key diagrams illustrating a heliostatic system had been reproduced erroneously, there were typographic errors, and an unauthorized preface was added. In contrast, Vesalius had arranged, supervised, and paid for the production of his woodcuts in Italy, which he sent over the Alps to the printer Johannes Oporinus, and then travelled to Basel himself in 1542 to supervise the printing. For a book of its size, it has remarkably few typographical errors, and it is clear from other evidence that Vesalius was a punctilious reader of his own text.[3]

What was the book about? The choice of the word "fabrica" suggests a skillful production, and the book was indeed about how the human body was made. It also presupposed that there was a maker of such a work – and Vesalius often refers to the Creator when he discusses intricate structures in the human body. The book was also about method. University physicians had lost the ancient art of first-hand dissection. Galen, a second-century physician working in the Roman Empire, and the prime authority on medical matters, had advocated in *Anatomical procedures*, a work rediscovered only in the sixteenth century, that physicians needed to dissect as many bodies as possible with their own hand in order to understand human anatomy. This was a project Vesalius took up with gusto, as he found out while studying in Paris that he was proficient at dissection. He tried to dissect as many human bodies as possible – as Galen had urged – and in the process realized that Galen had had only limited experience in dissecting the human body. Even correcting Galen in light of first-hand dissection can be deemed Galenic in spirit, since Galen himself had urged students not to take another's word on trust, but to dissect and see for themselves. Vesalius proceeded to correct Galen's numerous errors about human body, but none of these corrections challenged the general structure of the classical humoral body and its physiological functions.[4]

Vesalius was well aware that even if his book was Galenic in inspiration, his numerous corrections of Galen might attract censure, especially as he was relatively young, and without an established reputation in the scholarly world: he could be criticized as being ignorant (for not understanding Galen properly), negligent (for not looking at the body carefully enough) or arrogant (for daring to criticize Galen). Thus, *Fabrica* is not a simple compilation of dry, factual description of morphology and function as Vesalius found them, but rather a rhetorically charged polemic and defence, justifying his view against Galen and others at every turn. It is also remarkably vivid in description to help the reader visualize structures of the human body. For example, he described different types of muscles using visual analogy:

The seventh muscle of the eye, which is inserted into the root of the eye, resembles a pyramid or a spinning-top. The muscle that draws the eyelid downward resembles the letter C. In the back of the lower leg near the heel occur muscles whose shape resembles a butcher's cleaver. ... If you examine the muscle on each side to be numbered second among those that move the scapula [musculus Trapezius] you will assert that the Franciscans, Jacobites and especially the Benedictines borrowed the shape of their cowl, not from the form of the Satan who tempted Jesus in the wilderness but from the form of these muscles – at least insofar as it covers the back and shoulders.[5]

Equally important for presenting Vesalius's view of the human body was the images. *Fabrica* is of course well known for its spectacular images. They are woodcuts. The woodcutter cuts away from a woodblock the parts that appear blank on the page, and the raised parts left from the cutting are inked and produce the lines and hatching on paper. Woodcuts work well with metal types whose raised lines produce the letter forms, as they can be fitted into the same forme for printing text and image together on the same page. The woodblocks – which remarkably survived until the Second World War – were blocks of pear wood, cut parallel to the grain and treated with linseed oil.[6]

In this period, the person who drew the original sketch was not always the person who cut the woodblocks. So a number of craftsmen must have been involved in producing the woodcuts for *Fabrica*. We alas do not know for certain who these people were. Titian's name has sometimes been invoked in this context, but there is no evidence that he was. However, it is likely that artists within Titian's circle may well have been involved, such as Jan Stephan Calcar, who did help with Vesalius's earlier publication of anatomical tables, and Domenico Campagnola, known for his drawings for landscapes and ruins.[7]

The images in *Fabrica* were not, however, without precedent. In *Isagoge Breves* (*Short Introduction*, 1523), Berengario da Carpi, a surgeon and a keen collector of art, included a muscle figure based on Michelangelo's David set against a landscape, and a dorsal view of a skeleton in front of an open stone coffin. Vesalius too set his muscle figures against a landscape, used the Belevedere Torso in one of his illustrations, and deployed the contrapposto gesture throughout the book. Showing the progressive stages of the dissection of the brain is a convention Vesalius picked up from Johannes Dryander's *Anatomia Capitis* (1536). The famous frontispiece of *Fabrica* may well be a caricature of a dissection scene found in *Fascicolo di medicina* (1493).[8]

Vesalius had learned motifs, settings and conventions from earlier anatomical publications, but the figures in *Fabrica* are extraordinarily better in quality, helped partly by the size – the larger the image, the easier it is to include more details – in addition to the shadings and hatchings used to represent the three-dimensional body. The figures are, above all, posed to show the movement the human body is capable in life, and are angled in such a way to include as much information as possible. They are executed supremely in the style that Martin Kemp has called the "rhetoric of the real." They are naturalistic renderings of a dissected (and dead) body in animated gestures to persuade the reader how the human body works in life. Vesalius cleverly tied

Vesalius, Andreas. *De humani corporis fabrica libri septem*. (Basel: Johannes Oporinus, 1543), page 164. Courtesy of Universitätsbibliothek Basel.

together his text and image through a referencing system, to ensure that his readers understood what it was that they were looking at, and what the part of the body described in his words looked like.[9]

Perhaps the most famous image of all in Vesalius' *Fabrica* is this image of the skeleton, shown contemplating a skull placed on a sarcophagus or altar, on which the skeleton places its elbow so as to rest its weary head in its hand, a gesture akin to the one in Albrecht Dürer's "Melencolia I". Another, more explicit connection with an engraving by Dürer is the Latin line written on the side of the sarcophagus: "Vivitur ingenio, caetera mortis erunt". Dürer used this phrase in an engraved portrait of his friend and patron, Willibald Pirckheimer. The line comes from an elegy believed at the time to have been written by the Roman poet Virgil (1ˢᵗ century BCE) on the death of his patron Maecenas (we now know it cannot have been by Virgil, since Virgil died before him). "Ingenium" could mean natural inclination, innate capacity, talent or wit, and when contrasted with death, it could suggest something like spirit, and thus an appropriate line for a portrait with a message about the ephemerality of life. The line can be translated roughly as "One lives on by the spirit, the rest shall pass away." Skeletons were frequently associated with the theme of "memento mori (remember you shall die)," so Vesalius's use of the line is apt here. This sense of ephemerality of life was certainly picked up in Paul Reichel's design for a triptych shrine for Archduke Ferdinand II, Charles V's nephew.[10]

Death, after all, is the pre-condition of an anatomical study based on first-hand dissection of human bodies. In a time where there was not yet a specialized convention or style for "scientific" imagery, images from Vesalius's *Fabrica* captured something about the expressiveness of the human body in its many cultural meanings. This is perhaps the reason for the enduring appeal of the images from Vesalius's *Fabrica*.

## References

1.  For Vesalius's biography, O'Malley, C. D. (1964). *Andreas Vesalius of Brussels, 1514-1564*. Berkeley: University of California Press, is still the starting point. For more recent biographical sketches, see Nutton, V. (2014). Historical Introduction. In *Vesalius, Andreas. An annotated translation of the 1543 and 1555 editions of De Humani Corporis Fabrica Libri Septem*. 2 vols. Transl. D.H. Garrison & M. H. Hast. (vol. 1, pp. LXXV-CIII). Basel: Karger; Vons J., Velut, S. (2008). Biographie. In J. Vons & S. Velut (Eds.), *Vesalius, Andreas: Résumé de ses livres sur*

*la fabrique du corps humain*. Translated by J. Vons (pp. VII-XXXVI). Paris: Les Belles Lettres.

2    These are rough estimates, as surviving copies tend to have been trimmed down over the years.

3    For the making of Copernicus's book and its distribution, see Gingerich, O. (2002). *An annotated census of Copernicus' De Revolutionibus* (Nuremberg, 1543 and Basel, 1566). Leiden and Boston, MA: Brill. For a census of *Fabric*, see Margócsy, D., Somos, M., Joffe, S. N. (2018). *The Fabrica of Andreas Vesalius: A worldwide descriptive census, ownership, and annotations of the 1543 and 1555 editions*. Leiden: Brill. For Vesalius's correcting habit, see Nutton, V. (2012). Vesalius revised. His annotations to the 1555 *Fabrica. Medical History*, 56(4), 415-43.

4    For Vesalius's use of classical terms, see Pigeaud, J. (1990). Formes et normes dans le "De Fabrica" de Vesale. In J. J. Céard & M-M. Fontaine & J-C. Margolin (Eds.), *Le corps à la Renaissance: Actes du XXXe colloque de Tours 1987* (pp. 399-421). Paris: Aux amateurs de livres. For Galen's life, see Nutton, V. (2004) *Ancient medicine* (pp. 216-247). London and New York, NY: Routledge. On Vesalius as a Galenist, see Cunningham, A. (1997). *The anatomical Renaissance: The resurrection of the anatomical projects of the ancients* (pp. 88-142). Aldershot: Scolar Press; Siraisi N. G. (1997). Vesalius and the reading of Galen's teleology. *Renaissance quarterly*, 50(1), 1-37.

5    Vesalius, A. (1998-2009). *On the fabric of the human body: A translation of De Humani Corporis Fabrica Libri Septem. Book I: The bones and cartilages.* Transl. W. F. Richardson & J. B. Carman. 5 vols. (vol. 2, p. 124). San Francisco: Norman.

6    The re-discovered woodblocks were reprinted in Vesalius, A. (1934). *Andreae Vesalii Bruxellensis icones anatomicae.* Munich: ex officina Bremensi. See also Wiegand, W. (1952). Marginal notes by the printer of the icones. In Lambert, S., Wiegand, W., & Ivins, W. M. (1952). *Three Vesalian essays to accompany the Icones Anatomicae of 1934* (pp. 25-42). New York, NY: Macmillan.

7    For the lack of evidence for Titian, see Simons, P., Kornell, M. (2008). Annibal Caro's after-dinner speech (1536) and the question of Titian as Vesalius's illustrator. *Renaissance Quarterly*, 61, 1069-97. For the quality of the artists involved, the best discussion is Kemp, M. (1970). A drawing for the Fabrica: And some thoughts upon the Vesalius muscle-men. *Medical History*, 14(3), 277-88.

8    For Berengario's figures, see the "Historical Anatomies on the Web" at the National Library of Medicine, Bethesda. Retrieved June 9, 2020, from  https://www.nlm.nih.gov/exhibition/historicalanatomies/berengario_home.html ; for the classical sources of Vesalius's figures, see Harcourt, G. (1987). Andreas Vesalius and the anatomy of antique sculpture. Representations 17, 28-61; for the Fascicolo, see Bylebyl, J. J. (1990b). Interpreting the Fasciculo anatomy scene. *Journal of the history of medicine and allied sciences*, 45, 285-316.

9   For visual styles as forms of rhetoric, see Kemp, M. (1996). Temples of the body and temples of the cosmos: Vision and visualization in the Vesalian and Copernican revolutions. In B. S. Baigrie (Ed.), *Picturing knowledge: Historical and philosophical problems concerning the use of art in science* (pp. 40-85). Toronto, Buffalo and London: University of Toronto Press, 1996. For Vesalius's use of image and text, see Kusukawa, S. (2012). *Picturing the book of nature: Image, text, and argument in Sixteenth-century human anatomy and medical botany* (pp. 178-233). Chicago: University of Chicago Press.

10  For this phrase, see Bialostocki, J. (1989). Vivitur ingenio. In S. Füssel & J. Knape (Eds.), *Poesis et pictura. Festschrift für Dieter Wuttke zum 60. geburtstag* (pp. 223-233). Baden-Baden: Koerner; Segonds, A. P. (1994). A propos d'un emblème de Tycho Brahe dans le *Mechanica*. In W. D. Hackmann & A. J. Turner (Eds.), *Learning, language and invention* (pp. 261-272). Aldershot: Variorum. See also the on-line exhibition at the University Library, Cambridge. Retrieved June 9, 2020, from https://exhibitions.lib.cam.ac.uk/vesalius/. The triptych shrine by Reichel may be found in the Kunsthistorisches Museum, Vienna, Kunstkammer, 4450. Retrieved June 9, 2020, from http://www.khm.at/objektdb/detail/90457/.

# BODILY EKPHRASIS
James A. W. Heffernan

Ekphrasis is an ancient rhetorical term that has been lately reawakened in academic studies of art and literature. From the ancient Greek rhetoricians who gave us the term we inherit a range of meanings. What is probably the earliest definition comes from Ailios Theon of Alexandria, generally assigned to the first century of our era, who defined ekphrasis as a way of describing just about anything visible so as to set it figuratively but also vividly before the eyes. Budding orators were made to practice their art by recreating in words the sight of a ship or a mountain, for instance, as vividly as possible, making me wonder if today's medical students should be likewise made to channel Vesalius by describing the parts of the body. Leaving that question to the deans of medical schools, I pause just long enough to note that by the fifth century of our era, the art of describing visible objects in general had inevitably morphed into the art of describing something quite particular: visual art, works of painting or sculpture. But the original meaning – the much broader meaning – never disappeared.

As a result, ekphrasis now has a variety of meanings. In the Oxford Classical Dictionary, it is called "the rhetorical description of a work of art." In a scholarly book on the relation between the "sister arts" of poetry and painting, Jean Hagstrum traces *ekphrasis* to its Greek roots *ek* (out) and *phrazein* (tell, declare, pronounce), and thereby defines it as poetry that makes a silent work of visual art "speak out" (Hagstrum, 18n), like the ancient statue of the Egyptian Pharoah Ozymandias (Ramses II) in Percy Shelley's famous sonnet of that name. Since the statue has been shattered, the altitudinously arrogant words inscribed on its base – "Look on my Works, ye Mighty, and despair!" – seem to come from the twisted lips of a head half-sunk in the sand and thus to express, willy-nilly, the despair of Ozymandias himself.

At the opposite extreme from this art-based definition of ekphrasis stands one furnished by Richard Lanham in 1968: "a self-contained description, often on a commonplace subject, which can be inserted at a fitting place in a discourse" (Lanham 39). And finally, though I have hardly exhausted all possible meanings, Murray Krieger has defined ekphrasis as "word-painting," the verbal *counterpart* of visual art. Defying the temporal flow of language and the arbitrary character of words, which hardly ever look like what they mean, ekphrasis is said to be a verbal icon, "the verbal equivalent of an art object sensed in space" (Krieger 9-10).

It is not easy to say just when or how the description of a visible object becomes a verbal icon, an art object made of words. Yet something like this effect emanates from at least some of the poems – or prose poems – composed for this volume. In "Behind the Curtain," a poem prompted by Vesalius's drawing of "The Beginning of the Portal Vein, and its System of Branches," the poet finds within the drawing "a swamp of roots" hanging down "from the manicured tree in the sky," "a jelly Medusa," "a maze," a "curtain," and a "secret room" (Coulehan 129 in this volume). Here is not so much a verbal picture of the nervous system as a palimpsest made from overlapping metaphors, or from what another Vesalian poet in this volume calls a "fountain of literary metaphor" (Ofri 139 in this volume).

This poem thus exemplifies what happens just about every time I sit down to write about ekphrasis: it becomes a moving target. Some twenty-five years ago, I defined it as "*the verbal representation of visual representation*" (Heffernan 3). Also, channelling the memory of my father, a Boston-based ob-gyn who during his long career delivered some eight thousand babies, I ventured to call ekphrasis an obstetrical narrative, a piece of writing that delivers from the still moment of visual art the story it implies.

Thus defined, ekphrastic writing invites comparison with art criticism, and specifically with its rhetoric. This move may seem a detour from the high road of literature – especially if art criticism entails art history, the compilation of facts about painters and paintings and schools of painting and the sequence of pictorial styles. But the line between literature and art criticism starts to blur as soon as we consider the kinship between Homer's description of the shield sculpted for Achilles in the 18th book of *The Iliad* – the founding instance of ekphrasis in Western literature – and the *Eikones* or *Imagines* of Philostratus the Younger, who might be called the father of art criticism. A Greek-born teacher of rhetoric who flourished in the third century of our era, Philostratus demonstrates for his students the rhetorical art of description by describing a number of paintings that he claims to have seen in a luxurious seaside villa outside Naples. But Philostratus' descriptions of the paintings are actually interpretations of a distinctly literary kind: exfoliations of the stories they implicitly tell.

Typically, Philostratus interprets a painting by turning it into a narrative: not the story of its making, as in Homer's account of Achilles' shield, but the story suggested by its shapes, which are identified with the figures they represent. Though he never explains just *how* the episodes of a story are depicted or arranged in a painting, he aims to make the work "confess itself" – in the late Leo Steinberg's memorable phrase (Steinberg 6) – through the inferred speech of its characters. He sometimes tells us what painted figures are saying to each other and what sounds they signify, such as shouting and piping.

To see more fully how Philostatus generates words from a picture, consider his commentary on a painting of Narcissus standing over a pool. Philostratus treats this painting as a metapicture, a painting about painting. In so doing, he anticipates Alberti, who later calls Narcissus "the inventor of painting," and who asks, "What else can you call painting but a similar embracing with art of what is presented on the surface of the water?" (Alberti 64). Philostratus likewise begins by reading the reflected image of the youth as a painting within a painting. "The pool paints Narcissus," he writes, "and the painting represents both the pool and the whole story of Narcissus" (Philostratus 89). Unlike Alberti, however, Philostratus does not consider Narcissus himself a painter. On the contrary, he sharply distinguishes Narcissus from the painter and – just as importantly – from the viewer of the painting that represents him.

Philostratus first praises the verisimilitude of the painting in traditional terms: a bee shown settling on flowers looks so realistic that we cannot tell "whether a real bee has been deceived by the painted flowers or whether we are to be deceived into thinking that a painted bee is real" (Philostratus 89-91). Leaving this question open--perhaps only a risky fingering of the bee could decisively settle it – Philostratus treats the painting as a study in illusion. For him Narcissus could hardly be the inventor of painting because he does not even know how to *look* at a painting, or in this case at a visible metaphor for painting: a reflected image. As the bee (if real) mistakes painted flowers for real ones, Narcissus mistakes the natural "artifice" of his reflected image for another person. And instead of moving his own head or body to view this picture-like image from various angles, he waits – transfixed – for the other to move.

Consider now the viewpoint of Philostratus himself. In viewing this painting of Narcissus, Philostratus does not simply receive its illusionistic effects. He assumes a position of dominance and judges those effects. He sees only too clearly how Narcissus is deceived. Almost contemptuously, he asks of the painted figure gazing on his reflection: "Do you then expect the pool to enter into conversation with you?" Yet this very question destabilizes Philostratus' critical stance. The speaker's question is "rhetorical" in presupposing its answer, and the speaker clearly sees that "this youth does not hear anything we say." Yet to interpret the painting, Philostratus must embrace the illusion that he *can* converse with it. If "we must interpret the painting for ourselves," as Philostratus says, we must also, paradoxically, enlist the help of our painted companion (all quotations from Philostratus 91).

This is what Philostratus does in the rest of his commentary – with a curious combination of confident inference and hesitant speculation. The spear held by the painted figure shows that he has "just returned from the hunt" and he is said to be "panting." But not everything about the figure speaks to the viewer clearly:

Whether the panting of his breast remains from his hunting or is already the panting of love I do not know. The eye, surely, is that of a man deeply in love, for its natural brightness and intensity are softened by a longing that settles upon it, and he perhaps thinks that he is loved in return, since the reflection gazes at him in just the way that he looks at it. . . . The youth stands over the youth who stands in the water, or rather who gazes intently at him and seems to be athirst for his beauty. (Philostratus 91-93)

Sliding from assertion to tentative inference, from "surely" to "perhaps" and "seems," Philostratus hears and transmits as much as he can of the painting's confession. He not only tells the story it implies (a youth just returned from the hunt stands entranced by his own reflection in a pool); he also articulates the feelings signified by the silent figure, and in so doing, he inevitably imputes to it a conscious, sentient life. So the Narcissus wrought by this commentary is considerably more than the deceived "Other" exposed as such by the knowing, sophisticated Self of the viewer, as W.J.T. Mitchell has observed (Mitchell, *Picture Theory* 333). Though not the inventor of painting, he is, if anything, a figure for the interpreter of it. Like Narcissus, art critics gaze on a still and silent image to which they impute an independent life and from which they seek to solicit a voice, to hear a confession. But no matter how attentively they listen, the voice is inevitably their own, a product of their own reflections.

Like Philostratus' *Imagines*, ekphrastic poems traditionally presuppose both the stillness and the silence of the object they represent – be it a painting of Narcissus or the sculpted figures of the Grecian urn famously apostrophized by John Keats. This assumption permeates the most influential of all treatises on the relation between poetry and painting: G.E. Lessing's *Laocoön*, first published in 1766. Taking arms against the claim that poetry and the visual arts are fundamentally similar, and especially against the notion that poetry is a kind of painting, Lessing argued that visual art – sculpture as well as painting – fundamentally differs from poetry: while poetry is essentially *temporal*, representing a succession of actions, visual art is essentially *spatial*, representing fixed forms juxtaposed in space. "Succession of time," Lessing writes, "is the province of the poet just as space is that of the painter. It is an intrusion of the painter into the domain of the poet, which good taste can never sanction, when the painter combines in one and the same picture two points necessarily separate in time . . ." (Lessing 91).

By means of overtly territorial terms such as "domain," Lessing's decree severely restricts the stories that visual art can tell. Visual art can tell a story, he writes, but only by depicting its "most pregnant" (*prägnantesten*) or "most suggestive" moment: the moment that best recalls what precedes it and best anticipates what follows it (Lessing 78). Representing, for instance, the

Virgilian story of how Laocoön was killed, the famous ancient sculpture of the Trojan prophet and his sons (now in the Vatican museum) shows them fatally gripped by the pair of giant serpents who have just slithered up out of the sea and will shortly leave the three men dead. Yet even though this sculptured group evokes what came before and implies what follows, Lessing insists that no one work of visual art can combine "two points necessarily separate in time" without violating "good taste." But does Michelangelo really affront "good taste" on the ceiling of the Sistine Chapel, where he depicts in a single fresco both the original sin of Adam and Eve and their expulsion from paradise? Even if paintings like these could be somehow categorized as aberrational departures from the mainstream tradition of one-point perspective and unitemporal art, we may well ask ourselves if any such essentialist theory of the arts can survive in an age when all arts have been digitized, when all texts and pictures are ultimately reducible to digits, pixels, or dots—the stem cells of all printed words and reproducible images, most of which and soon all of which, no doubt, can be readily called up on our computer screens. If Lessing's laws can hardly accommodate Michelangelo's depiction of the Temptation and Fall, what would he say about works of digital art such as Ori Gersht's *Pomegranate* (2006)? When examined for more than a few seconds, this would-be still life of a pomegranate, a cabbage, and a pumpkin turns out to be a high-definition film of the pomegranate struck by a bullet and then exploding its seeds in slow motion.

The anatomical drawings of Vesalius are of course not moving—except perhaps in the emotional sense, rousing our sheer amazement at the almost inscrutable intricacy of the human body. The poems in this volume bear eloquent witness to that intricacy as well as to the virtuosity of Vesalius himself, so I can only marvel at what these poets have wrought, beginning with Amit Majmudar's striking couplets on the frontispiece of *De humani corporis fabrica*, where the disemboweled body at the center is identified with Vesalius's own book: a Book "Opened without religious scruples / Before a Throng of breathless Pupils" (55 in this volume). It is also fascinating to see how Vesalius' drawings can be made to "speak out" here, as in Nina Siegal's "What Man Am I," where the body in question turns out to be actually that of a woman "splayed on the table / breasts pancaked to my defiled frame, legs spread / guts spilled from their coils like the petals of my lower lips" (56). This volume radiates both horror and wonder, and there is a marvelous moment of the latter in Kelley Jean White's "Anatomy of the Hand," where Vesalius's drawing of a pair of skeletal hands prompts White to remember the amputated hand that her doctor husband kept in a pickle jar filled with preserving fluid in the basement of their house. As the nails yellowed and the skin frayed, she says,

I wondered at the status

of tendons and tendon sheaths, at the
(I hoped) preservation of the majestic,
magnificent, miraculous, angelic mechanism
by which the fingers tap. (74-75 in this volume)

As a literary form, ekphrasis is nearly three thousand years old. But just as artists and sculptors keep surprising us, keep pushing the envelope of what constitutes "art," these new practitioners of ekphrasis offer startlingly new ways to look at and think about the work of a pioneering anatomist who was also a Renaissance artist. Collectively, these poets invite us to join the crowd of pupils shown on the frontispiece of Vesalius' book: the pupils who – unlike the skeleton "look[ing] / Away in horror," as Majmudar says (55 in this volume) – remain forever fascinated by watching the master at work.

## Works Cited

Alberti, L. B. (1966). *On painting*, Trans. John R. Spencer (RevEd). New Haven: Yale University Press.

Hagstrum, J. (1958). *The sister arts: The tradition of literary pictorialism from Dryden to Gray*. Chicago: University of Chicago Press.

Heffernan, J. A. W. (1993). *Museum of words: The poetics of ekphrasis from Homer to Ashbery*. Chicago: University of Chicago Press

Keats, J. (1982). Ode on a Grecian urn. In J. Stillinger (Ed.), *Complete poems* (pp. 282 - 283). Cambridge, MA: Harvard University Press.

Krieger, M. (1992). *Ekphrasis: The illusion of the natural sign*. Baltimore: Johns Hopkins University Press.

Lanham, R. (1968). *A handlist of rhetorical terms*. Berkeley: University of California Press.

Lessing, G. E. (1984). *Laocoon: An essay on the limits of painting and poetry*. Trans. Edward Allen McCormick. Baltimore: Johns Hopkins University Press.

Mitchell, W. J. T. (1994). *Picture theory*. Chicago: University of Chicago Press,

Philostratus, (1931) *Imagines (Eikones)*. Loeb Classical Library. Trans. Arthur Fairbanks. London: Heineman.

Shelley, P. B. (1977) Ozymandias. In D. H. Reiman & S. B. Powers (Eds.), *Shelley's poetry and prose* (p. 103). New York, NY: Norton.

Steinberg, L. (1972) *Other criteria*. London: Oxford University Press.

## Further Reading

Keefe, A. (2011). The ecstatic embrace of verbal and visual: 21st century lyric
        beyond the ekphrastic paragone. *Word & Image*, 27(2)(June), 135-147.
Mitchell, W. J. T. (1994). Ekphrasis and the Other. In *Picture theory*
        (pp 151-181). Chicago: University of Chicago Press.

# PROLOGUE

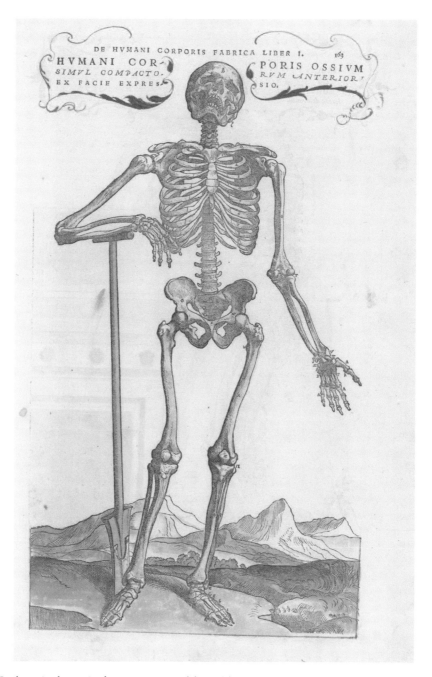

1. Vesalius, Andreas. *De humani corporis fabrica libri septem.* (Basel: Johannes Oporinus, 1543), page 163. Courtesy of Universitätsbibliothek Basel

## The Fabric: A Poet's Vesalius
Heather McHugh

Some etymologists give the Greek "to see for oneself" as the source for the English word "autopsy." An alternative, "seeing into oneself," is hard to overlook when one studies the work of the sixteenth-century Belgian anatomist Vesalius. I gaze on these *ecorché* figures with an exquisitely doubled (or divided) sense of looking.

Take the suffering skeleton (i), for instance. Very detailed, down to the tailbone, an excruciated figure: wailing away under the auspices of the clinician. But the artist has been at work in this presentation too. For the facts are mysteriously informed by feeling, and as the brain can make us feel, so too the heart can make us think.

Vesalius had his drawings done by Titian and his studio. (Some scholars attribute the work to only one artist, Calcar. For economy I refer to Titian himself, since I hold him responsible for his atelier.) There is some graphic footage here. The images rivet and reveal us as no list of facts could do. And the shocks are carnally compounded when (in the muscleman series) flesh adds its suggestiveness to gesture, even though overall, thanks to the depth of Titian's gifts, the images cannot remain merely voyeuristic.

Only a lifetime after Gutenberg died, Vesalius delivered to the printer for production and reproduction his *De humani corporis fabrica*, the extraordinary volume that contained these images and many more. What wows us in them now must once have wowed that printer too, the moment he laid eyes upon such beautifully belabored (and bedeviled) bodies, their lines and delineations studied to a fault. So carnal an exactitude! Even more than this work's forthrightness, its artifice assails us: the skeletons' figures are figured – down to the numbers of their fingertips, or, more precisely, down to the letters of their digits. And so they enter the realm where sign and design, science and art, conspire.

Drawn as surely to the drawn-and-printed as to the drawn-and- quartered figures (and as surely to the syntactics of the situations as to the semantics) I found I couldn't get enough of them. My senses fell to feasting. What exactly is that skeleton wailing over? As he mourns his lot, we see his lot is, not least, that one bit of real estate he's stuck on. His situation in time and space, unnatural though it is, moves us by analogy, or sympathy: we know, in time, we can't go back; he seems to know he can't go on.

However disposed we may be, in the face of such a foreground – in the face of such a *face* – to ignore the circumstantial background, nevertheless it bears regarding. (A casual eye is tempted away from it — as from those bowers and beaches of Victorian photographic studios, stylizations so conventional they lose the power to refer to anything but convention itself: their branches and waves seeming merely those of a weary imagination. But here the backdrop is no ordinary lover's lane. Our human being, our human has-been, stands on a bleak landscape, premises of hill and hole. He's either just come from, or is just now going toward, the very earth whose parts we tag for parts of our own anatomies: at the foot of a hill, at the mouth of a hole, this figure pauses to be figurative, and there to mourn the unrecoverable.)

Much is not to be recovered in the realm of the suffering skeleton. Flesh, for example. Beckett says "tears are liquefied brain," and catches the pain in a language pan. This guy has cried his eyes out too.

The peaks and pits nearby appear reduced, by perspective, to the overlookable — the hill is barely knee-high, and the hole is hardly intimated. This skeleton's particular dugout (at the lower-left corner of the page) is one of the smallest features of the artist's rendering, but it may well be, in the purview of the wailing skeleton, one of the largest geophysical (or psychoactive) features around, a hole too big for him ever to fill. (As soon as the hole is finished, perhaps he'll have to occupy it ... At last? Or again?) Perhaps then all his letters will migrate to a headstone.

You notice that Mr. Mort himself is equipped with a shovel, that armrest we at first glance might have taken for a branch or (more mortifying by far) a crutch. The shovel's head is improbably small, and its crossbar of handle is at right angles to that head; we might well *not* at first identify it as a digging tool. (Misprision, judiciously administered, can be indispensable to the protocols of art. At its best, it cannily administers the motions of the senses, makes a map of takings in, and of mistakings; a fever of identifications — first, false, and final. In the literary arts, the placements and displacements of our readerly regards can become a narrative of its own.)

Since a skeleton is itself a sort of apparatus of crutch and buttress, the shovel's shaft on first glance may well resemble a long bone, not only in shape and size but also in its involvement in the figure's posture — a proverbial third leg (subliminal allusion to the missing thrust so prominent in the flesh and consciousness of living men!). But then on second glance we realize: this is a shovel, not a body part, and this hapless figure seems to have dug his own grave. Or, sadder still, dug his way out of it. (After all, it's the image of no realistically fresh corpse on his way in. Because it isn't dripping flesh, this bone-man, though he seems to suffer, is far less troubling to the eye than are the Vesalian musclemen I'll look at soon, whose meat melts down from fingers and whose flesh is calving from their lower legs. It is flesh we find repellent, not bone. If cleanliness is next to godliness, rot is not. And nothing cleans a body up like dirt.)

So maybe this figure's wailing betokens a terrible disappointment at the world into which he has, again, so haplessly emerged.

Above the earth's own hills and holes, his unearthed pelvis hovers, in heavy lepidopterousness – an impression to which the recumbent skeleton, the naturalistic skeleton, would never give rise (there only the lowliest flies might have come to rest). Perhaps the exposed geologies of his own structure make us conscious of the hole-and-hill-work in the world. The pelvis (seat of so much heat and haunting, in a human life) has always made some mountains out of molehills – being itself a potent terrain for man's self-knowledge. (It's where knowledge got its hotter senses.)

Much of the power of this picture, taken as a whole, comes from a fundamental trope: the restoration of an animated attitude to the thought of bones — the skull and pelvis and patella marked by the human alphabet, and the kneeling and writing bones letter- bedeviled, letter-beset, as if it were language itself that had eaten the flesh away, as if even now a writer's pestilence of letters were attacking what is left of this suffering skeleton—the letters having, moreover, a particular taste for ligatures and joints. The semantics are antic; the syntax attacked.

Among readers, I suppose, poets are a materialistic sort. As soon as I detect the sign of the x at work, I'm near a buried treasure. (Hence the power of the figures of chiasmus.) You make the mark of the x because to elaborate – to literate – beyond that mark would dimish its meaning. How paltry or profane by comparison it is to write out the word "kiss," or the word "Christ," or in big black letters above the earth's own secret curves: SEE CHEST (or HEART) OF GOLD INSIDE. Take note: The bonds of such a materialism are deeply unconvertible: As an artist, I'm likely to love the x better than I love the gold. Or more precisely, for me there is no greater gold than that unexplicated x.

For as the logos becomes more and more explicated (through the successive ministrations of priests, philosophers, professor-postmodernists and PR men) more and more it loses for me the secret riches of its double nature. I'm talking language here, as much as anything, that logos – its capacity to radiate non-lexical senses. Perhaps that's why I am by nature a poet, and not someone more – well, more well-meaning.

The folio-feel of things, the crossfolds themselves, the quarto and verso of things, the physical implyings of the brain, not its big ideas, but its brooding broccoli, its coddled cauliflower, the mysteries of its material, lurking there in a brainpan – all mean more to me than any foistings of explainery. You can no more beard the world than make its meaning bald: no sooner prove a god to me than analyze an eagle. Yet eagles amaze us, alighted or aloft: and that gives us faith.

<br>

Let's not forget our shoveller. The bones don't seem to realize yet they're dead, or at least they haven't lost some living capacities to rue it. Meanwhile the shovel's head (what bites the dust) is peculiar in having a reinforcing or protective sheathe (something the skeleton himself no longer possesses). And the shovel is ready to undermine what a crutch might support. Leaning on the very instrument of its own engraving (ah, shades of penmanship!), this is a self-mourning, self-referring figure − i.e. the figure of art, figure of figures, with its ribs rigorously numbered and its companion, its comfort, its Eve, not apparently forthcoming: for this is the anatomist's art, and not the theologian's: of this man's ribs, not one is missing.

But he's missing almost everything else: and *the feeling* of loss is about him, heavy as stone. What metaphorically lumps in the throat, what wells up in the eye, what gets broken in the spirit, what drags the heart down − has its reality in the force of feeling, which brings to the subject's loss the object's weight. Our subject here becomes his own accusative.

This gravedigger faces skyward − of all the skeletons, he's the one who expresses the greatest inclination toward heaven, a figure who has been unearthed only to wind up grounded. If he's dug himself out, he's come to the place where he can't dig any further up − the air is all hole from there on out, and after the grave has been escaped, gravity will still keep him down. This poor soul cannot fly. He's looking up, but things are not.

And then (in the long now of a book) he's an object to *be* looked up. Unable even to die, he lives on, exposed to the view of those early medical students (who studied him once and who now bear him even more likeness, in structure if not in gesture), and lives on in our views as well; we too will die. Such is autopsy: it's yourself you're looking through, and at. The likeness that was buried in them as they regarded him is now buried in us as we regard him. (Inside every man of flesh is a man of bone just dying to escape.) The past we work to reassemble we'll resemble soon. With this handful of letters, we try to recover him—maybe even cover him up again. But we can't ever really recover *from* him.

What have I gotten into? the wailing skeleton seems to ask. (Figure of the long-suffering reader!) But also: What haven't I gotten *out* of? His nakedness is manifest and manifold − for the clothing of muscle, the fabric of nerve, the weave of arteries and veins are a carnal attire of which, layer by layer, Vesalius has elsewhere stripped him, in loving excruciation, in a kind of mortal tease.

By contrast the sidewise skeleton (2) seems calm and contemplative, the man of thought rather than the man of feeling. He's contemplating someone *else's* skull, his personal Yorick, and in one print of him there is inscribed, upon the stone sarcophagus or lectern, the words: *Vivitur ingenio, caetera mortis erunt* (Genius lives on, all else is mortal). He rests one hand upon the skull, perhaps affectionately, perhaps to keep it in its place. The foot is very lettered, which may be why I feel entitled to make my poet's reading of it. And there on the table, beside the skull he's contemplating, are bones from jaw and inner ear – poetry's parts. Half-turned away from us, the figure addresses an empty head, a numbskull. (Unlike his own, this skull is the merely mindless kind: it has no

2. Vesalius, Andreas. *De humani corporis fabrica libri septem.* (Basel: Johannes Oporinus, 1543), page 164. Courtesy of Universitätsbibliothek Basel

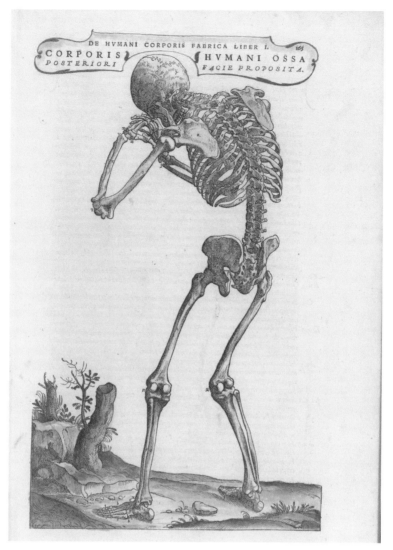

3. Vesalius, Andreas. *De humani corporis fabrica libri septem*. (Basel: Johannes Oporinus, 1543), page 165. Courtesy of Universitätsbibliothek Basel

associated remains, no anima or matter to hook up with, no connections for making a gesture. In other words, the skull he contemplates is realistically dead – a noun alone: semantics without syntax, bone without brain. Only in life, or in art, may the parts cohere, conspire, aspire into a whole that's greater than their merely arithmetic sum.)

In the second of the bone-man frames, there's no longer a hole in the ground. Instead there's a kind of Parnassus: the figure stands upon a high place, all else falls away, except the objects of his contemplation lying atop a solid structure which – if it's a sarcophagus – might otherwise have contained them. This bone-man is the cooler, perhaps more comic, figure; where the others have tensions, he has pretensions. An artist may make an altar of art while bringing some sarcasm to a sarcophagus.

After the second bone-man, his sidewise stance of an encomiast, we get the last, and posterior, skeletal figure (3). Where the middle one was distracted from his own condition, and stood in a high place, this one by contrast is most downcast, in the very attitude of sobbing. Unlike the gaze of the first frame's petitioner (which is toward heaven), this figure's attention seems fixed on the earth itself – where stands a pitiful lopped-off tree. Maybe that's what this bone-man mourns the most – that arboreal figure of life cut short (despite its promising little side-branch). Maybe it's the tenacity of life he grieves, as the tree survives. Maybe he's suffering Adam's punishment for sex (which was mortality). As a corpse, perhaps it is precisely sex he misses – he can't, after all (for all his bones) ever again have a boner.

Maybe he's the wisest of all the three: certainly he is the one most turned away from the likes of us.

---

There's plenty of tease in Vesalius's muscleman strips – a macabre combination of the comic, the erotic, and the horrific. Just cast a glance across the sequence of musclemen seen from behind (4) – they're nothing if not showy, with the strutting self-display and seductive gesticulation of models, hookers, pumpers of iron. Balletic yet self- mocking, pseudo-seductive, the next-to-last figure is visibly buckling in the right leg; the flesh hangs off in a grotesque parody of tattered clothing, and the knees are about to *need* the praying stone they'll get, just one frame later.

That the brain, too, undergoes a striptease suggests its own gruesome humors: here the seat of thought and imagination, philosophy and poetry, is split, like any inferior seat (5). The moment you publish so literal an insight as this, the gulf between mind and brain is forever and humiliatingly revealed. These head-strips seem especially unnerving because what's on our minds, what's in our brains (usually considered in the figurative and facile sense, a mere gloss on everyday transactions) is here by contrast lugubriously literal: we asked for the lowdown on the seat of intellect and we got a den of worms; at best a higher intestine.

We are not used to treating mind as matter. We prefer to set the two apart, as contraries. But there, in harrowing artistic fidelity, just beneath the awful opened skull, are patches of an all-too-familiar face — an ear, a nose — and even (worst of all, because it suggests the flair of individuality, of style) that Lothario's moustache.

Among body parts, faces are special cases. (In everyday commerce, they tell the most about the interior life of the emotions; in death it's especially

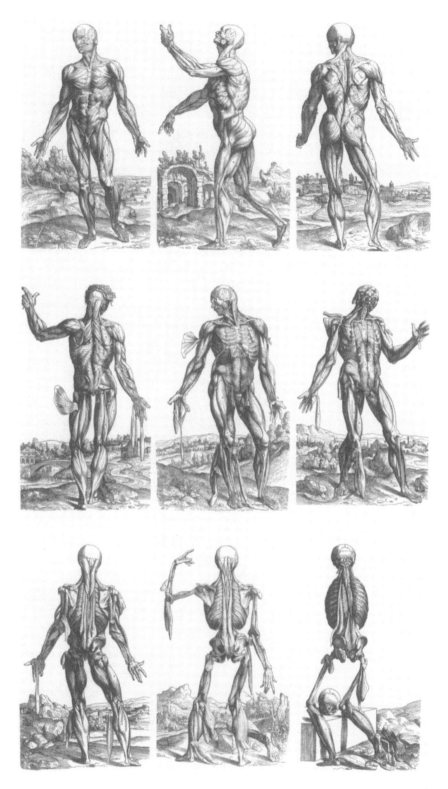

4. Collage of images from Vesalius, Andreas. *De humani corporis fabrica libri septem*. (Basel: Johannes Oporinus, 1543)

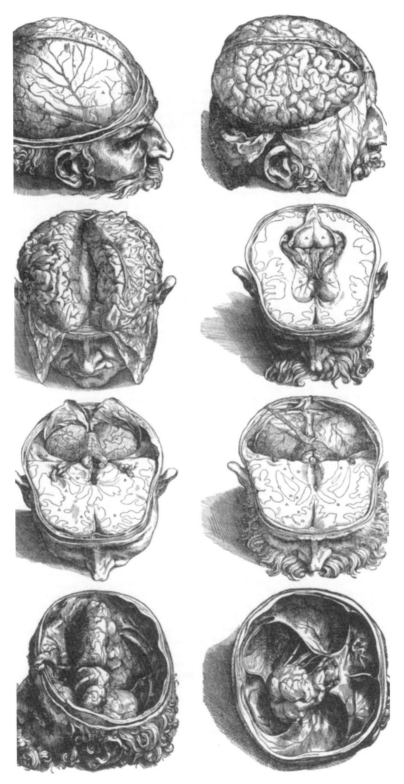

5. Collage of images from Vesalius, Andreas. *De humani corporis fabrica libri septem*. (Basel: Johannes Oporinus, 1543)

unnerving to see them turned inside out.) The records tell us Vesalius got his heads from criminal executions; he needed them fast and fresh in order to make certain circulatory observations; the guys in these cranial and cerebral stripteases were more than figuratively hot.

In some Vesalian frames you see odd or floating body pieces, suspended above — or posed nearby—the central and coherent figures (which are by contrast clearly subject to the force of gravity). Above that most crucified of musclemen, for example (6c), floats what looks like some sea creature, skate or ray, almost a comment on the meaning of the current. (The musclemen's tale is one of some liquefactions, after all, since it drips with flesh, in time.)

This airborne oddity is a human diaphragm. (Hung up in air, the diaphragm's a structural reminder of the air that once was hung up in it.) Our most intimate parts come to the surface unforeseen, like gilled or underwater oddities: we don't recognize them because we do not know ourselves, no matter how sharp are the scalpels or saws, the lenses or legends, we bring to our occasion. (On occasion the subjective genitive overwhelms the objective genitive.)

In this same panel of the all-but-crucified muscleman, we get the single most gorgeous botanical detail we'll see up close in all Vesalius's offerings; under the diaphragm and hand (now dripping whole armlets of flesh) an exquisite flowering seems to thrive, embodying the gardener's law of exchange: decay for beauty, beauty for decay.

---

In the progression even of just these three figures (6) I've used to exemplify the muscleman series, you can tell there's a clear program, as muscles are stripped away, layer by layer. As good readers we quickly grasp Vesalius's pedagogical arc, we see the meaning of the sequence: its inquiries move from outermost to innermost, by progressive incursion. (The excursive qualities in the landscape I'll treat later: but they do not enter into that first wallop of the visual impression.)

Most people will be shocked, at first look: in the transactions of everyday life, our innermost selves remain unexposed. We can't afford such insight − either about death, or, say, about the autonomic nervous system. (Thank the heavens something keeps us pumping through the night, so we can rest.) The ripping away of the veil, the violation of that integrity, especially in the muscleman sequence, where pieces of muscle hang like gaiters and gloves from deepening improprieties of flesh, feels sometimes painfully sexual.

The essence of this impropriety isn't moral: it's mortal. It occurs at the conjunction of the living pose and the fatal exposé: if this is a strip show, the

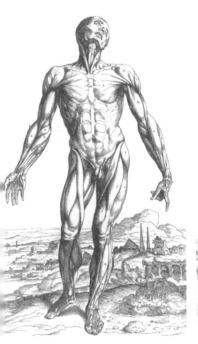

6.   (From bottom: a, b, c) Vesalius, Andreas. *De humani corporis fabrica libri septem.* (Basel: Johannes Oporinus, 1543)

seduction will come to its climax in gaping horror. Culminating the frontal series is a macabre carnage, in which the figure's bones are visible through its last scraps of flesh, as its skull and right shoulder are hoisted by a noose of rope (6c). Behind it is a wall whose shaded edge appears, to the casual glance, like the upright timber of a crucifixion scene. This illusion is carefully fostered: only at the ground, and half obscured by vegetative flourish, might the lateral line of a foundation be detected, and that line establishes the entire space of the right half of the panel to be a wall, not a sky.

But the proportions militate against our so identifying it: More than two-thirds of the panel - everything above the figure's knees (in short, the area we commonly take for central) - conspires to make the shaded area appear to be a wooden post. Only a scrupulous student of the the arts of earth will gravitate toward that telltale line. If the heavenly gaze falls earthward, air will turn to stone, and the ray is nailed. But if the terrestrial gaze moves upward, stone turns air, and the ray flies free.

Of course that's an artist's lyric version of things. In the clinician's view, that item I'm calling a ray, as if it were some sun-spear or flying fish, remains a human organ. The two seers, let us call them Titian and Vesalius, collaborate in deepening and dividing our insight and our plight.

In the culminating illustration of the posterior musclemen series (4), the figure is abandoned by whatever spirit up until now made it able to stand and present itself in living postures: it falls to its knees upon a stone knee-rest. The musclemen at the end of the series need supports (whereas in most Vesalian poses even without skin or hearts or nervous systems, these pseudo-people are able to stand and gesture and display emotion) – so the effect is of a very strange natural science, with laws selectively pertaining to the animated dead. The sequences make narratives in which these dead figures too have life spans, and can decay. Even the dead can mourn. And even they must die.

Perhaps in Vesalius's Titian one most vividly sees the historical moment at which art branches off from theology – and realism from the realms of the original *res*, its theological ideal. To put it indelicately, this plate suggests a history of crucifixion images, but with a crucial difference: this guy (we think) won't rise again.

What Titian brings to Vesalius is what Dickinson brings to ornithology; the art of her invitation (to "split the Lark" to "find the Music" in it) foregrounds a necessary irony and suggests the danger in too literal a mechanism of analysis. The principal medical motive of the illustrations is (of course) to show how organs work in active (not dead) figures. The artistic genius lies in Titian's solution to the problem of the literalist: namely, the reanimation of the human figures in their erstwhile higher spirits.  The cooperative enterprise of art and science that results is as darkly ironic as brightly informative.

And even in these most grotesque of the excruciated musclemen there are signs of spirit. The hands' stripped skin and flesh suggest a melting materiality, a melting that leads the eye via gravity (through the downfall from the figures' fingers) into the vertical axis, axis of simultaneities, where it can dwell for a while out of the domain of the horizontal lines and historical progressions. (The vertical prevails again when gravity requires the final figure to be dragged up from above by rope and pulley. Perhaps, in the heaven of anatomy, God is the one with the winch.)

And indeed you can see a kind of wing on the second frontal figure (6B): look at the splay of muscle in the upper right arm which fans out just where, in other paintings of the time, you'd find an angel's most uplifting featherwork. (Elsewhere a muscleman sports the more Mercurial form of this wing, on one leg.) In the center frontwise muscleman, a phallic cross-section reveals what otherwise would have remained hidden by skin: a kind of clover shape of fig leaf in the patterns of a severance. Hints of higher and lower worlds are artfully inscribed in this, of all the panels: for the fig leaf which, in Genesis, would hide the skin is now shown in a perverse reversal to have been there all along, hidden by skin. Thus do mortal dilemmas becomes moral ones (like that of Chekhov's character who had too little skin to cover her face: in order to open her mouth she had to shut her eyes, and vice versa.) These are jokes that hurt, jokes that reveal. In our gapings, our apings, our flesh, how deep can a nakedness go?

Even while deeper and deeper inside information is revealed, wider and wider outside information unfolds. I've given you only selected panels, so you can't see the effect entire, but the landscapes behind these individual figures aren't repeated: they are continuous. The background terrain of the series, taken in the ensemble, forms a geographic panorama. Researchers have actually identified the stretch of Italian countryside to which this background scenery corresponded. Such circumstantial coherence proposes peculiar paradoxes: it requires us to consider whether the human figures are those of many men, or one.

For if our first impulse had been to see, in cinematic sequence, the successive stages of de-muscling in a single being, now instead (noticing the continuity of the landscape) we might be forced to think of them as different men all lined up in one moment. Time, too, is implicated: for if the lineup is of one man progressively stripped, then time must pass between shots, so he can move along the landscape's frame. Whereas if these are many men caught in a fortuitously progressive line of muscular disinvestiture, then the whole is a snapshot, not a moving image. Is it many still men, side by side; or over time a single man who moves? Is time a situation in which we're all engulfed together or a vector passing through each being's isolate experience?

This contest of interpretations manages to be reminiscent of some of the theological arguments of the time (is life one or many? is divinity concentrated or distributed? is it a material or a force?). To my mind the question catches something of a great unsolvability about our nature as living beings – about Being distributed through beings. (Is it a similarity that runs through all our differences? is it a differing that now and then falls into patterns of resemblance?) Thanks to the collaboration of Vesalius and Titian, we can't readily exclude either possibility. It isn't so much either/or as both. Not long after Vesalius was dead, Pascal would write, "the series of men may be considered as a single man, living forever, and continuously learning."

I'll end with only one more set of hints at my favorite twist of matter. (But I warn you: it's a twist like a Moebius strip. It's endlessness's twist.)

In the era of information technology, bedeviled and bedigited by a proliferation of facts and instances, its intellectual life reorganized along lines laid out by the instruments it creates, its lookers scanning stats, its oglers Googling globes, all in the game for an answering glance, all on the trail of that certain other one-and-onliness (doomed enterprise), even in such an era, the Era of Everything, there is something untallied. Or let's say there are at least − and perhaps only! − two kinds of everything, two all-at-oncenesses.

One of the two is additive. Its piling up becomes occlusive, numbing, essentially mechanistic. The other is comprehensive. Its overlays are translucent, generative, essentially metaphysical. Where Kant discerned four kinds of Nothing, I propose (as an amateur in these realms) to distinguish only two kinds of everything. One everything is accomplished by the sheer patient summing up of all its component parts. (This sort of everything, when aimed for by technology, makes for amazing computations at amazing speeds. It is achieved at the ideal end of a pile of information, a sum beyond the capacity of a mind to contain it. It is instrumental, and indeed spreads instrumental diseases like wildfire, then has to adapt its own conceiving to create safeguards and search mechanisms sufficiently selective across a prolix, detail-bedeviled field.) Scholars, theorists, historians, mathematicians may be blessed with such gifts. To reach a given point, they build the road by which they get there − painstaking, legalistic, cumulative, horizontal.

Meanwhile the poet or intuiter, a metaphysician or feel-meister, will have fallen off a cliff, and reached the same point. A sudden vertical gets him there: an unforeseenness. The critic speaks of authorial intention; he thinks the artist means transitively. But the poet doesn't mean to mean: he writes to find out what he means, in some less transitive sense. In any sense in which an artist makes it, a seer's claim is not to a power, but to a vulnerability. Few would wish it: he must remain open to unbidden stimuli, suffer (without preconception or prescriptive filter) the sheer perceptual onrush. The second of the two everythings is of suddenness, not horizontal accumulation. It arrives in a slant of light, a snap of understanding across a field of patterns already richly there in a single moment's field. This other everything is holistic, not additive, as completeness is distinct from totality.

---

One feels for the facts in *De humani corporis fabrica*. The scientist's preparations deepen the satirist's sense of preposterousness; and the scientist's

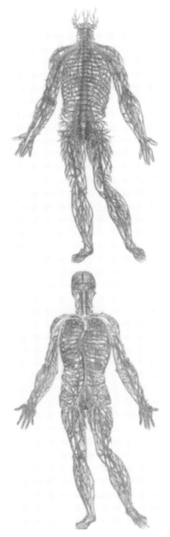

7. Vesalius, Andreas. *De humani corporis fabrica libri septem.*
(Basel: Johannes Oporinus, 1543)

points become the artist's poignancies. In all these representations of the body, the place where *least* you feel the whole human being savaged, where least it seems reduced to the strutting stuff of a stripper's boudoir or the hoisted meat of the butcher's abattoir, and where the human figure seems not only whole but greatened somehow beyond mere sums of parts – is in the representations of the circulatory and the nervous system (7).

The body's blood network wraps a man into his shape, keeps him bound in influences, fluencies. It is the tree of our family system, with one trunk and many branches and twigs curved about in interlocking bonds, a place of humming hammockwork. It's a comforting figure. When you look at circulatory man, you see why humans had to hug.

But when you look at neural man, you see why humans had to fly.

For the nerve ends, taken altogether, make a complete human shape, while pointing with their flametips away from drags of gravity and heft, toward open air, as if into space. They make the man appear to be on fire, not so wrapped inward as circulatory man, but radiating outward, especially at loin and crown.

Despite etymology's insistence on a respiratory figure for spirit, it is rather the neural map, out of all the anatomical cartographies, that best matches our human intuitions of angelic form. The head is an aspiring crownwork, with its ring of flames upleapt; the meat is gone from mentality, and *mens* means mind again, in a way now clarified. Here in neural man the exposed mind turns out to be not a pitiable gaping of stuff or an unlidded cistern (as in all those autopsies of gray matter we saw before), not looping and self-centering but instead like our idea of an open mind, with its indicators pointing up and away from the self and the grave.

In Vesalius's work a cool, unflinching eye for physical truths meets Titian's hot, imaginative flair. Just where we might have feared that the inexpressibility of human being would be reduced to mere mechanics, or mere fancy, instead we find our attentions rewarded with a wealth of a spirited self-revelation, an extension rather than an abridging of the mysteries (mysteries which lie at the very heart – or maybe synapses – of our happening at all, in time and space). To my mind, the ultimate gift from Titian and Vesalius working together is the kind of evidence no mere theories of brotherhood, no willfulness of theology, can match. Revealed right there in graphic terms, both in the flesh and past it, are the matters that must matter most: blood's embrace, and nerve's release. You may be homely on the one hand, dying on the other, what remains is not to fear it. You can still look well. For what's beyond us is within us: look at the fact and the art, the mark and the remarking. There you'll have it: loving's fabric, and the evidence of spirit.

Images courtesy of Daniel Garrison, Malcolm Hast, and Northwestern University. For more information about the Vesalius Project, visit: vesalius.northwestern.edu.

# EKPHRASTIC WORKS

# FRONTISPIECE

Vesalius, Andreas. *De humani corporis fabrica libri septem*. (Basel: Johannes Oporinus, 1543),
frontispiece. Koblenz: Courtesy of Bibliothek des Staatlichen Görres-Gymnasiums

## Random Thoughts On Anatomy And Vesalius

F. Gonzalez-Crussi

The body is arcane, enigmatic, and multifaceted. Between the simplicity of inanimate objects and the astounding complexity of living flesh, the contrast is immeasurable. A stone, observed the Spanish philosopher Ortega y Gasset, is all exteriority: break it, and the inside becomes the outside; depth and surface are all one. A mineral's inside is "relative interiority." But a living organism is never like that. No matter how we cut it, its inner portions will never become its outside. The body's interior is "absolute interiority." And in the case of the human body, the situation is compounded. For behind the concrete body there is an intangible psyche, a spirit, or a consciousness – what used to be called a "soul." We see the external man, but this one is inhabited by an inner man whose life is made of dreams, emotions, hopes, fears, conflicts, and yearnings that we can never know with accuracy. Thus, the vital core of a man, his deepest interiority, becomes enormously potentiated and enriched by his soul. Hence the mysterious quality of the body: its multi-stratification, the "onion-skinning" of its significations, one layer behind the other. Everything we see in the body signifies more than what we see.

This complexity of the body is intimidating. Most people experience this dread or intimidation with regard to the dissection of corpses, which is seen as a violation of an ineffable mystery. This explains the refusal to permit the donation of organs of a recently deceased relative. This explains also that curious "selective blindness" of those who, in the course of history, looked at the interior of the body. Overawed, they flinched at the sight and focused on symbols and metaphors. The nuns who opened the body of St. Chiara di Montefalco after her death did not see the muscular pillars (trabeculae carnae) that crisscross the cardiac chambers. They saw the cross that the saint claimed she carried within her heart. The Aztec sacrificers who held thousands of smoking hearts in their hands never saw a heart. Instead of a muscular four-chambered organ, they saw a beam of energy, a repository of cosmic force whereby the sun could be made to move along the firmament: the Aztec version of a powerful nuclear reactor.

To the ancient Greeks goes the glory of having turned their vision away from constructs of the imagination and toward concrete nature. Still, they gave no systematic description of anatomy. Hippocratic medicine favored physiology at the expense of anatomy.[1] "Their ignorance of anatomy, both human and animal, was fairly comprehensive," wrote an eminent historian.[2] There followed a number of learned men who, hankering after new knowledge, looked at the inside of the body. But their gaze was almost always distorted or blurred by philosophical systems that saw the organs as manifestations of something else, as symbols of a transcendent reality, not as real entities in their own right. At still later times, their gazing became transient and hurried, out of fear of transgressing the religious prohibition against cutting the human body.

Among the ancients who searched for truth in the recesses of the body, one man stands apart from the rest: Galen of Pergamum. The sheer volume and diversity of this man's endeavors has ever been a source of amazement. Galen's opus is as immense as it is multifarious: his complete works comprise twenty-one thick volumes or about 20,000 pages.[3] Anatomy, physiology, pharmacology, therapeutic, philosophy, and literature: nothing escaped the attention of this gifted mind. Admirable is the fact that this immense and diverse work constitutes a system harmoniously coordinated in every one of its parts. But it is precisely the love of system that ended up precipitating him into deplorable errors. It has been justly observed that Galen wished to fit nature into his system, rather than bending his system to accord with the observations of nature. Even anatomy, "a positive science if there ever was one,"[4] Galen bent to fit his preconceived ideas. He imagined the structure of man from that of animals, and he guessed it so precisely, that he succeeded in making the top scientists of his time believe that the human corpse had been the base of his demonstrations. He dominated the science of anatomy as absolute ruler for 1,400 years. There is no other example in medicine, or in any scientific field, for that matter, where one man should have exerted so complete a domination for so long.

Who would dare to oppose a system admitted without debate for 1,400 years? Who would have the mettle required to undermine the dogmas protected by the prescription of centuries? Fate had decreed that this task should fall to a young man, a 23 year-old citizen from the Southern Low Countries: Andreas Vesalius. It was appointed that his should be the glory of accomplishing what has been appropriately described as the "discovery of a new world."

That he had the courage needed to venture into unknown worlds is easily inferred from the dauntlessness, the audacity, and even the swagger and bravado with which he cuts unwarranted allegiances, dismisses uncritical servility, and faces hostile opposition. Thus, sallies such as this one may be read in his major opus, the *De Humani Corporis Fabrica*:

Our doctors, who follow Galen's ideas, describe however the structures of the kidney in an uncritical and false way. Where they do not take into account the distribution and localization of the vessels they invent many things, among them sieving membranes. Others, having an aversion to the practice of dissection sit on their high chairs, self-sufficient as Prometheuses ["ipsis mirificé placentes Promethei"] and consider their assignment as fulfilled after having created a human body by means of their imagination.[5]

Commentators and historians have descanted endlessly about the fact that the illustrations of *De humani corporis fabrica*, (in which some think that Titian may have had a hand), contributed in a major way to the success of this epoch-making book. This is a felicitous circumstance that, far from diminishing the merit of Vesalius's work, greatly enhances its value. Rarely have art and science come together in such accordant manner to generate one of the milestone accomplishments of humankind.

It has been said that the illustrations showed the anatomical structures, for the first time, in living attitudes of the body. The leg muscles, for instance, are represented while the subject is walking. Not in the usual passive, inert posture of traditional anatomical atlases. But this is not the feature that most entrances the viewer. The unique, extraordinary aspect of the illustrations is that they go to the very "heart of the imaginary," to borrow the expression of an eminent art critic.[6] Thus, in a chapter on osteology, which Vesalius considered fundamental to the practice of medicine, we are not shown a simple skeleton, but a "thinking skeleton": the figure represents a skeleton that is clearly in a meditative pose; it reclines on a tomb that bears the inscription *Vivitur ingenio, caetera mortis erunt* ("Genius lives, everything else is mortal"); it stands with its lower extremities elegantly crossed, and holding in its right hand ... a skull! In other words, we are presented with a skeletized Hamlet evoking a "poor Yorick," except that in this case the conflicted Prince of Denmark, having been reduced to a mere scaffolding of bones, finds himself in a plane of perfect equality with the Yorick he knew so well.

Something of the sort occurs in the other chapters. The different muscles are shown in corpses whose skin has been peeled off, and nonetheless they stand in various elegant or even coquettish poses. Detached from one or more of their insertion sites, the muscles hang down like tatters or loose ribbons. One would think that the person who suffered such a horrible torture would be howling in pain, agonizing under a pain greater than any mortal man can bear. Instead, the corpses of Vesalius's *Fabrica* go about their occupations as if nothing had happened. Human beings recently flayed like the mythical Marsyas disport themselves in utter nonchalance. A skeleton holds a skull while seeming to meditate on the transience of human existence. The book's illustrations could be a museum of unspeakable horrors, the iconographic record of tortures of the Inquisition. And yet, to judge by the poses adopted by the victims, they might as well be in a picnic, in a pub, or reposing on a couch in the comfort of their living-rooms.

It is highly significant that a book devoted to a science that demands utter precision and strict accuracy of description should happen to be illustrated under the inspiration of unbridled imagination. The depiction of the anatomical structures is rigorously true to nature. Never before had iconographic representation been so faithful. But the poses of the models, the dream-like setting, and the background are baroquely fantastic. Their world is surrealistic.

Here lies much of the imperishable, transcending strength of Vesalius's *Fabrica*. The contrast between scientific descriptive accurateness and free artistic imagination produces a tension that fills us with an inexpressible uneasiness. It is the same disquiet or intimidation that we experience when we consider the complex "fabric" – in the sense of framework or underlying structure – of which we all are made. The figures in Vesalius's book incarnate this very tension. These skeletons – these flayed, sectioned, or disemboweled men and women – seem to be telling us: "If your gaze stops at the surface, it will seem to you that this is how we are made. But if you reflect ever so little on what you see us doing, you will realize that we are also made of dreams, ambitions, projects, passions, joys, and sorrows." Only these things are not visible, but lie behind the exterior. For the human fabrica is essentially multi-stratified: one layer behind the other, like the onion skin.

## REFERENCES

1. Bonnard, J-B., Doherty, L. E., Cuchet, V. S.  (2013). Male and female bodies according to Ancient Greek Physicians. *Clio*, 2013, (1), 21-39.

2. Singer, C. J. (1956). Introduction. In Galen. *On Anatomical Procedures: Peri anatomikn enkheirsen. De anatomicis administrationibus*. London: Oxford University Press.

3. This, in the authoritative edition of C. G. Kuhn (Galen, Kühn, K. G., Assmann, F. W., & Nutton, V. (1821). *Claudii Galeni opera omnia*. Lipsiae: Prostat in officina libraria Car. Cnoblochii), which appeared in Leipzig from 1821-1833. And we must take into account that some of Galen's works have been lost!

4. Daremberg, C. (1854). *Œuvres anatomiques, physiologiques et médicales de Galien: 1* (page viii). Paris: Baillière. (Author's translation)

5. Translation from *De humani corporis fabrica*. In De Broe, M. E., De Weerdt, D. L., Ysebaert, D. K., et al. (1999). The low countries −16th/17th century. *American Journal of Nephrology*, 1999, (19), 282-9.

6. Caillois R. (1965) *Au coeur de fantastique*. Paris, Gallimard.

## HUMAN ATLAS

Marianne Boruch


Because the body really
is Mars, is Earth or Venus or the saddest downsized
Pluto. Can be booked, bound, mapped then.
Or *rendered* like something off the bone, fat just under
the animal skin, to lard,
cheaper, quicker than butter, like stillness
belies restlessness, like every yes
was or will be never, no,
                      none of that.
Such a book keeps
the skeleton so untroubled. To narrow in, to say
*femur, rib,* − a suspension, a splendor −
to stare like that
stops time. Or slick pages and pages given over
to slow the blood, remake muscle, to unsecret
that most mysterious *lymph*, its arsenal
of glands under the arm, at groin, at neck, awful
ghost lightning in it. Inscrutable.
                      Complete: because
the whole body ends, remember?
But each ending
goes on and on. Complete: because some
minor genius with a pencil, with ink, with drastic color
makes that arm you've known for years
raw, inside out, near wanton run of red vessel and nerve,
once a sin to look, weirdly now,
what should be hidden. Oh, it's *garish*
                    equals *austere.*
Compute. Does not compute. Tell me.
Then tell me who that
*me* is, or the
*you understood,* the any of us, our precious
everything we ever, layer upon
bright layer.

# Poem on the Frontispiece to Vesalius's
## *De Humani Corporis Fabrica*

Amit Majmudar


The little that we know, we've read
By spreading the covers of the Dead
Dust-jacketed, clothbound, designed
To stand upright on nerve-rich Spines.
Death is the Frontispiece and Rubric
Of *On the Human Body's Fabric*,
Which having rent and reckoned with,
We find ourselves as strange as Myth.
A Skeleton, meanwhile, looks
Away in horror from this Book
Opened without religious scruples
Before a Throng of breathless Pupils.
Some cling to Pillars, gazing deep
Into the Body's castle keep
For twenty Centuries inviolate
Dissected into reds and violets,
Diffracted into Gut and Spleen,
Nothing unknown, nothing unseen
For anatomic Theaters
Have no Fourth Wall; we are immersed
As Vesalius, with a subtil Knife,
Sculpts from a Corpse the shapes of Life.
To see this from a higher Place
The Monkey clambers past a Face,
This Page's only other Sound
A whimpered protest from the Hound.

## What Man Am I?

Nina Siegal

What man am I?
He, whose body twists away, revolted by the scent or sight?
He, in thick cloak, hands pressed close in prayerful kiss;
He who hovers low, curious and unabashed;
or that bold man of *scientiae*, upright and steadfast?

I am a woman, so I am not alive in this scene,
(unless I am the shrouded figure by the pilaster, peeking in)
A dog is here. A pet monkey too. But women are not allowed.
Observance in the name of truth is strictly for the men.

Since I am a woman, I am she, splayed on the table
breasts pancaked to my defiled frame, legs spread
guts spilled from their coils like the petals of my lower lips.
No hope of self-composure here, no right to pose and preen
That frail cloth I used to cover myself, crumpled underneath.

He slices, prods, and pulls; they plumb my core
gaze into that gaping place of lore – black hole
to see if butterflies flitter in my womb, or rabid boars.
To know how frightened they might be, should their seed
be planted in me, and I become supple and engorged.

As a woman, my body is criminal by Nature
weak by constitution, secretive, withholding, wrong.
As a convict – for what crime? – I am twice damned.
They'll pay more for a woman, twice for a pregnant one.
But I am a Medusa's head – do they dare turn to stone?

Centuries pass, and still they peer into this hole,
authorial, in the guise of science, medicine or art.
And yet the truth eludes them, while they stand there,
grappling with our bloody entrails, our uterine walls.
Our souls, there they go: flickering from our wombs and out the open door.

# THE ANATOMY THEATER AT PADUA

Michelle Boisseau

title page, *De Humani Corporis Fabrica*, 1547 [sic]

As there's no malice in science, there's nothing
personal about this rowdy crowd. One student
brought in a dancing dog, another a monkey
who spills orange rind on the men's velvet feet.
Such a horde of jubilation you'd think

the opened body had released them
like that minor god and his sack of pent up winds.
In the etching's center a skeleton rides
a railing. One jostled boy peers through
the low spy holes of the pelvis:

guess who? guess who? a barn owl
whirring in a hollow tree. Amid the scholars
down on stage, their beards hanging
like spades above their robes, the author
Andreus [sic] Vesalius illustrates the true

method of dissection, the fabric
of the human body. The corpse's skin
folds back neatly on louvered doors,
showing the crowded room
we each are, the perfect fit.

But who could you be? Some poor soul
dragged from the steaming hill beyond the city gates?

Your face is turned aside as if in modesty.
You're the only one naked among them,
a woman. I see now the artist's attention
to shading, the scratches on the copper plate
that indicate the rise of breasts, the dark nipples.

And this blur is your flowery uterus.
Shoulder to shoulder they hover above the opened
place they way men gather to dip
their dippers in a rain barrel or call
into a well when someone has fallen in.

# INVITATION TO EKPHRASIS

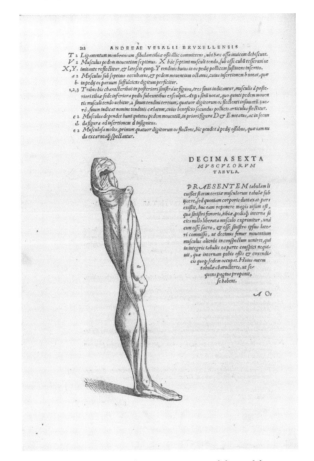

Vesalius, Andreas. *De humani corporis fabrica libri septem.*
(Basel: Johannes Oporinus, 1543), page 212.

# PRAEFATIO

Vesalius, Andreas. *De humani corporis fabrica libri septem.* (Basel: Johannes Oporinus, 1543),
portrait of Andreas Vesalius. Courtesy of Universitätsbibliothek Basel

## Eye Contact

Richard M. Berlin

A ghostly glow
frames the face of a man
with nothing to hide,
his vision honed
on the graceful heft
of charnel house bones
poached from the hangman's
noose and Cemetery
of the Innocents.
His fierce eyes
lock on ours, confident
as we stand beside him
witnessing the dissected truth
of a sternum's three bones,
a sacrum's six, the singular
presence of a ductus arteriosus.
With nostrils grooming death,
and a flayed cadaver at hand,
his eyes compel us to plumb
*The Fabrica's* woodcut
skeletons dressed in flesh
flaunting deltoids gaudy
as epaulets, each sartorious
ribboning a lusty thigh
of pained, praying souls
that mirror his heart and mind,
men muscled hard as gods
whose beauty turns
a blind eye toward death.
*Come closer*, his gaze
commands. *Abandon fear
and Galen's dogma.
Confirm my work to find
in the body's design
the naked truth
your own eyes can see.*

# INVITATION TO EKPHRASIS

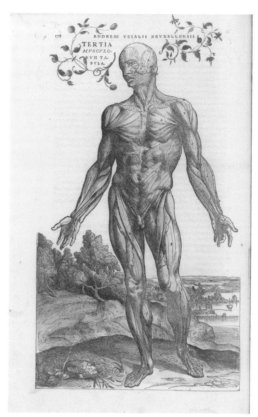

Vesalius, Andreas. *De humani corporis fabrica libri septem.*
(Basel: Johannes Oporinus, 1543), page 178.

# Book I

Vesalius, Andreas. *De humani corporis fabrica libri septem.* (Basel: Johannes Oporinus, 1543), page 18. Courtesy of Universitätsbibliothek Basel

# No Men of Grace

Dennis Barone


All five had walked into a bar
On Carmine Street: three Montagues
And two Capulets. No need to

Guess what happened. A fight
Broke out and somehow all five
Got themselves killed. In their

Likenesses one sees their skulls
Shorn of hazel skin. Boaz says
Long-head Italians become round

Headed after a single generation
On Manhattan Island. Study the skulls,
Professor. Environment will not

Displace inherited traits. These
Italians had demonstrated their
Proficiency with the knife.

They are by nature this way
And no other. Titian, the artist,
Likewise: study his etchings,

Their fine cut lines; yet
Distrust so idolatrous a scheme:
This beauty paid for in blood.

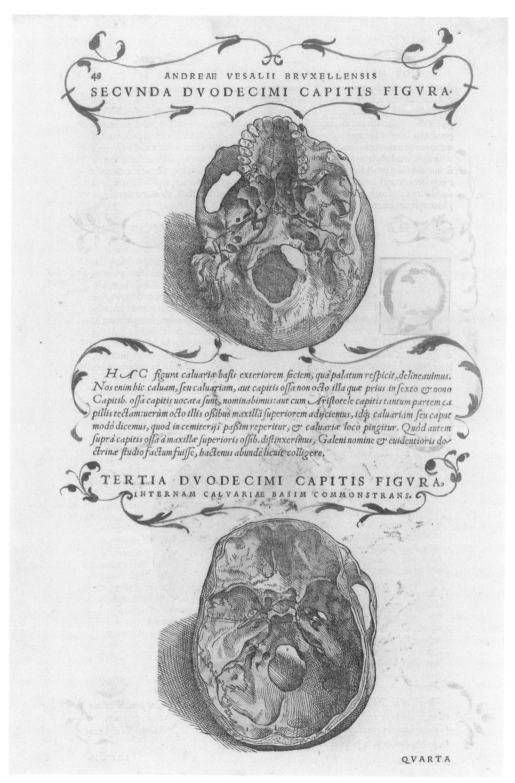

48   ANDREAE VESALII BRVXELLENSIS
# SECVNDA DVODECIMI CAPITIS FIGVRA.

H *AC figura caluariæ basis exteriorem faciem, quà palatum respicit, delineauimus. Nos enim hic caluam, seu caluariam, aut capitis ossa non octo illa quæ prius in sexto & nono Capitib. ossa capitis uocata sunt, nominabimus: aut cum Aristotele capitis tantum partem capillis tectam: uerùm octo illis ossibus maxillâ superiorem adijciemus, idq́; caluariam seu caput modò dicemus, quod in cemiterijs passim reperitur, & caluariæ loco pingitur. Quòd autem suprà capitis ossa à maxillæ superioris ossib. distinxerimus, Galeni nomine & euidentioris doctrinæ studio factum fuisse, hactenus abunde licuit colligere.*

## TERTIA DVODECIMI CAPITIS FIGVRA,
### INTERNAM CALVARIAE BASIM COMMONSTRANS.

QVARTA

Vesalius, Andreas. *De humani corporis fabrica libri septem*. (Basel: Johannes Oporinus, 1543), page 48. Courtesy of Universitätsbibliothek Basel

## SEAT OF THE SOUL

for Cora Lee Tucker, Decatur Island, WA
John L. Wright


I'm walking to the Saturday market – dirt road, hilly, one and a half miles –
when you, an octogenarian, drive up in a golf cart with friends and offer me a
ride. Thanks, I say, hopping on the carriage deck. When you tell where your
friends live, I say, Years ago I was offered the endocrine position at the clinic
there. *That must be an interesting field*, you query. If Descartes is right about
the pineal gland, I say, it's the specialty nearest the soul. Then, after bantering
about the soul's where-a-bouts, you admit, *I don't know where the soul resides
but I know when it's not there.* I had never considered that a diagnosis but what
else explains so well those lost years in the slough of despair? I hike home at
ease, my backpack full of produce and a baguette, my soul, for the moment,
comfortably seated.

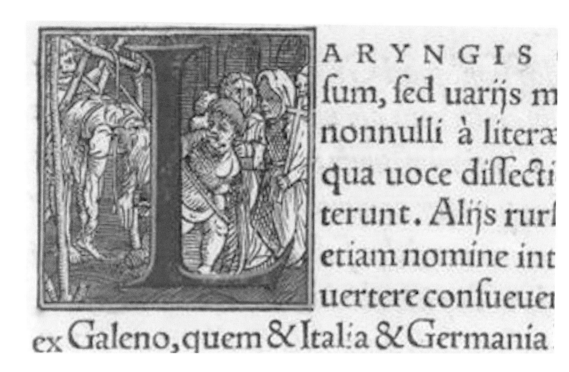

A R Y N G I S
ſum, ſed uarijs m
nonnulli à literæ
qua uoce diſſecti
terunt. Alijs rurſ
etiam nomine int
uertere conſueuei
ex Galeno, quem & Italia & Germania

Vesalius, Andreas. *De humani corporis fabrica libri septem.* (Basel: Johannes Oporinus, 1543), page 55. Courtesy of Universitätsbibliothek Basel

## VESALIUS AT THE GIBBET OF MONTFAUCON

*Near Paris, 1535*
Clare Rossini

He heaves himself onto the crumbling mortar platform. *God,*

*The stench!* Holds a scrap of stained linen to his mouth

As he cranes his neck back, eying the slumped shapes

Swaying between him and the stars. This one's

Been edited by wind and sunlight to a skull

Hitched to a trail of vertebrae,

The next one, still whole, still fleshed and clothed

In a flutter of rags, but the poor soul's face, how is it —?

A cavern

Shagged with hair. *Quickly, man!*

If the watchman he's bribed wags his tongue to the priest,

That dung-heap Deputy to the Chief Inquisitor — sacrilege

To steal the bones of the dead, even from such sorry

Ones as these.   *Ah!*


He says to the moon.

Here's a fellow


The crows have plucked almost clean, the tendons still holding

The delicate collation of bone together. Look,


Not one is missing –

(Reaches up, grabs the skeletal foot).


Every tiny bone-jot in place.

He laughs aloud at the pleasure, the luck of it.


Then stands on his toes – he's a small man –

Grasps the dangling femurs, tugs –


A shudder passing up through the airy skeletal shape, the noose

Giving way, the chains made tender by frost and rain,

It falls

        he staggers

                lands in a heap

Of ilium and humerus, clavicle and tibia, the skull's bare grin

To his warm wet cheek.

Man and speci-

Man and wind

Browsing both, speaking to itself aloud, as wind does and will,

*Why, it's a bundle of bones*

*In love*

*With a bundle of bones.*

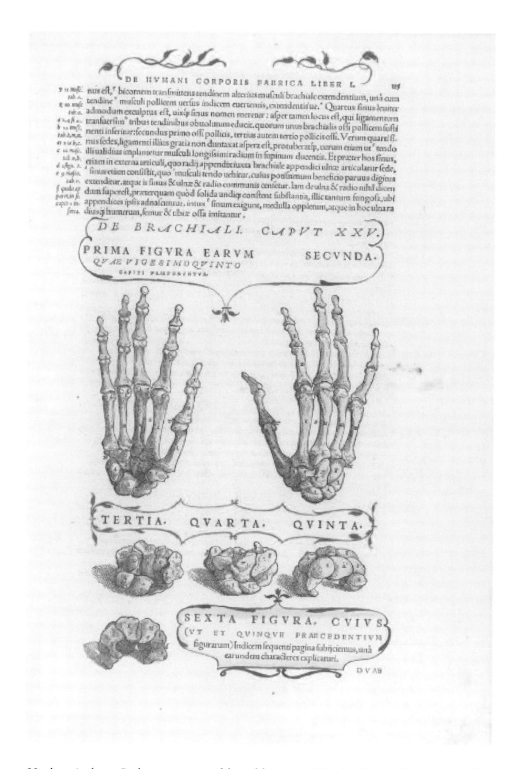

Vesalius, Andreas. *De humani corporis fabrica libri septem.* (Basel: Johannes Oporinus, 1543), page 115. Courtesy of Universitätsbibliothek Basel

# OF HUMAN HANDS

Wynne Morrison

These hands are like a ghostly specter's claws,
drawn upright with nothing left but bone;
tendons, muscle, skin all gone – the scars
of a life's labor stripped away.  They could
be Charon's narrow fingers glimpsed within
the shadows of his sleeve where they wrap
around the long pole of his boat. The bare
*ossa metacarpi*, with the palms removed,
stand like ancient temple columns with no roof.

At first I thought the hands were right and left,
facing each other supplicant, like branches
of a tree stretched up to draw life from the sun.
On closer look, I see the artist drew
a right hand front and back – both sides to show
all facets of the bones. Thoroughly numbered,
both art and teaching tool, an epoch in every
Latin-labeled finger. Crosshatching makes
the thumbs recede into a different plane;
the opposable thumb that marks a human,
hands that can grasp a knife, a pen, a child.

My hands and fingers, held up side by side,
begin to show their age as if to say
this flesh is but a temporary form.
Freckles have been replaced with large brown spots,
and blood swells in my veins not far below.
My breath flows with that blood to my still-beating
heart, and echoes in the murmured touch
of skin to skin. Living or dying, both
are ways of changing. Unlike those bones forever
fixed upon the page -- they have aged past
the fleeting softness of connections
and need a finger's touch to give them life.

## ANATOMY OF THE HAND

Kelley Jean White

A long time ago when I was married
my husband, the plastic surgeon, came home
from the hospital late one night with a human
hand wrapped in newspaper like a fish.
There had been an urgent amputation,

a tumor of the forearm that did not affect
the hand.  The patient wished to contribute
to the advancement of science.  It was thought
that perhaps my husband could use the hand
in study. At first he placed it in the freezer

but being concerned that the babysitter
might inadvertently unwrap it he moved it
to a pickle jar filled with preserving fluid. It sat
downstairs on his workbench among paint
cans and assorted screws another project

not finished or truly quite begun.
Even I would be taken in occasional surprise
turning with a basket of clean laundry, headed
for the steps.  It must have been quite
difficult on the sitter.  It waited.

Like an extreme merit badge project:
woodworking, fire craft, skeletal finger lore.
At first it was fat, swollen, but month by month
it aged, skin bleached, nails yellowed, bits of
skin frayed.  I wondered at the status

of tendons and tendon sheaths, at the
(I hoped) preservation of the majestic,
magnificent, miraculous, angelic mechanism

by which the fingers tap.  It was the left
hand. Tonight I wonder: Did it

hold a child?  Did it wear a wedding
band? Did it touch a man?  What work did it do?
Knitting?  Typing?  Filing?  Weeding?  Did it play
the piano?  Did it bake bread?  I do not want
to think of the woman, alive, I see her

body unwieldy like mine, the thin
cotton print dress, the empty sleeve.  Or worse
I see her dead of the tumor and buried, bereft, while
the jar's top is thick with dust and cobwebs.  It became
a mummy's hand, curling, reaching for the door,

the children brought their friends, switched
off all but a flash light, ran screaming away, delighted.
It is a long time since I lived there.  I do not know where
the hand is now.  He may have thrown it away.  Alone
I wish it the dignity its service should command.

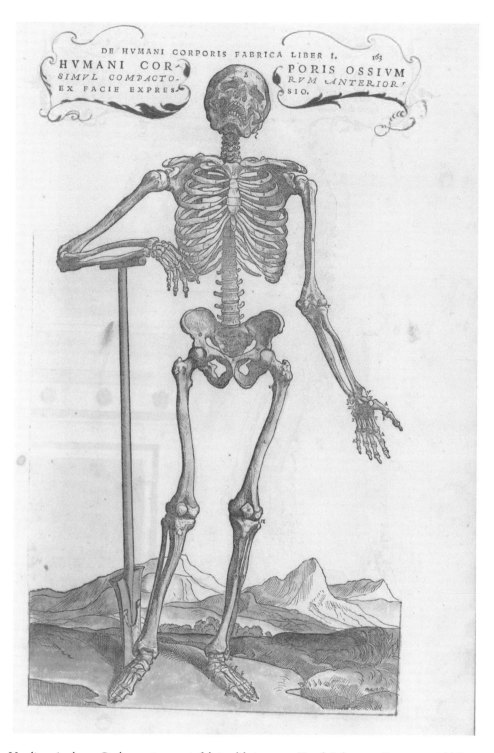

Vesalius, Andreas. *De humani corporis fabrica libri septem.* (Basel: Johannes Oporinus, 1543), page 163. Courtesy of Universitätsbibliothek Basel

## MAN WITH A SHOVEL

Cortney Davis


I am alone on this hill – they
fled when they saw all that I have
suffered, heard wind through this body Vesalius pierced
and stripped of flesh.  The ravens and crows wait, my
cries fall on arid gullies and mountains, on these empty hands
and useless shovel.  Pity my anguish, and
help me dig what will be my
own grave.  Bless my hollows, look to my feet,
see how I cry to those who were to help me – they
             all departed, and now I have
only this flimsy spade, only the odd and anguished numbered
curses he imposed, counting my knuckles, my hours, all
in vain!  I have neither allies nor company; my
final pit will soon be home.  I dread the scattering of my bones.

## JAKOB KARRER VON GEBWEILER

Andreas Vesalius, *De Humani Corporis Fabrica*, 1543
Marc J. Straus


They took me from the stockade, marched me
to the foot of Mittlere Brücke, the sun striking the new copper
roofing on the Basel Bibliothek, a small girl
in a wide pink dress eating a sticky candy, everyone
here to see the execution, and for what, I was thinking,
for wielding a knife at the throat of my wife, which
I tell you was never true; after all her uncle is a chief
magistrate, and my wife claimed I was married with a second
family, and I tell you that also isn't true — yes perhaps
a dalliance or two, but to lose my head when
the very magistrate, the good mayor, the councilmen — they
frequent the establishment just off Rheinsprung, an elegant parlor
overlooking the river, and here in this city of penny pinchers,
usurers, thieving bankers, and linen merchants, they call me
a thief because I refused to repay a loan falsely made,
and it came to an end on May 12 of 1543 and like any *petty* criminal,
executed on such a sunny day in front of laborers eating a mid-day
meal, in front of housewives and whores and little girls licking
candy, my remains would have been pieced together and thrown
into a common grave in a field in Otterbach, and what of my children
who would never know nor care where I lie, except that on that same
day came Andreas Vesalius, a young Flemish doctor in Basel
working with a printer on *De Humani Corporis Fabrica*,
which I know so well, published the same year,
plates of anatomical dissections which upended much of Galen,
which became the important basis for human anatomy till this day,
and it was because of *me* he understood the correct structure
of the mandible, the sternum, the small bones in the feet, because of me,
my plate, where I lean skeletally on a shovel, left hand extended down,
head tilted slightly back, less weight on the right foot,

just thinking, I suppose about that great subject
of posterity, an etching with a deep ravine and then the Alps
behind, thinking that I will be seen for centuries, yes, stripped
down, but where is the Magistrate, where is the wayward wife,
where is Vesalius, who died penniless in Greece, but
who immortalized me, one Jakob Karrer von Gebweiler.

# Urgency

Boris Veysman, MD

I've been out for over a year. Not from prison, not from combat duty. But close. From being a night shift ER doc - the graveyard shift of my profession. For a decade, I treated the full spectrum of trauma, heart and brain emergencies, life and limb threats of every kind. The academic regional ER where I practiced is a magnet for the sickest patients. Needles and knives, defibrillators and tubes, scanners and pharmaceuticals were my tools for keeping people out of graves.

Today, only a few miles down the road from that ER, I am a suburban urgent care doctor. It's a tiny place between a nail salon and a shoe store. Most of my patients simply have too much snot, anxiety, or chronic and annoying discomforts or dysfunctions. They cough, sneeze, clog up and ache all over. They suffer fatigue and worry, pinched nerves and worn joints. Some need forms signed off for work, some want quick labs or refills on basic meds. Almost no one is dying. Yet to paraphrase the Roman Stoic philosopher Seneca, who insisted that "we die every day", many of my current patients are habitually "busy dying." Tobacco, alcohol, and various psychoactive prescriptions -- chemical coping tools for an unbalanced stressful life devoid of sufficient rest and exercise. Disinterest in and resistance to controlling blood pressure or blood sugar. Resigned refusal to be active or eat sensibly.

Vesalius's image of a skeleton who has dug his own grave stands before me, resonating with my "busy dying" patients. Just like the skeleton, they don't seem to mind what's happening, grinning in annoyance as I ask about the habits of activity or inactivity they know are "bad for" and "killing" them.

"Doc, I've heard it all before, thank you." My prompt reassurance that "I get it, life is for living" puts them at ease that I'm letting it go. I move on to the stuff they came for, between the lines gently dropping hints for ways out still available to them and what I can do to help. Often, as I reach for the doorknob, the skeleton looks up from the grave and asks, "You really think I can?"

I've been out for over a year. But for my patients, the doctor is in. I no longer miss most of the circus-worthy pyrotechnics my life-saving in the ER was all about. I found something no less thrilling. A few good words, a look of encouragement and a nod of approval can say "I know you can do it" and bring about a change of heart not unlike a defibrillator. The graveyard shift taught me much about a sense of urgency. In my urgent care, we seize the day and get "busy living."

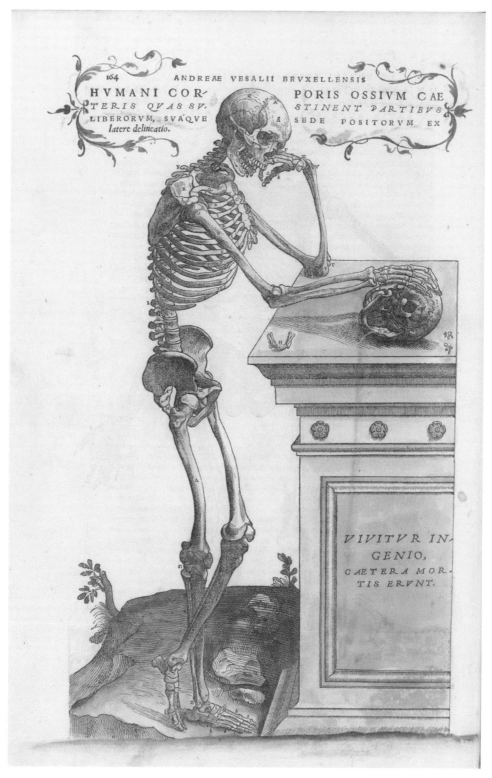

Vesalius, Andreas. *De humani corporis fabrica libri septem*. (Basel: Johannes Oporinus, 1543), page 164. Courtesy of Universitätsbibliothek Basel

# ARTIST STATEMENT

Jenna Le


At the age of 3, I hunched
over the coffee table's staggered
glass panels under a sizzling
yellow lightbulb and, grinding
my pencil's soft proboscis
into a quarter-sheet of tomato-
tinted paper, produced
my first drawing: a bird
with zigzag wing serrations,
3 stick-like toes radiating
out from each foot. I declared
myself an Artist and, to punctuate
my brag, drew a second
bird, and then Bird the Third,
and would have kept churning
out replicas like a hack
if Mom hadn't confiscated
my paper stack, witheringly
informing me All Artists Starve.

And so I grew up to be
a doctor instead, but struggled
to find my niche until I heard
(like the voice of that skew-scribbled
bird) the field of radiology
chirp my name. That summer,
I hauled Hale's *Drawing
Lessons From the Great Masters*
off the plastic shelving unit
slouched against the wall and asked
myself: was I up to this task?
Could I learn the body as thoroughly
as Leonardo, each twist

of bone, each slab of meat?
For a radiologist must cultivate
knowledge of anatomy so complete
as to compete with Rembrandt,
with Goya. And recalling my caw-scrawl,
I relished this challenge.

Midway through Hale's book,
there are reproductions of 7
Vesalius woodcuts of the human
figure, considered state-of-the-art
in the 16th century, though modern
experts know better, know
the lumbar spine has a concave
curve and the carpus
never hangs as low as the knee.
Each print depicts a skeleton,
muscles stripped and swinging
like banana peels from his bones,
walking about in nature,
unashamed to lack a skin.
One leans on a tomb carved
with Latin words I paraphrase
to say, "Yes, All Artists Starve,
and all beings die someday,
but ingenuity finds a workaround."

## St. Thomas at His Desk

Marilyn McEntyre

St. Thomas wrote his *Summa Theologica* standing at a desk built for the purpose, leaving it between long Latin sentences to walk his cell, relieving the labor of binding thought to thought with logic tight as a sailor's knots. Hawthorne wrote *The House of the Seven Gables* the same way, standing for hours by an attic window, imagining. Thomas Wolfe stood to write his copious novels on top of an icebox. Six feet six inches, he leaned a little even there, tossing completed pages on the floor. Some thoughts require that we stand, the way worshippers do to speak sanctified words, the way subjects rise and wait before the king.

Vesalius knew this – how the body participates as we think, assuming postures that have proven conducive to thought. We lean and loaf (if we are Whitman). We rest our cheek on a hand, gazing into middle space. We cross our legs at the ankles, resting our weight on one foot and then the other, learning how posture changes perspective. The whole body, I have learned, is where thinking happens – not just in the nerve-riddled brain with its lobes and folds and fissures, but in the muscles of the athlete and the quick eye of the hunter and in the very bones that hold us in place when a thought arrives, positioned to receive it, hold it, let it move through memory, descend through the centers of feeling, turn to energy and fuel fingers that write or strum or spin. We recognize those moments:  fingers drumming on the chin, idling over an idea; pencil in the mouth; foot wagging; spine stretched backward over the chair while the body waits for insight to alight.  Feeling finds its way into our very structure: "My bones are troubled," the Psalmist writes, and elsewhere that his bones "rejoice." Oliver Sacks, among others, wrote about how the blind learn to "see" with their bodies, how versatile and available the body is not only as instrument but as an extension of the mind.  There are things we know in our bones, sheathed, protected, buried and held, deep secrets of the body, seldom fully fathomed.

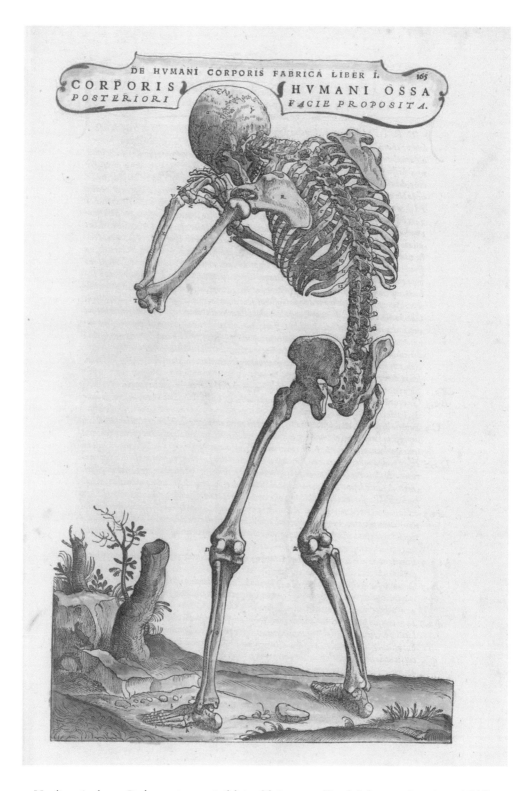

Vesalius, Andreas. *De humani corporis fabrica libri septem*. (Basel: Johannes Oporinus, 1543), page 165. Courtesy of Universitätsbibliothek Basel

# CORPORIS HUMANI OSSA, POSTERIORI FACIE PROPOSITA

Hugh Blumenfeld

The red fibers that make a muscle's belly gather into
a thin white tendon, which, detached
carefully from the bone and pulled away from the dissection,
reveals what's underneath. We say that it is reflected.
And so we see in the muscle men of Vesalius
not anatomies, but mirrors of our inner selves,
laid open, as if flayed, to the stare of centuries.
We find ourselves in a world of stumps and stones,
our habitations close enough to suggest our social nature
but beyond help or shelter, leaving us to our chosen pose,
the attitude we cop toward man, toward God.
The muscle men cast an upturned eye, or look askance,
revealed - they stand without their skin, their power
drips from them - and emasculated,
genitalia too tiny for successful copulation, as if a penis dangling
in its true proportions would distract us from the existential loneliness
they wear like strength, like sinew, like complete men.

I am not one of those.
I am a bone man, a walking talking
memento mori, not the famous thinker
with one hand curled beneath his chin, the other resting on a dead man's
skull,
but the one who wrings his hands, back bent in sorrow
or supplication. Or both. I do not reflect, but bear the weight that buckles my
knees unquestioningly.
So totally beyond sex, beyond companionship,
beyond need am I – I have no belly even – and yet
I sway before a nameless stump that once was dead,
that once was dead but now sends sunward a single green shoot
Is it too much to ask?
Is it too much to ask?
Is it too much to ask?
I sing, like a cricket.

## IN THE VALLEY OF BONES

Marilyn McEntyre


*Son of man, can these bones live?*
In a dry land, in a desolate place,
under the heat of the pitiless sun
they remember they are dust.

They bend under the weight
of sorrow.  Made of earth,
they begin their return, curving
around all that is unforgotten,

unforgiven.  What is bred
in the bone is borne there until,
multiplied by years, it begins
the great unburdening, sheds

flesh first, unravels what was knit
in the womb, releases mind
from mattering.  What tethers
bone to bone dissolves.

What is left is rubble. Chop-fallen
and clattering in the wind, these bones
bespeak the secrets they protected once
from every gaze but God's.

# BOOK II

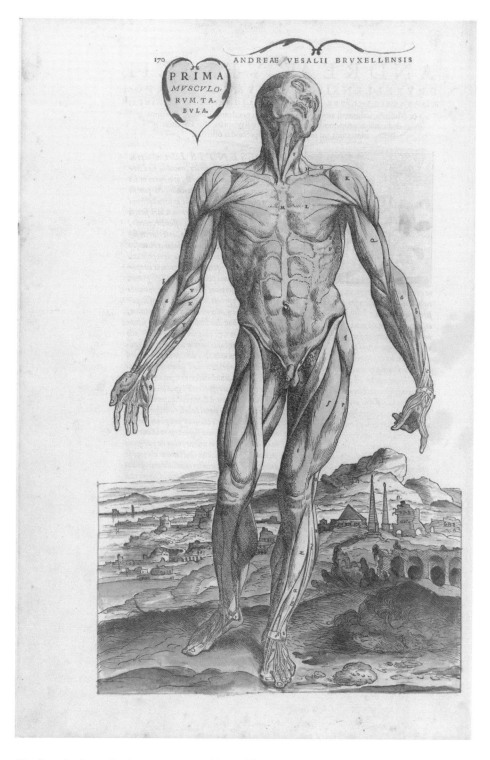

Vesalius, Andreas. *De humani corporis fabrica libri septem*. (Basel: Johannes Oporinus, 1543),
page 170. Courtesy of Universitätsbibliothek Basel

FABRIC

Scott Cairns

> *— Whatever this was to them,*
> *it is all yours now.*

What matters most is most infused
within the patent matter of the host.
What matters most is often lost
whenever one sees fit to parse *the one*
into a splay of bright constituents.

Observe, just here, the keen degree
to which a honed indifference attains
its edge, and pares away what may
have kept us innocent and sick. The trick
lies yet in severing one's sense of *he*

from him whose glib humanity
proved impediment to excavation
heretofore. We must admire what
special art obtains for us so clear, such
obvious advantage, the price of which

– by all appearances – was one man's soul.

## Saint Bartholomew

Margaret Lloyd

I did not, like Marsyas,

lose a contest with Apollo,

to be flayed by the knife grinder.

Once under the fig trees

I was seen and known and I followed.

Each muscle, sinew, bone

in the body I came by

I gave to Christ. Now my skin

which held my life together

as I walked the dust of the world

is held out for you to see.  Look

into its folds and find

what you are:

artist, martyr, lover,

worker toiling in the vineyard.

Alone and apart,

the way you came into this world.

Perhaps you are no different from me –

flayed every day

with a gathering of pain

in which God makes

himself more visible,

or unwrapping your skin

for love. It was ecstasy

I tell you.  I was never

more fully alive, weightier,

closer to desire

hunting me down,

than under the knife.

Vesalius, Andreas. *De humani corporis fabrica libri septem*. (Basel: Johannes Oporinus, 1543), page 174. Courtesy of Universitätsbibliothek Basel

## PRETEND TRUTH

Chuck Joy, MD


who could fail to be charmed

presented with a man walking

gaily, having just tossed a thing,

a ball or a coin or his fate?


but wait! he is no man

he is skinless carcass


fooled again . . .

Anatomy obscures the truth that it pretends

# THE MUSCLE CADAVER

Kelley Jean White

Relaxed? I say not: he stands, thicker than a wrestler,
more solid than a boxer, stolid as a dray horse,
one hand raised as if to ask for sunlight, for air, for breath,
the other pointing to the tomb, each set of fingers
pulled by the marionette strings of his questioning mind.

Think, the biceps contract, the triceps, deltoid, as the spade
is lifted, quadriceps tug to set the foot against the blade,
hamstrings slam it into packed earth, buttocks clench, abdominals
ripple to dig his grave. And here am I, losing muscle mass,
bones thinning beneath atrophic breasts. The first cut

a circling of the nipple, (saved for a later study), as the students
begin to learn dissection; they remove fatty tissue, bare
the chest wall, the pectoralis, the sternocleidomastoid, scalenus,
scalenus, external oblique. Who wove his shroud? Who wrapped
his winding cloth? Who laid him in? Who tossed the first clods

into the gaping hole? Whose feet trod, tamped the soil? Who
set the unmarked stones at foot and head? And who will do
these last honors for me? For my shriveling brain, my
edentulous smile, the brittle hair braided against dry scalp.
Will they plant a cedar tree, a poplar, a pine? An avenue of trees
to lead me to his arid windswept country.

## INVITATION TO EKPHRASIS

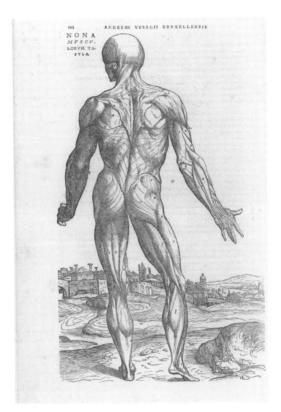

Vesalius, Andreas. *De humani corporis fabrica libri septem.*
(Basel: Johannes Oporinus, 1543), page 194.

Vesalius, Andreas. *De humani corporis fabrica libri septem*. (Basel: Johannes Oporinus, 1543), page 181. Courtesy of Universitätsbibliothek Basel

Vesalius

Karl Kirchwey


I turned ten that year.
Our new house rose from the raw wood
of a suburb said to have
engaged in a successful skirmish
for the zipcode 01776.
Spring stole up the Sudbury River
as if out of a captivity narrative.
My teacher was Nancy Hanks
(same name as Abraham Lincoln's mother).
My mother was ill, and some days could
not rise from her bed for anguish.

I decided I would become a doctor.
I built model after plastic model.
*The Visible Man* was my favorite.
I loved the rattling treble sound
of the molded parts on their tree
in the box, and how everything fit.
I mixed colors for the nestled viscera,
and on the inside of the body's clear shell,
with a whisker brush and a steady hand,
in red and blue I traced the vascular
system ramifying endlessly:

oh, the breathless grace of it when

the paint did not smudge and clot!

I wanted a title in Latin

for my fifth grade science report.

My mother rallied long enough to improvise

*On the Fabric of the Human Body.*

But he was years in my future, Vesalius,

filleting truth patiently

from the body's desecration

with his bloodstained blade,

and the whimsy with which he laid


out the buskins of muscle dangling

from the knees of an executed criminal

in a meticulous dishevelment on

some imaginary stage set

far from our New England village,

while that flickering ravenous snout

caused the outraged nerves to thrill

as her every attempt at negotiation

succumbed to kidnap and ravage

— for I had no idea, not yet,

that her life was not a containment, but a flaying.

# THE MUSCLES ON THE MUSCLE MAN

Michael Salcman

Think of them as flaming sarcomeres, of wings,
As anything but meat spilled in an abattoir,
Think of them as freed from gravity, from age
From death, from all the ailments angels fear
And run from, from adrenal dystrophy and polio
From myasthenia, from central core disease
From all and anything that stops us on our way,
These mighty agents of movement unspooled,
Their severed tendons hanging like bandages,
Like scarves in the wind or ribbons won
In a race long ago ended, the motors of the body
Gigantic placed in a landscape by Leonardo,
The head turned away in grief at so many secrets
Revealed, hung by a pulley hung from a beam.

## Observing Third and Fourth Dimensions in a Masterpiece

Ian Suk

Dimensions in Art can reveal the true nature and intent of both the artist and the artwork. And the more dimensions the work demonstrates, the deeper the storytelling and levels of thinking the artist can elucidate. The 3rd dimension is length x width x **depth** which gives a volume in 3-D space. The 4th dimension is **time**. Observing 3rd and 4th dimensions is particularly helpful in appreciating a good drawing or artwork.

One of the most striking aspects of Vesalius's images is the absolute sharpness and clarity of the prints themselves. At first glance, they are 2-dimensional line prints that show a voluminous amount of anatomical and scientific knowledge. It is remarkable how crisp and detailed the physical printing is, even compared to today's advanced printing methods.

Nearly five centuries ago, they were created either by cutting into woodblocks or by etching a metal plate surface. They were essentially 3-dimensional relief sculptures. The ink collected in the valleys where the artist (Jan Steven van Calcar) made cuts/etchings, and every single valley made a line when it was pressed against paper or vellum.

What we are seeing, therefore, is a dimensional sculpture of dark lines printed on a flat surface where the artist originally gouged out a deep valley. One marvels at the near impossible precision required by the artist to carve each line. This 3rd dimension is evident in the later editions of Vesalius's prints where, after repeated pressing of the plates, the microscopic crisp edges of the valleys wear out and the printed lines appear visibly softer.

The 4th dimension is time, and the Vesalius prints invite the observer to imagine the colossal amount of time used to dissect this cadaver in a methodical step by step process, but they also make us appreciate the effort required to condense the anatomic information graphically and aesthetically as a teaching tool. Today, the modern medical illustrator expends great effort to compress time—to compress several different steps of surgery or deeper levels of anatomy for a final comprehensive illustration.

Reviewing this Vesalius plate, one can not only see the genius of scientific knowledge required to depict *in situ* details of musculature, splayed out diagrammatically, but one can easily imagine the mental gymnastics required by the artist to simplify, organize and omit information for clarity. Michelangelo famously said "The sculpture is already complete within the marble block, before I start my work. It is already there, I just have to chisel away the superfluous material."

Sculptures obviously live in the 3rd dimension. A 2-dimensional picture of a sculpture does not accurately capture its full aesthetic value. Neither does an original oil painting printed as a photo or an illustration in a magazine. Observing an original oil painting necessarily involves, and is affected by, the given lighting conditions, distance and angle from view, ambient colors in the room, et cet.  One is looking through the numerous collective layers of paint and through light reflected and refracted from each glazed pigment. It is reported that the Mona Lisa has over 27 layers of paint in some areas. The richness of all those translucent layers perceived by human eyes is far superior to seeing even the highest-resolution digital or printed photo. Like a sculpture, a few paces in any direction of the painting changes its physical perception.

I've long wondered what draws people to stare at a masterpiece in a gallery. It's interesting to observe people observing art. Beyond the prosaic curiosity of witnessing such a famous and valuable masterpiece or perhaps academically trying to correlate the artist's history or symbolism or personal emotional evocation, what are people really thinking? Since I am more inclined to technical and procedural challenges, the 4th dimension, **time**, is always at the forefront of my imagination. What are the sequential events that led Vesalius's artist Van Calcar to depict the structures and how did he compress steps for the final comprehensive figure? A mental exercise of imagining how the entire piece was rendered from start to finish whether in a Vesalius or Mona Lisa is a fun way to explore insights and thought processes of the artist. And this chronologic analysis can reveal the deliberate, methodical, genius thinking of the artist/anatomist even centuries after its creation.

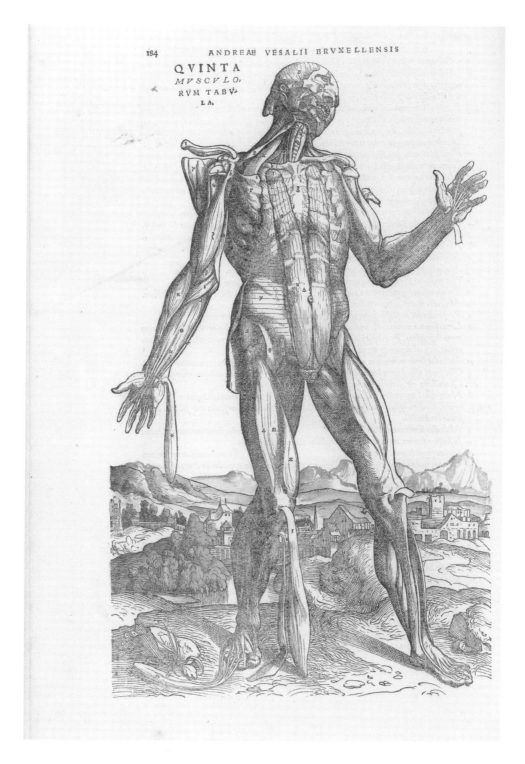

Vesalius, Andreas. *De humani corporis fabrica libri septem.* (Basel: Johannes Oporinus, 1543), page 184. Courtesy of Universitätsbibliothek Basel

# Candid Cadaver

Brian Zink


You have fabricated, Master,
Scarecrows of anatomy,
Road signs of dissection

So each of us,
In the clan of muscle men,
Has our cross to bear,
Death to ponder,
Landscape to memorize

My muscles, once luscious,
Hang loose in the Paduan breeze
Useful perhaps for swatting the flies
Drawn to my decomposition

But all you care is that Galen was bested
As we eternally hold these positions

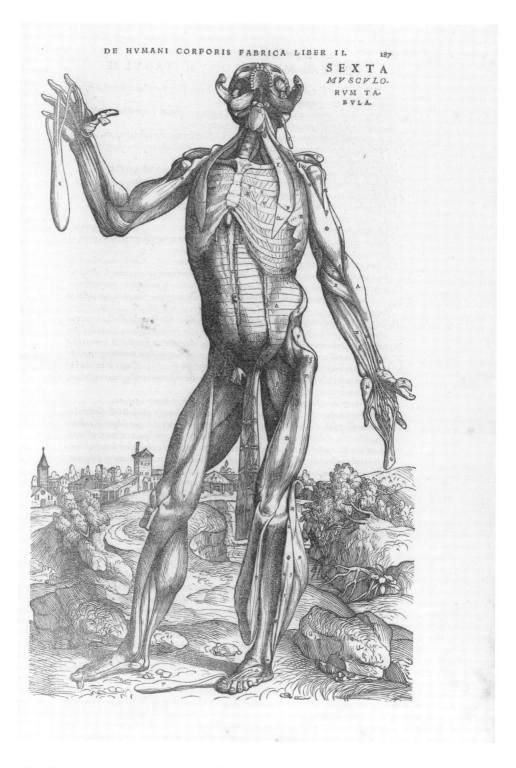

Vesalius, Andreas. *De humani corporis fabrica libri septem.* (Basel: Johannes Oporinus, 1543), page 187. Courtesy of Universitätsbibliothek Basel

# Skinless Figure

Jeffrey Harrison

This one is truly a monster, more frightening
than any creature from mythology,
horror movies, or the imagination
of Max Ernst, and your first impulse
is to quickly turn the page. Instead,
you stare, transfixed by the way his head,
tilted back and sliced into, reveals
a hideous face, lobed with exposed organs,
whose few recognizable features
are incongruously placed: the upper teeth
forming a small Romanesque arch
between the pupil-less walnuts of the eyes,
while the lower teeth and jawbone
have been severed in the middle and
the two halves swiveled out to each side
like the horned mandibles of an insect.

You might take him for a torture victim,
his skin flayed away to the raw muscle
that braids his limbs or hangs in meaty flaps
or, between the legs, the long veined sash
that must be the penis unfurled.
Yet his stance is open, almost casual,
not clenched in pain or crouching to hide
from that quaint village in the background…
so that his raised right hand
(a fleshy pendant dangling from the fingers
by four tentacles, like a limp squid
or cat's cradle of muscle gone slack)
begins to seem less a gesture of sad dismay
than a friendly wave hello or good-bye—
and you feel the muscles in your own hand
flexing themselves to wave back.

## Proud Flesh

Peter Pereira

Largest organ in the human body, our skin
sketches a map so large it cannot fit upon
a single page. From grooved philtrum
crowning the upper lip, to the soft creases
behind each ear, gently stroked by a fingertip's
swirling gyri. From smooth rolling
dunes of breast, buttock and thigh, to the umbi's
lake eye, scrotal raphe, purple labial wings.
So much a part of us, we imagine it *is* us —
knitted forehead, raised eyebrow, crow's foot,
crooked smile. Every nick and bruise, wrinkle
and scar. Each port wine stain, *café au lait* spot,
freckle or nevus. From soul patch, wattle, dowager's
hump, to calloused heel, ticklish toe-web, swollen
ankle — a bag big enough to hold us together,
contain us. Elastic enough, tough enough
to carry us through our days, this self-sealing,
self-healing, sling. Where our travels
become imprinted and old wounds show
clearly as words written upon a page.

# INVITATION TO EKPHRASIS

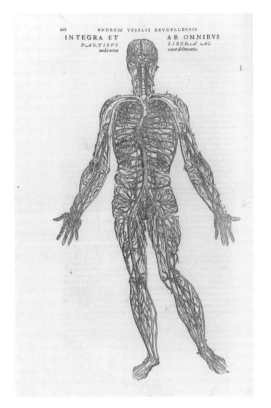

Vesalius, Andreas. *De humani corporis fabrica libri septem.*
(Basel: Johannes Oporinus, 1543), page 268 [368].

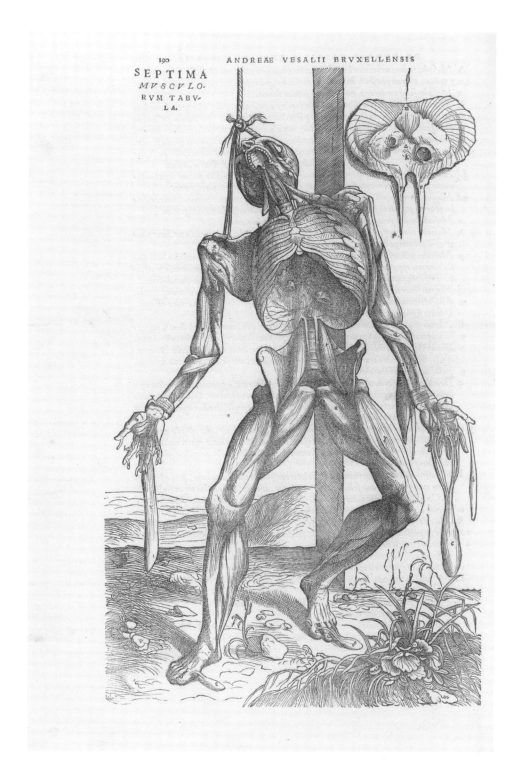

Vesalius, Andreas. *De humani corporis fabrica libri septem*. (Basel: Johannes Oporinus, 1543), page 190. Courtesy of Universitätsbibliothek Basel

# Twice Hanged

Richard M. Ratzan

The man Vincenzo paid for me to kill
That he might keep the dead man's loving wife
Was but the half of two, a double life.
I did not know his mirrored brother 'til
I plunged my knife into the wrong twin's breath
Then heard the wife with sobs my error cry.
To claim my fee the true twin had to die
As well. Two brothers stabbed, a double death.
The trial was short, the shame was long, but not
As long as sturdy rope with sturdier knot
Placed firmly 'round my neck: I dropped. I died.
I am now hanged again, this time from hooks,
The better for Vesalius inside
To probe: my second life is now in books.

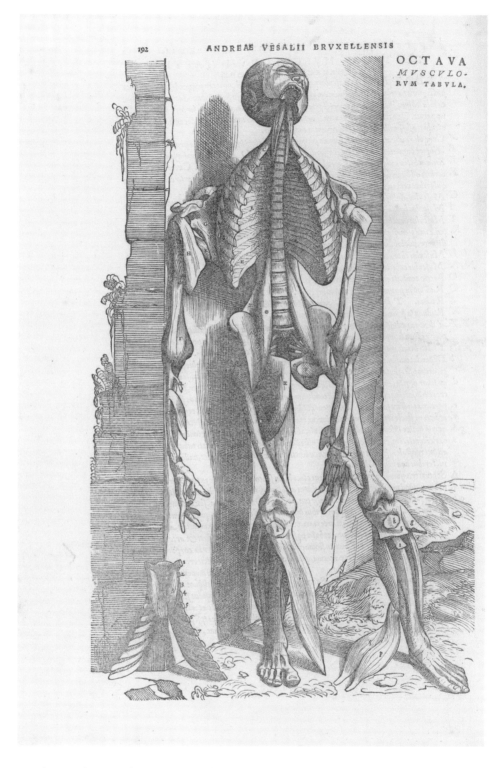

Vesalius, Andreas. *De humani corporis fabrica libri septem.* (Basel: Johannes Oporinus, 1543), page 192. Courtesy of Universitätsbibliothek Basel

# Anatta

Rosalyn Driscoll

*Anatta*, 2010, Steel, glass, rawhide, 80" x 38" x 37"

Vesalius, Andreas. *De humani corporis fabrica libri septem.* (Basel: Johannes Oporinus, 1543), page 200. Courtesy of Universitätsbibliothek Basel

# Last Words of Saint Anthony of Padua

Margaret Lloyd


I lift my arm over the city I love.
Do not look away. The world left me
breathless and I can no longer live.

I have come, Padua, to say goodbye.
Goodbye to the sleek fish and the river lilies,
goodbye to the hills rocking in their green sea.

Goodbye to the castles, the clear air that binds us.
One more shining day and one more night
to find what you have lost. Now I am skinless

while bells in their towers ring, ring, and the light
reveals how life has shaped my toiling muscles,
sailing in penance, working my way back

in late spring to the start of my last loss.
Muscles change, then skin begins forming
growth around them.  All the world is flesh

of the God I walk in each early morning,
praying, praising, longing. Do not leave.
Listen. My tongue is for you and it is singing.

God is crying within. You can believe
in the attention of rushing water, touch of pardon,
shelter of walnut trees in your grief.

See the white stars in your hidden garden.
Closed like small hands in prayer all day,
blooming in night under the one heaven.

I am tired of separation.  I make my way
seized and fasting in my last earthly grip.
My palms face you. Look at me today.

## The Physical Exam as a Work of Art

(adapted from the unpublished novel NIKKI)
L.J. Schneiderman

Now, after so many hundreds, perhaps even thousands, of patients, after so much practice, I take pride in having mastered not only the weapons of high technology but the simplest skills as well, my own bodily senses, whose exercise gave me a particular aesthetic pleasure. Here too I fancy myself a kind of performance artist, having brought to a high polish a pattern of actions involving eyes and ears and hands and even my nose, integrating them with a kind of athletic, musical grace. Like a slow-motion tumbling dive, a figure-skating routine, a drive to the hoop, although for me it is more like surfing, an almost sensual meeting of two bodies. I enter a patient with a kind of flowing movement, the way I enter an oncoming wave.

First I have them reach toward me with their hands. I look for tremor, weakness, drift, scan the fingernails, the palms, the arms, searching for odd marks and discolorations, meanwhile slipping my hands over both wrists to take note of the pulses, then up to the elbows, pressing the pulses there as well, lymph nodes, checking the rough patch of skin, then up over the shoulders to the neck – trachea mid-line, both carotids pulsing, no swollen lymph nodes there either – then up to the skull, through the hair, around the ears, my fingers sweeping along the surface, alert as a safecracker to odd clicks and interruptions.

Then in unbroken motion to my instruments – the ophthalmoscope and otoscope and tongue blade – and into the ears, the eyes, the nose, the mouth, my face right up against theirs, my nostrils sniffing – this is when I spot the closet alcoholic.

Then I move behind the patient, my fingers again skimming the surface of the body, comparing its minutest variations to categories common to all human bodies, assessing its normal range of humanness, caressing, feeling for lumps, textures, asymmetries, awaiting the unexpected jolt that will violate the ordinary and announce something interesting, pressing the thyroid, penetrating the little craters behind the clavicles.

Then to the chest, percussing the ribbed keyboard with a high-prancing staccato clarity modeled after my guru in these matters, Glenn Gould, then out with the stethoscope and into my ears, my eyes meanwhile checking the shapes, swellings and contractions of breathing: In. Out. In again. Out again. Upper lobes, lower lobes, right middle lobe. Down stethoscope, but let it hang. Gently punch over the kidneys (Does that hurt?). Then down the spine (Does that hurt?). Then to the front, patient down: Check the breasts, treading flat-fingeredly across them, tamping them down while feeling for lumps all the way to the armpits, then pause where the heart strikes the ribs. Then up stethoscope again and listen: systole, diastole, the valves, the arteries in the neck, down stethoscope and check the arteries in the legs and feet (All peripheral pulses palpable).

Then to the abdomen, listening and probing, then to the genitalia, the joints, the reflexes, and finally the last deepest and most moist intimacy, the patient, submissive now, even presenting, not forgetting to hand the patient the box of Kleenex to wipe himself of the KY jelly. Or if it's a woman, the nurse is called and the pelvic and rectal are done together.

All of this achieved as I take pleasure in observing myself, the practiced, supple, sweeping grace of my hands and fingertips, as though I were a connoisseur savoring a Brancusi statue, my hands transformed into a mobile work of art by another work of art. All of it had become a deeply satisfying routine, the way I imagine the best of lovemaking to be − sensual and seamless, familiar yet stirring, enjoying one's animate self as well as the other. Until I know the patient's body in a matter of minutes the way I get to know a wave − with that consummation of sense and spirit, a less ecstatic, but no less pleasurable slide through the fleshy texture of another surf.

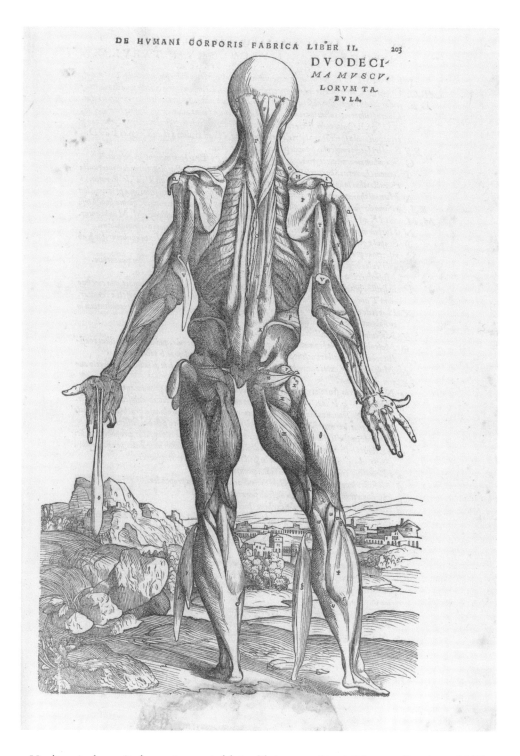

Vesalius, Andreas. *De humani corporis fabrica libri septem*. (Basel: Johannes Oporinus, 1543), page 203. Courtesy of Universitätsbibliothek Basel

## SURGERY

Rafael Campo

After they handed out our new white coats,
which during the solemn ceremony
in the wood-paneled auditorium
made me feel less innocent as I pulled
on mine, they took us down to the basement.
They called it the anatomy lab, but
to me it seemed more like just a morgue, white
floor tiles, white fluorescent lights, white bodies
wrapped in plastic sheets.  I thought briefly of
Casper the Friendly Ghost, but I knew
this was medical school now and they were
cadavers, not people, and certainly
not benevolent spirits.  On the walls
huge prints of those famous Vesalius
drawings writhed, dissected human bodies.
Back then, I thought I'd become a surgeon,
eager to wound others to make healing
possible.  I gaped up at them blankly,
saw they weren't all drawn from the same body,
and yet they were in the profoundest sense
the same body.  They all wore their muscles
like rags, yet their poses suggested
not poverty, but aspiration.  My
white coat became a disguise, hanging on
me like loose skin.  They were criminals and
beggars, dead for centuries, yet how they

lived, how they must have suffered but were

deprived of rest – and still, how they opened

themselves to us, to our disgusted awe.

One in particular beguiled me,

unnamed except for the designation

*DUODECIMA Musculorum*, his back

to us, caught in the act of putting his

hands up, as if he wished to demonstrate

not the flayed fibers of his existence,

through which we could see the guilty white day,

but instead cooperation, the pain of

the impossibility of escape.

## LANDSCAPE GLIMPSED

Terry Donsen Feder

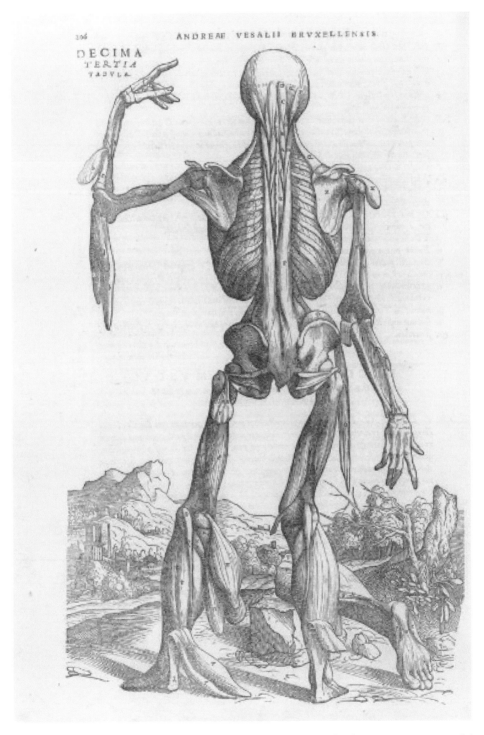

Vesalius, Andreas. *De humani corporis fabrica libri septem.* (Basel: Johannes Oporinus, 1543),
page 206. Courtesy of Universitätsbibliothek Basel

Landscape Glimpsed through Limbs

Watercolor 9 $^1/_4$" x 6"

Landscape Glimpsed through Limbs on Closer Examination

Watercolor, 7" x 4 ³/₄"

DE HVMANI CORPORIS FABRICA LIBER II.   235
237

## DE INSTRVMENTIS, QVAE SECTIONI-
bus adminiſtrandis parari poſſunt.   Caput *VII.*

### ANATOMICORVM INSTRVMEN-
TORVM DELINEATIO.

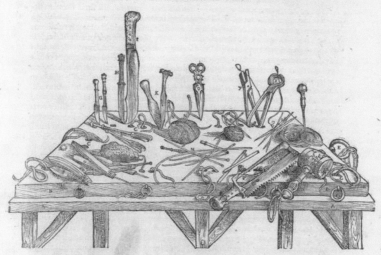

CHARACTERVM SEPTIMI CAPITIS FIGVRAE INDEX.

PRAESENTI *figura menſæ cuidam incumbentem finximus aſſerem, quo in ut uorum ſectionibus opportunè utimur, dein huic aſſeri omnia propemodum accōmodauimus, quibus in diſſectionum adminiſtrationibus, adeoꝗ tota Anatome quis poſſet uti. Quo autem ſingula leuiori opera aſſequaris, huic etiam figuræ characteres, ac demum eorum indicem adhibere non grauatus ſum.   Indicetur itaꝗ*

A,A  *Menſa, cui reliqua omnia modò ſeriatim indicanda ſuperſternuntur.*
B,B  *Aſſer uiuis ſectionibus adminiſtrandis idoneus.*
C,C  *Varia foramina, quibus laqueos pro animalis mole adhibemus, quſi femora et brachia uincimus.*
D,D  *Eiuſmodi anuli, ſummis manibus pedibuſꝗ ligandis adaptantur.*
   E  *Huic anulo maxilla ſuperior, libera inferiori, catenula alligatur, ut caput immotum ſeruetur, ac interim neꝗ uox, neꝗ reſpiratio uinculorum occaſione præpediantur.*
F,F  *Diuerſa nouacularum genera, quibus ſpongia accumbit.*
   G  *Cultelli ad earum ſpeciem formati, quibus calami adaptantur.*
   H  *Vulgaris qui menſæ adhibetur culter.*          I.  *Grandis ac ualidus culter.*
   K  *Cultri è buxo parati.*          L  *Hamuli.*          M  *Varij ſtyli una cum ſiphone.*
N,N  *Obliquatæ acus cum filo craſſiore, quibus literarum faſciculos colligamus.*
   n  *Minores acus, quas uulneribus ſuendis accommodamus.*
   O  *Serra.*          P  *Forficula.*          Q  *Malleus ligneus.*
   R  *Arundines inflandis pulmonibus, & alijs quibuſdam partibus idoneæ.*
   S  *Filum æncum, oſſibus nectendis aptum.*          T  *Subula forandis oſſibus parata.*
V  *Varia ſubularum ferra.*          X  *Forpex intorquendis filorum extremis comparatus.*
Y  *Forpex, quo intorti, & oſſa iam committentis fili reliquias præſcindimus.*

V  4          QVAN-

Vesalius, Andreas. *De humani corporis fabrica libri septem*. (Basel: Johannes Oporinus, 1543), page 237[235]. Courtesy of Universitätsbibliothek Basel

# ANATOMY AT THE DINNER TABLE

Leslie Adrienne Miller

Vesalius advises us to notice as we pluck
at table the cooked meat from the neck
of a calf, piglet or kid, the yellow ligament
so tough it's offered only to dogs.
The only ligament in the body unfit
for human consumption, it's offered
he says, in Brussels to young girls
because its pale yellow color is not
unlike the color they desire in their hair,
and the ligament itself diffuses its fine
strands into other parts of the body.
Not unusual then, to recommend
that one eat what one desires to wear
in the flesh, Beauty, we suppose,
being its own invitation to a meal.

## INVITATION TO EKPHRASIS

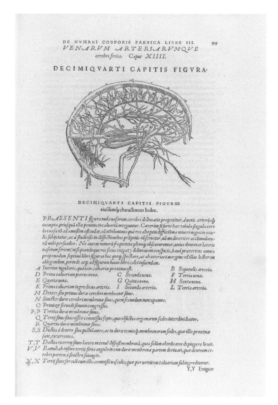

Vesalius, Andreas. *De humani corporis fabrica libri septem.*
(Basel: Johannes Oporinus, 1543), page 305 [405].

# Book III

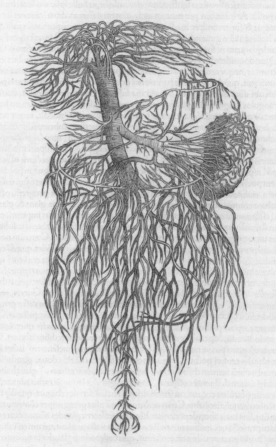

262        ANDREAE VESALII BRVXELLENSIS
*VENÆ PORTÆ ORTVS, IPSIVSQVE*
*propaginum series. Caput V.*

## VENAE PORTAE AB VNIVERSIS QVI-
BVS COMMITTITVR PARTIBVS LIBERAE, INTEGRA
delineatio, in ea proportione expreſſa, ad quam ſecundùm præſentem figuram aliquis iecur, bilis ueſiculam, uentriculum, lienem, omen
tum, meſenterium & inteſtina ex illorum magnitudi
ne, ac inſuper in ſuo ſitu depingeret.

NVDAE VENAE PORTAE DELINEATIONIS
characterum Index.

*A, A etc.*     QVINQVE *his characteribus portæ uenæ propagines indicantur, per iecoris*
*corpus diffuſæ, & hic ueluti iecoris formam ſecundùm cauam ipſius ſedem exprimentes.*
*1, 2, 3, 4, 5  Numerus iſte quinq; portæ uenæ ramos (niſi ſubinde etiã pauciores ſint) notat, ex quibus ipſius*
*caudex quodãmodo proximè cõſtituitur, aut in quos is primùm in iecoris ſubſtantiam digeritur.*
Venæ

Vesalius, Andreas. *De humani corporis fabrica libri septem.* (Basel: Johannes Oporinus, 1543),
page 262 [362]. Courtesy of Universitätsbibliothek Basel

## BEHIND THE CURTAIN

Jack Coulehan

A swamp of roots hangs down
from the manicured tree in the sky
to shield its solar plexus
from the eye.

Floating with infinite grace,
a jelly Medusa buds a clone
while it waits to digest
what floats in.

The map I sketched at sixteen
of Delaney's Cave
multiplied and turned
into a maze.

If every pathway led me home
to a central vein, where I'd
be shorn of my burdens
and made clean,

I'd step behind the curtain
into a secret room.

## self-portrait as a baby

Irène Mathieu

if lifted from the body
the belly's veins resemble
mangroves: equatorial thicket of spleen,
wrought biliary root like sappy filigree –
half water or blood,
half pillow-shaped sponge.

if I press my finger to a baby's
pulse while she writhes and
pitches toward mother
I am testing her like a compass,
and all the iron in her body
floods northward.

if eighteen years later
she is found maneuvering
backwater tributaries
without a paddle, call her
brackish wanderer,
call her lost in blood.

if her age quintuples
but her liver remains the
same, say she has a
lucky swamp inside.
*what do you carry? what do you carry?*
my hands ask the baby's skin.

every vein ferrying something, every
child hurrying through the swamp
with what will kill her
tucked under her stomach.
arms wrapped around my own trunk
I cannot see through water this murky.

*look anyway*, I tell her. the baby
holds a mirror to my face.
      the silt thins.
at the bottom something gleams.

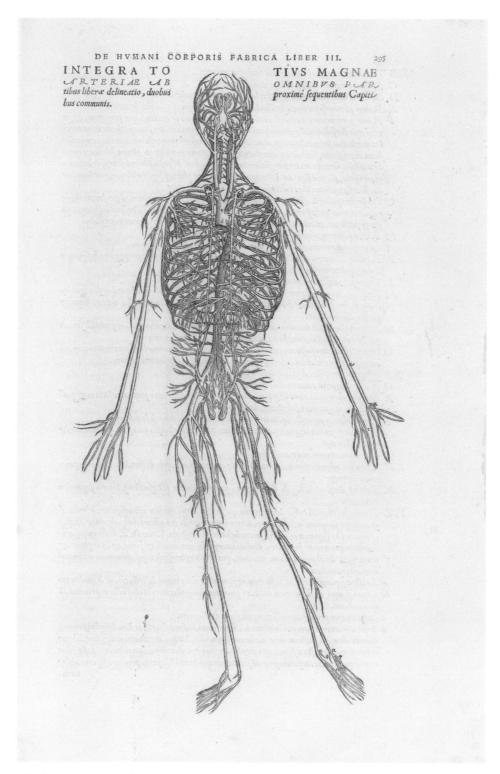

DE HVMANI CORPORIS FABRICA LIBER III.    *295*

INTEGRA TO                              TIVS MAGNAE
*ARTERIAE AB*                          *OMNIBVS PAR*
*tibus liberæ delineatio, duobus*       *proximè sequentibus Capiti*
*bus communis.*

Vesalius, Andreas. *De humani corporis fabrica libri septem.* (Basel: Johannes Oporinus, 1543),
page 295 [395]. Courtesy of Universitätsbibliothek Basel

## BONE HOUSE

**bone house** *n.* *(a) the human body; (b) a building or vault in which the bones of the dead are placed, a charnel house.*

Christine Montross

The day my son asks how many blood vessels
        we have in our bodies is the day
my patient shouts at me that he knows

        his deep vein thromboses will paralyze him.
*A stroke killed my father,*
        the deluded man says when I try

to explain that there is no anatomic pathway
        by which a venous clot could travel to his brain.
*If you don't send me out*

        *of this effing psych ward to a real*
*emergency room then I'll break the doors down*
        *to get there.* In both moments −

        in my son's earnest inquiry and my patient's
fury and fear − my mind conjures
        the beautiful Vesalius woodcuts in which so many vessels

        dive and circumambulate.
*Profundii*, I want to say to both of them
        for the sheer beauty of the names.

*Circumflex. Saphenous.* Instead, once home I pull
        my weighty reproduction of the *Fabrica* off the shelf.
Flip pages until I find the drawings of the faceless man

who nonetheless faces us, arms spread with vigor and audacity
in equal measure.  Palms held outward – toward us really –
        as if to say, *Do you see now what is within?*

My son traces the woodcut's lines, asks over
        and over again:  *What happens if this one gets cut?*
pointing first to the tiniest, most distal vessels

        and then to their wider, more critical origins. *Band-aid,*
I say at first.  Then: *stitches,* as he works
        his way upstream.  When he points to the aorta

with its lovely, looping arch I cannot bring myself
        to say the word which is the answer:
*catastrophe.*

        I know, in truth, what they both ask of me,
my son and my patient.  Both seek
        reassurance of their safety.  Both want the lie

that the vascular man with his jaunty stance
        is peddling: that life persists,
that animation does, and spirit.

        That our bodies, too, are mere vessels;
superfluous receptacles which hold some formless essence
        of the self, unlocatable, unable to be laid bare

even by Vesalius, that relentless master.
        They reach – my patient and my boy –
for the same elusive hope that I do –

        that despite these mortal frames
we exist somehow, in some form, with permanence,
        impervious to clot and wound.

# BOOK IV

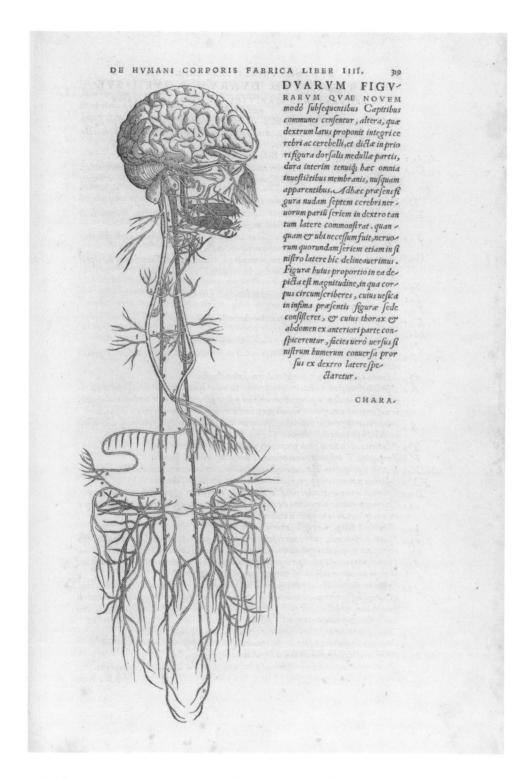

DE HVMANI CORPORIS FABRICA LIBER IIII.   319

**DVARVM FIGV-**
RARVM QVAE NOVEM
modó ſubſequentibus Capitibus
communes cenſentur, altera, quæ
dextrum latus proponit integri ce
rebri ac cerebelli, et dictæ in prio
ri figura dorſalis medullæ partis,
dura interim tenuiſ hæc omnia
inueſtictibus membranis, nuſquam
apparentibus. Adhæc præſens fi
gura nudam ſeptem cerebri ner-
uorum pariū ſeriem in dextro tan
tum latere commonſtrat. quanquam & ubi neceſſum fuit, neruo-
rum quorundam ſeriem etiam in ſi
niſtro latere híc delineauerimus.
Figuræ huius proportio in ea de-
picta eſt magnitudine, in qua corpus circumſcriberes, cuius ueſica
in infima præſentis figuræ ſede
conſiſteret, & cuius thorax &
abdomen ex anteriori parte con-
ſpicerentur, facies ueró uerſus ſi
niſtrum humerum conuerſa pror
ſus ex dextro latere ſpe-
ctaretur.

CHARA.

Vesalius, Andreas. *De humani corporis fabrica libri septem.* (Basel: Johannes Oporinus, 1543), page 319 [419]. Courtesy of Universitätsbibliothek Basel

# FLOATING FIGURE

Jim Finnegan


I float through space, these streets,
dragging a net of nerves beneath me.
Things may be caught up, entangled
in these strands, but I know not what.

I feel everything yet I'm incapable
of the kind of sense that apprehends,
that holds and realizes: experience.
What I touch I immediately forget.

Passing a stranger, or someone who once
knew me, I'm a puppet dragging its strings,
let loose in the world. He brushes by me,
a slight tingle, an infiltrating breeze.

## The Nerve Center

Danielle Ofri

"Oh, Oh, Oh, To Touch and Feel a Guy's Vas deferens Sometimes Helps." This was the mnemonic we used in anatomy class to memorize the twelve cranial nerves (and to counter the more prevalent version that referred to a woman's genitalia). This was also the first thing that popped into my mind when I gazed at Vesalius's rendering of the nervous system. It starts with the brain and cranial nerves on top and reaches downward, pretty much to the vas deferens.

Seeing the nervous system entirely disembodied is revelatory. While we typically envision the brain as a palpable whole, the spidery latticework of nerves is a more ephemeral affair. At best the nerves come across as limp linguini, flopping languidly over whatever bone, muscle or organ offers a convenient landing pad.

Vesalius's version offers heft and independence to these humble nerves. The nerves stand on their own two feet, as it were, rightly illuminating their commanding role of the body.

What I love about this particular view is that it dispenses with the thorax and the limbs. Vesalius has other drawings depicting the nerve supply to these parts but for this particular figure I imagine him shrugging off the thorax as mere scaffolding, and the arms as mere mechanical tools. The real meat of the human enterprise – Vesalius might be saying – is the face, the gut and the groin.  This is where the action is, and it is the nerves that corral these three regions into intimate acquaintance and action.

The face – our interpreter and communicator for the outside world – is a hotbed of nerves. Like a great Oz, the brain sits right behind the face jiggering and rejiggering facial expressions. It soaks up the sights, sounds, and tastes, and oh oh oh those smells. (The aquiline nose depicted by Vesalius is particularly enriched with nerves.)

As Vesalius shows us, these senses, emotions, and expressions are knitted inextricably with the machinations of the abdomen and pelvis. Direct neural highways run north and south, ensuring that our gut feelings do indeed hurtle from our gut to our brain, that butterflies invade our stomachs when we feel skittish and that nerve-wracking situations send us scrambling to the bathroom.

Vesalius's drawing affirms the primacy and vigor of the nervous system. Even with the numerous inaccuracies modern anatomists have pointed out, it's clear that Vesalius got the basic construct correct. Thoughts, emotions, and feelings may swirl in our heads, but they dwell in the pit of our stomach. Sensory input may be processed north of our neck, but the reactions erupt from our gut. Without such connections between the emotional and the physical (and the resultant fountain of literary metaphor thus available) our lives would be dull mechanistic transactions. And legions of poets would likely end up employed as accountants.

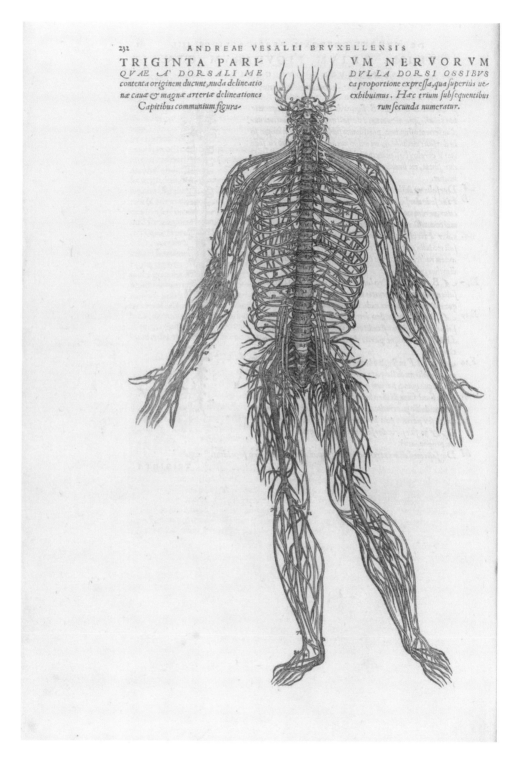

Vesalius, Andreas. *De humani corporis fabrica libri septem*. (Basel: Johannes Oporinus, 1543),
page 232 [432]. Courtesy of Universitätsbibliothek Basel

## PLATE 50: TO A NAKED DELINEATION OF THE THIRTY PAIRS OF NERVES

Jessica Greenbaum

Standing before us with arms out to the side
as if illustrating the length
— *About this long* —
of your whopper of a fish,
and one knee lightly bent
as if shifting weight
because you've been there for some time.
*What can I do*, your stance might ask,
*I've nothing more to offer*
*than these thirty pairs of nerves,*
your posture calm as if to dowse a spat,
*It's only me, and all I've got.*
As for your vines of nerves
their frilly ends could be an ocean plant
that flutters to mere whispers
of the tides, and from up close
are not unlike these penciled
lines that wave and sway with hopes
our alphabet might register the touch of life —
But let's get back to you
and the argument you're in;
those nerves that fit around
your absent skull
poised like an open setting for a ring
without its gem, they also bring
short flames to mind, while you
still at a cordial tilt continue
your entreaty: *I'm so sorry*
*if I lost my head and hit a nerve — ha ha —*
*but dear, come now; if you'll*
*forgive me we can do the wild*
*math that adds us up to sixty.*

# INVITATION TO EKPHRASIS

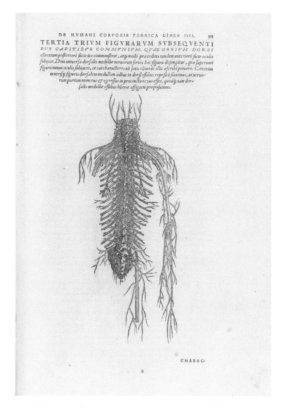

Vesalius, Andreas. *De humani corporis fabrica libri septem.*
(Basel: Johannes Oporinus, 1543), page 333 [433].

# BOOK V

M,M *Glandulæ uaforum diftributionibus interiectæ, quæ uafa in ipfo per mefenterium ad inteftina moliuntur progreffu.*

## VNDECIMA QVINTI LIBRI
### FIGVRA.

VNDECIMAE FIGVRAE EIVSDEM´QVE CHA-
racterum Index.

H I C *duntaxat ipfum delineatur mefenterium è corpore exemptum, omnibus q partibus ipfi connatis liberum, præterquam ab inferioris membranæ omenti portione, qua colon dorfo inibi colligatur, ubi fecundum inferiorem uentriculi fedem id procedit.*

K *Character K, ut & in decima figura, mefenterij indicat centrum.*

L,L *Hi quoque characteres fimiliter atque in decima, glandulofum corpus notant, totius mefenterij maximum.*

M,M *Glandulæ notantur illis interpofitæ uaforum diffectionibus, quæ iam inteftinis appropinquant.*

N,O *His characteribus mefenterij circumfcribitur pars tenuia inteftina dorfo alligans.*

P *P ad Q ufq mefenterij indicat portionem, colon inteftinum dorfo affirmantem, qua id à dextri renis fede ad cauum ufq iecoris protenditur.*

Q *Q ad R ufq inferioris omenti membranæ partem notat, quæ colon tota illa fede dorfo commit tit, quà id fecundum uentriculi exporrigitur fundum.*

R *R ad S ufq mefenterij infinuat portionem colo inteftino tota ea fede propriam, qua id à lienis regione ad rectum ufq inteftinum pertinet.*

S,T *Quod S & T intercluditur, mefenterij pars eft rectum inteftinum dorfo nectens.*

V *Hac fede mefenterij naturam exprimere conati fumus, quandoquidem unam mefenterij mem-*

X,Y. *branam ab altera unguibus diuulfam pinximus: ut X nimirum una fit, altera uerò Y infcriba- tur. Atq in harum membranarum medio mefenterij uafa excurrunt, & ipfius adeps, ut & glã dulæ etiam continentur, quemadmodum quoq in uigefima quarta huius libri figura eft cernere.*

DVO.

Vesalius, Andreas. *De humani corporis fabrica libri septem.* (Basel: Johannes Oporinus, 1543), page 364 [464]. Courtesy of Universitätsbibliothek Basel

# To dissect

et.stark

·to dissect:

    i.      Vivisection is the unraveling of live matter. To bisect is
to·separate.
          Conscientiously the devotion of time to separating a skull and
          witness of

          the compartmentalization of that which remains,
becomes:
a life goal.

          The righteous is only·righteous in
          retrospect.

          Nothing that has come to pass will come
up·again.
Claim an eye to·something.
          There is vitreous fluid, a benign sample of
          the·vilified.

i.

So many bodies come to represent the progress of what is ill·defined
within a sphere of:
craniotomy contains the potential·to adjust.

          ii.     Split the dermis.
          Form a subcutaneous understanding of:
          what should·be·there.

          Stand simple,
          I have created a cavern of what is hands·off.
               The adjustment of features comes solely from
               an understanding of what has come·to·pass
               off.

          So we rob graves.
          So we violate the inviolate.
               Anatomy is so much more·than:
               taking what is·not·yours.

ii.

          Viscerally speaking a synapse is a microcosm
          version of taking letters as letters
          to·and·from:
          bodies.

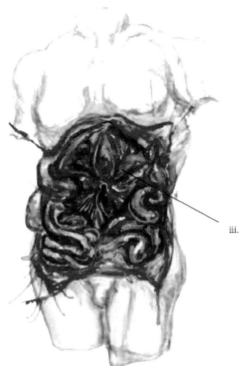

iii.

iii.    Let's question the ethics of what it means
to-steal,
take it upon-ourselves to capture:
the value of a human-being.

       Flesh-and-bone does not exist without inaction
       but is crafted by the active shapes of something
       that becomes dead-over-life,
like an egg or:

       a venous structure that claims color
       where there used-to-be
       none.

The illustration of a letter does not contain:
From-or-to-

# INVITATION TO EKPHRASIS

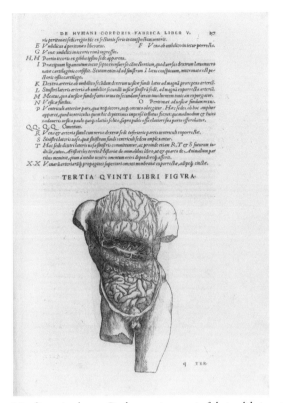

Vesalius, Andreas. *De humani corporis fabrica libri septem.*
(Basel: Johannes Oporinus, 1543), page 357 [457].

DE HVMANI CORPORIS FABRICA LIBER V.    365

## DVODECIMA QVINTI LIBRI FIGVRA, QVAE

*IAM PRAEPOSITIS INTEGRIS FIGVRIS SECTIO-
nis serie succedit. Habet enim dissectū peritonæum, & omentum quoq; in hac ablatū est, & hic
costas aliquot etiã effregimus, quō iecoris cauū opportunius delineari posset. Hic namq; conspicitur uniuersum iecoris cauū, ipsusq; iecoris forma. Dein uĕtriculi quoq; apparĕt orificia. Inte-
stina autĕ perinde ac uentriculū in sinistrū latus depressimus, ut in cōspectu esset mesenterij pars,
ac uenæ portæ in ipsum series: dein bilis meatus in intestinū insertio, et si quæ sint reliqua quæ characteribus seriatim adnotabimus, mox atq; quid decima tertia ostendat figura, expresserimus.*

## DECIMATERTIA QVINTI LIBRI FIGVRA,
*NVDAM BILIS VESICVLAE EIVSDEMQVE
meatuum delineationem exprimens.*

CHA

Vesalius, Andreas. *De humani corporis fabrica libri septem*. (Basel: Johannes Oporinus, 1543),
page 365 [465]. Courtesy of Universitätsbibliothek Basel

# The Body Contains.

*Noah Ratzan*

But what?
The pulse it plays,
But curious minds,
never content,
cast a form.

In the hall, he sharpens his tools.
There, muscles bound in marbled white.
There his pen, his ink, his knife.
There, the apprentice lingers.
"Hold the light." and he lingers.

His fingertips search the page,
the sculpted corpus
And reflections of his mind,
For the thread that binds the body

But at last he plunges
into the white pulse where it beats
like a drum at the surface.

And what of it? On the inside?
Worlds - unfolding, falling, spilling
out onto the page.

What of it... and a pen searches.
Where to begin?

How do you contain an orgy? A feast of viscera?
A pulse without a source?

But the pen distills,
drawing the innards
into the cagey torso
from where they sprang

And he crafts them into a cornucopia
there on the table, held up long enough
for the ink to dry,

before it spills again -       lost       pulse     from
                                      the
                          to                    the
                                 it     life
                                                   pretends
                              spring     to          from

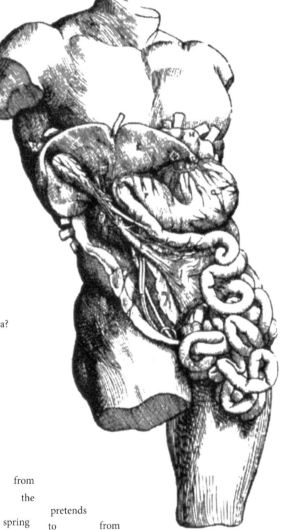

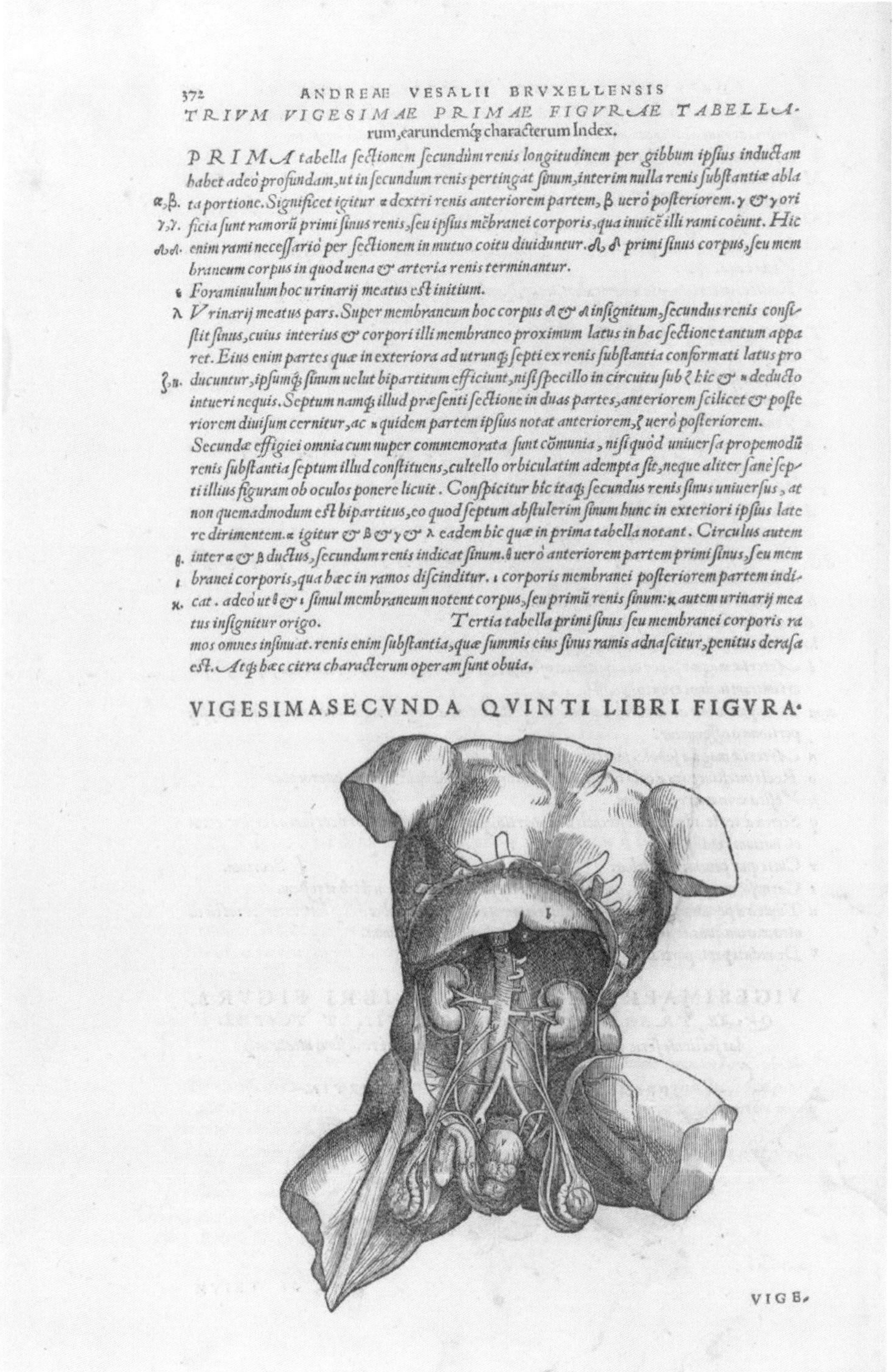

372 ANDREAE VESALII BRVXELLENSIS

TRIVM VIGESIMAE PRIMAE FIGVRAE TABELLArum, earundemque characterum Index.

*PRIMA tabella sectionem secundùm renis longitudinem per gibbum ipsius inductam habet adeò profundam, ut in secundum renis pertingat sinum, interim nulla renis substantiae abla-*
α, β. *ta portione. Significet igitur α dextri renis anteriorem partem, β uerò posteriorem. γ & γ ori-*
γ, γ. *ficia sunt ramorũ primi sinus renis, seu ipsius mẽbranei corporis, qua inuicẽ illi rami coëunt. Hic*
δ, δ. *enim rami necessariò per sectionem in mutuo coitu diuiduntur. δ, δ primi sinus corpus, seu membraneum corpus in quod uena & arteria renis terminantur.*
ε *Foraminulum hoc urinarij meatus est initium.*
λ *Vrinarij meatus pars. Super membraneum hoc corpus δ & δ insignitum, secundus renis consistit sinus, cuius interius & corpori illi membraneo proximum latus in hac sectione tantum apparet. Eius enim partes quae in exteriora ad utrunque septi ex renis substantia conformati latus pro-*
ζ, η. *ducuntur, ipsumque sinum uelut bipartitum efficiunt, nisi specillo in circuitu sub ζ hic & η deducto intueri nequis. Septum namque illud praesenti sectione in duas partes, anteriorem scilicet & posteriorem diuisum cernitur, ac η quidem partem ipsius notat anteriorem, ζ uerò posteriorem.*
*Secundae effigiei omnia cum nuper commemorata sunt cõmunia, nisi quòd uniuersa propemodũ renis substantia septum illud constituens, cultello orbiculatim adempta sit, neque aliter sanè septi illius figuram ob oculos ponere licuit. Conspicitur hic itaque secundus renis sinus uniuersus, at non quemadmodum est bipartitus, eo quod septum abstulerim sinum hunc in exteriori ipsius latere dirimentem. α igitur & β & γ & λ eadem hic quae in prima tabella notant. Circulus autem*
θ. *inter α & β ductus, secundum renis indicat sinum. θ uerò anteriorem partem primi sinus, seu mem-*
ι *branei corporis, qua haec in ramos discinditur. ι corporis membranei posteriorem partem indi-*
κ. *cat. adeò ut θ & ι simul membraneum notent corpus, seu primũ renis sinum: κ autem urinarij meatus insignitur origo.* *Tertia tabella primi sinus seu membranei corporis ramos omnes insinuat. renis enim substantia, quae summis eius sinus ramis adnascitur, penitus derasa est. Atque haec citra characterum operam sunt obuia.*

VIGESIMASECVNDA QVINTI LIBRI FIGVRA.

VIGE.

Vesalius, Andreas. *De humani corporis fabrica libri septem*. (Basel: Johannes Oporinus, 1543), page 372 [472]. Courtesy of Universitätsbibliothek Basel

ANATOMY LESSONS

David Hellerstein, MD

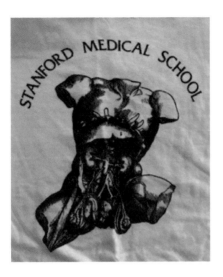

As first year med students, we struggled with scissors, scalpel, forceps, probes, the tools of nascent physicians. For a year, several hours per week, we hovered over our corpses, cautiously slicing and probing, recapitulating Vesalius's great work from centuries earlier, though we inhaled formalin instead of the stench of putrefaction. With awe, respect, fear and irreverence, we sliced the fabric of human flesh for the first time.

Vesalius's corpses were often stolen from cemeteries, or from the gallows mound at Montfaucon in Paris, 'where he once had to run for his life from a pack of wild dogs' – and included hanged prostitutes, suicides, executed prisoners, a stonemason fallen to his death, a beheaded man, a murdered woman. Ours, at Stanford Medical School in northern California in the 1970s, were donated – from elderly heart patients still bearing traces of unsuccessful surgeries, to old women with large abdominal tumors, to a small red-headed boy with no evident cause of death.

Perhaps it is no coincidence that the graphics of our med school T-shirt paid tribute to our great, long-dead teacher. First year, our blue freshman year T-shirt showed a skeleton, standing pensively at a stone pediment on which rested a skull, evocative of *Hamlet*. Our next year's T was blatant and provocative: a male cadaver, limbs chopped away and abdomen sliced wide open, testicles flung aside, baring its innards to every passerby. On sober reflection, we realized that the engraving depicted the urinary tract with the uncanny accuracy of first discovery – ureters, bladder and urethra … even the vena cava draining blood from the kidneys, as Vesalius correctly deduced function from anatomy.

Following the publication of Vesalius's anatomies, practicing doctors began to envision organs at work inside their patients. As they began to see through their patients' skins to imagine the workings of their organs, so too, our view of the human body was forever changed by those long afternoons – from then on, the bodies of everyone we encountered were transparent to us, whether classmates or patients or random strangers – we saw the flow of blood inside their hearts, the movement of food through their digestive tracts, the surge of hormones from their adrenal glands. Later, emerging into our own specialties, we envisioned our patients with special sorts of 20th century X-ray glasses, from skin to cells to organelles, and became cardiologists and orthopedists and oncologists using fantastically sophisticated means of exploring every bodily organ. Decades later, I am still touched by Vesalius. With fMRI, and magnetic spectroscopy and positron emission tomography, and other forms of dynamic neuroimaging, my fellow psychiatrists-turned-neuroscientists and I now see the brain as a working organ, and imagine neural hubs and networks activating for our patients with psychosis or mood disorders or posttraumatic stress disorder.

Back then, we wore our Vesalius torso while biking through eucalyptus groves or walking among the redwoods, or hiking in the sun-browned hills, or while lounging beside the glinting pool in our Speedos and aviator sunglasses. But as a shirt worn in 1970s Palo Alto, California, whether sported in The Good Earth Restaurant on University Ave., or at The Oasis burger joint down El Camino Real, it was edgy, boundary-pushing – evoking outrage, even disgust.

Which is why, after a few months, we shoved it in the back of a dresser drawer. It had made its statement: *We have arrived, our generation, we are opening the book of the human body anew – just wait to see what we'll discover!*

# INVITATION TO EKPHRASIS

Vesalius, Andreas. *De humani corporis fabrica libri septem.*
(Basel: Johannes Oporinus, 1543), page 562.

378    ANDREAE VESALII BRVXELLENSIS

Q,Q *His characteribus sinistræ lateris membrana notatur, quæ illi correspondet, quam nuper O,*
*O indicarunt.*

R,S *Vteri ceruicis anterior pars, inter R & S ea adhuc obducta tunica, quam peritonæi partes il*
*li offerüt, quæ ipsi uasa exporrigunt, deducuntq́, ac illum peritonæo adnectunt. Cæterùm inter*
*uallum inter R & S consistens, uteri ceruicis amplitudinem quodammodo significat. Rugæ ue*
*rò hic conspicuæ, illæ sunt quas uteri ceruix in se collapsa, neq; aliàs distenta, inter secandum*
*commonstrat.*

T *Vesica, cuius posterior facies hic potißimum spectatur. ita enim in figuræ huius delineatione ocu*
*lum direximus, ac si in corpore prostrato, posteriorem uesicæ sedem quæ uterum spectat, potißi*
*mum cernere uoluissemus. Si enim præsens muliebre corpus ita uti id quod modò subsequetur, e*
*rectum arbitrareris, etiam secus atq; res se habet, uteri fundum multo elatius ipsa uesica delinea*
*tum esse tibi persuaderes.*

V *Vmbilici est portio, à peritonæo inter secädum liberata, & unà cum uasis fœtui peculiaribus*
*hic deorsum reflexa.*          X *Portio uenæ ab umbilico iecur petentis.*

Y *Meatus à uesicæ fundi elatißima sede ad umbilicum pertinens, ac fœtus urinam inter secundum*
*& intimum ipsius inuolucrum deducens.*

Z,et & *Duæ arteriæ ab umbilico huc secundùm uesicæ latera prorepentes, atq; hac sede magnæ arte*
*riæ ramis pubis ossium foramina potißimum adeuntibus insertæ, seu continuæ.*

## VIGESIMAQVINTA QVINTI LIBRI FIGVRA.

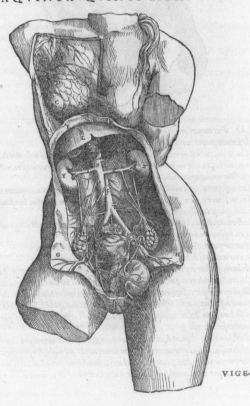

VIGE.

Vesalius, Andreas. *De humani corporis fabrica libri septem.* (Basel: Johannes Oporinus, 1543),
page 378 [478]. Courtesy of Universitätsbibliothek Basel

## Autopsy

Sarah N. Cross

Before the body was burned
it was cut apart, looking for an answer.
As if whatever was found there
could explain the five day death.
Those long summer days, the longer
nights, the bacteria stormed the shadows
of the body, besieged her.

The machines are turned off,
lines removed. Once they take
the body, all you can do is leave,
through the dark, hot city.

The autopsy report is brutal, full
of detail and unrevealing. This body,
that carried you forth, is disemboweled,
full of *Staphylococcus*. On each page,
organs are removed, weighed,
investigated with systematic reverence.

Finally removed are her ovaries, fallopian
tubes and uterus. Your very origin,
teeming with bacteria. Everything was
taken. Everything turned to ash.

# MEDIEVAL TORSO OF WOMAN, DISSECTED

for Katharine Park

Richard M. Ratzan


No longer can you see my deformed face,
a face my father said was only fit
for whores or easy raping which he did
before he sold me to Ercole, the price

one hundred lira and a birthing sow.
I sold cheap love to men with anger filled −
before Ercole and I them robbed and killed −
then threw their headless bodies in the Po.

Condemned to hang, "I am with child," I lied −
in life, not death, the only secret pried
from me. Now body op'd, of head bereft,

what is most truly mine you can not see.
A medieval peasant woman's life
was never mine to change or free to be.

# INVITATION TO EKPHRASIS

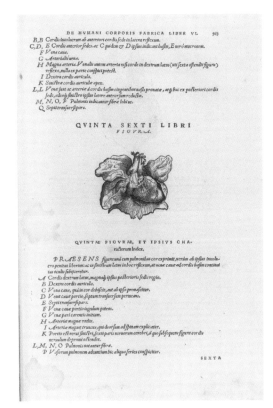

Vesalius, Andreas. *De humani corporis fabrica libri septem.*
(Basel: Johannes Oporinus, 1543), page 563.

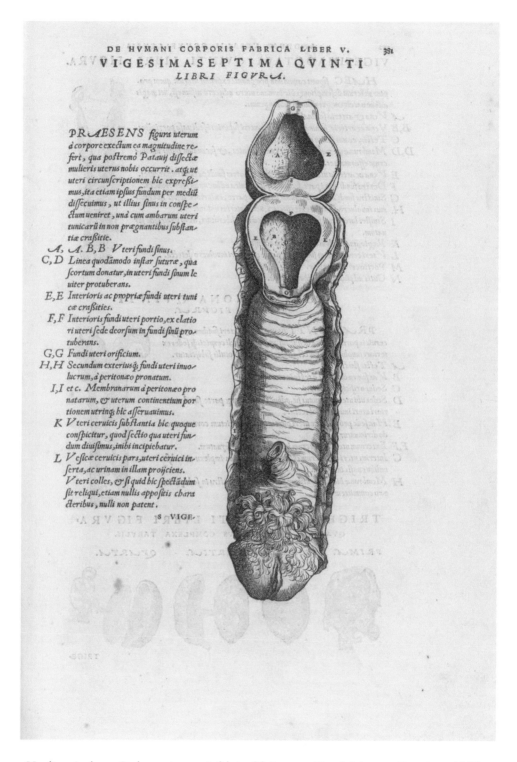

DE HVMANI CORPORIS FABRICA LIBER V.    381

## VIGESIMASEPTIMA QVINTI
### *LIBRI FIGVRA.*

PRÆSENS *figura uterum à corpore exectum ea magnitudine refert, qua postremò Patauij dissectæ mulieris uterus nobis occurrit. atq; ut uteri circunscriptionem hic expressimus, ita etiam ipsius fundum per mediũ dissecuimus, ut illius sinus in conspectum ueniret, una cum ambarum uteri tunicarũ in non prægnantibus substantiæ crassitie.*

A, A, B, B *Vteri fundi sinus.*

C, D *Linea quodãmodo instar suturæ, quà scortum donatur, in uteri fundi sinum le uiter protuberans.*

E, E *Interioris ac propriæ fundi uteri tunicæ crassities.*

F, F *Interioris fundi uteri portio, ex elatiori uteri sede deorsum in fundi sinũ protuberans.*

G, G *Fundi uteri orificium.*

H, H *Secundum exteriusq; fundi uteri inuolucrum, à peritonæo pronatum.*

I, I *et c. Membranarum à peritonæo pronatarum, & uterum continentium portionem utrinq; hic asseruauimus.*

K *Vteri ceruicis substantia hic quoque conspicitur, quod sectio qua uteri fundum diuisimus, inibi incipiebatur.*

L *Vesicæ ceruicis pars, uteri ceruici inserta, ac urinam in illam proijciens. Vteri colles, & si quid hic spectãdum sit reliqui, etiam nullis appositis charateribus, nulli non patent.*

Vesalius, Andreas. *De humani corporis fabrica libri septem.* (Basel: Johannes Oporinus, 1543), page 381 [481]. Courtesy of Universitätsbibliothek Basel

# MARKED

Leslie Adrienne Miller

*The vulva, vagina, and sliced uterus of a monk's lover*
*(Fabrica 1543, Book V)*

Now I see how much the thin flames of white
in a red tulip's arch and cave recall
the flayed corpse's wrap of muscle
on bones that cup the secrets of breath,
hunger, sex and the always mobile wand
of human fear. Even Vesalius was not
immune to copping a corpse or two
when the criminals and poor ran few.
And flaying, I always assumed, made
manifest the intricate handiwork of God,
the body's circling chains and gears
ticking off our days like beacon clocks
presiding over public squares. My tulips
are living souvenirs, gifts from my son's
pass through Amsterdam in summer.
"See," he says, "they're the special ones,
certified by royal stamp as safe to take."
*Carnaval de Rio, Semper Augustus*
*Queen of the Night.* Flaying, I learn,
sometimes had a simpler aim,
to make the dead woman nebulous,
wipe the life of markings from her skin,
and disconnect her from her kin,
so even a lover couldn't brush
her brow again and find the nick
only he could know, the tiny script
where the cooking pot's foot

wrote once, and only once,
whose woman she was. Now, of course,
we'd run a test, ask the DNA
to whom the flesh must be returned,
and the human art of reading marks
upon our own, felled by folly, force,
or transplant, becomes ancillary,
aesthetic, private enough to light
this small space, her torn bloom.

# BOOK VI

# ANDREAE VESALII
## BRVXELLEÑSIS, DE HVMANI CORPO-
### RIS FABRICA LIBER SEXTVS, CORDI IPSI'QVE
famulantibus organis dedicatus, ac mox in fronte figuras fibi proprias offerens,
quò minus & hîc quoq; eædem figuræ uarijs Capitibus
palsim præfigantur.

### PRIMA SEXTI LIBRI
#### *FIGVRA.*

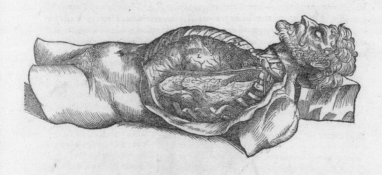

#### PRIMAE FIGVRAE, EIVSDEMQVE CHARA-
cterum Index.

*PRAESENS figura tantam hominis in dorso cubantis partem ex finiftro latere commonftrat, quantam oftendendæ thoracis fedi fufficere arbitrati fumus. Ab anteriori itaq; thoracis fede et lateribus, ac dein ab aliqua colli regione cutem fectionis ferie ademimus, ac dein mufculis qui coftis obducuntur refectis, coftarum offa à fuis cartilaginibus unà cum pectoris offe liberauimus, et coftarum offibus (uti inter fecandum fit ) effractis, coftarum cartilagines furfum uerfus dextrum latus attraximus, ut thoracis amplitudo, hancq; interfepientes membranæ, et pulmo, reliquaq; in conspectum uenirent, quæ modo in characterum Indice fignificabuntur.*

A,A    *Siniftri lateris coftarü indicatur cartilagines, unà cü pectoris offe, dextrofum furfumq; tractæ.*
B,B    *Intercoftales mufculi interualla cartilaginum occupantes.*
C,C    *Coftarum à cartilaginibus feiunctarum offa.*
D,D    *Intercoftales mufculi interualla offium adimplentes.*
E    *Clauicula hîc nuda, atque in fua fede adhuc afferuata cernitur.*
F    *Venarum, arteriarum, neruorumq; in axillam perreptantium feries.*
G    *Exterior iugularis uena hîc mox auulfa cute fecantibus occurrens.*
H,H    *Siniftra thoracis amplitudinem interdiuidens membrana, fuperficie ipfius finiftra hîc conspicua. quam etiam L,M,N et O indicant.*
I,I    *Septum transuerfum ea fuperficie hîc apparens, qua finiftram cauitatis thoracis fedem respicit.*
K    *Sedes ubi interdiuidentium thoracem membranarum finiftra septo connafcitur.*

Aa 4    Hæc

Vesalius, Andreas. *De humani corporis fabrica libri septem.* (Basel: Johannes Oporinus, 1543), page 559. Courtesy of Universitätsbibliothek Basel

OFFERING

Stacy Nigliazzo

The surgeon reads aloud, before the first cut

*Jack,*

*thirty-five years old*

    *with three sons,*

*loves fly fishing.*

    *He's giving three people his lungs and his eyes.*

SECVNDAE FIGVRAE, EIVSDEMQVE CHA-
racterum Index.

*PRAESENS figura, quam erectam, nõ autem humi proſtratam finximus, primam ſe-
ctionis ſerie ſubſequitur. etenim anteriori thoracis ſede & lateribus cute & muſculis qui illis ad
naſcebantur, denudatis, ac coſtarũ cartilaginibus ab oſsibus liberatis, ipſíſq́; oſsibus extrorſum
effractis, tandem pectoris os unà cum ipſi coarctatis cartilaginibus ab utriſq́; thoracem inter ſe
piĕtibus mĕbranis liberauimus, ſurſumq́; deduximus, ut illius interior ſuperficies obuia eſset, et mĕ
branarum thoracĕ interdiuidentiũ natura accuratiùs adhuc quàm in prima figura exprimeret.*

A,A  *Pectoris oſsis unà cum coſtarum ipſi commiſsis cartilaginibus interior, ſeu thoracis cauitatem
ſpectans ſuperficies.*

B,C  *Duæ indicantur uenæ á iugulo pectoris os petentes, ac præter frequentes quas diffundunt ramu
mulos, etiam ad elatiorem abdominis ſedem excurrentes.*

D,E  *Duæ arteriæ uenas nuper commemoratas ad umbilici uſq́; regionem concomitantes, nullibi tamĕ
ut uenæ ad cutem ſubeuntes.*

F  *Glandulæ ſub elatiſsima pectoris oſsis ſede in iugulo repoſitæ, ac uaſorum ſecuræ diſtributioni
à Natura præfectæ.*

G,G  *Dextræ thoracem interdiuidentium membranarum pars, quæ dextro pectoris oſsis lateri ad-
naſcebatur.*

H  *Dictæ modó membranæ dextra, ſeu pulmonem ſpectans ſuperficies.*

I,I  *Siniſtræ thoracis cauitatem inter ſepientium membranarum pars, quæ ſiniſtro pectoris oſsis lateri ante ſectionem connata fuerat.*

K  *Dictæ modó membranæ ſiniſtra, ſeu pulmonem reſpiciens ſuperficies.*

L,L  *Interuallum indicatur inter duas thoracem interſepientes membranas inibi conſpicuum, ubi humano pectoris oſsi continuantur.*

M,M  *Hæc protuberans regio cordis indicat ſitum. cór enim unà cum ipſius inuolucro immotum inter
membranas thoracem ſepientes collocatur.*

N,O, P,Q  *Pulmonis gibbum ſedeſúe coſtis contermina indicatur. neutra namque ex parte pulmonis partes in latera refleximus. Verum N & O duas fibras dextræ partis pulmonis indicant,
N quidem elatiorem, O uero humiliorem. atq́; ita etiam in ſiniſtro latere P & Q.*

R,R  *Septi tranſuerſi ſedes, quã á mucronata pectoris oſsis cartilagine hic S inſignita, & dein á car*
S.  *tilaginum quæ pectoris oſsi non coarticulantur mucronibus, liberauit.*

T,V  *Cutis deorſum à thoracis anteriori ſede, euerſa, atque ea ſuperficie conſpicuà, qua muſculis
obducebatur.*

## TERTIA SEXTI LIBRI
*FIGVRA.*

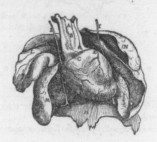

TER-

Vesalius, Andreas. *De humani corporis fabrica libri septem.* (Basel: Johannes Oporinus, 1543), page 561. Courtesy of Universitätsbibliothek Basel

# By All Accounts

Rebekkah E. Depew

Attempted resuscitation of the dead was
once punishable by lightning strike. Now we
are the ones who unfold hearts like flowers,
tugging at the coattails of Morpheus as if the
gods were butterflies we could pin to the
back of a picture frame if only our hands had
thick enough callouses. And still

we play requiems in concentration camps,
watch the darker sides of major chords dance
down the lightning fibers of the heart like its
own pulsations, electric and real, mirrored by
rhinestone teardrops on our plaster faces
while we flay open hearts for what exactly.

Next time you carry a dying heart in your still-
fluttering hands, tell us how it feels to hold
heaven back, if only briefly. One would think
that playing god would keep us humble. But
our history holds us to a different story,
bow poised over the *deus irae*, bowing out
before the cup and bread. And still,

you know me well, so you wait for the *and yet*.
And I will give it to you: hearts beat, unnoticed
mostly, inside our origami chests. And there is
a doctor on the seventh floor who plans
his rounds every Thursday morning so that his
loneliest patients can meet an Irish wolfhound
named Will.

## INVITATION TO EKPHRASIS

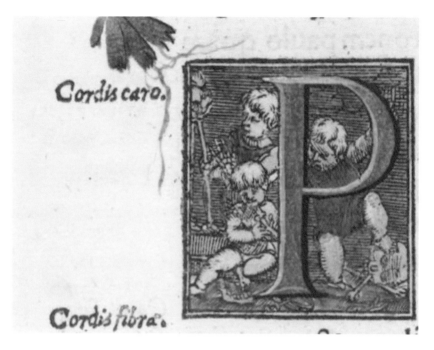

Vesalius, Andreas. *De humani corporis fabrica libri septem.* (Basel: Johannes Oporinus, 1543), page 586.

# BOOK VII

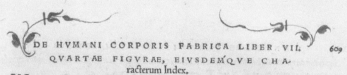

DE HVMANI CORPORIS FABRICA LIBER VII.    609
QVARTAE FIGVRAE, EIVSDEMQVE CHA-
racterum Index.

IN *quarta figura omnes duræ tenuisᵹ membranarũ partes resecuimus, quæ in prioribus figuris occurrerunt, ac dein dextrã sinistramᵹ cerebri portionẽ sectionis serie ita ademimus, ut iam cerebri uentriculi in conspectũ uenire incipiãt. Primũ nanᵹ secundùm dextrũ callosi corporis latus, ubi sinus altero M in tertia figura notatus cõsistit, longã duximus sectionẽ, quæ per dextrũ cerebri uentriculũ ducta, dextræ cerebri partis eam portionẽ abstulit, quæ supra sectio nẽ habebatur, qua orbiculatim caluariã serra diuisimus. Atᵹ quum idem quoque in sinistro la tere absoluimus, hic ad sinistrũ latus sinistrã cerebri partẽ ita reposuimus, ut superiorẽ sinistri uentriculi sedem aliqua ex parte cõmonstraret, calloso interim corpore in capite adhuc seruato.*

A, A,   A  *Cerebri adhuc in caluaria relicti pars dextra.*        B, B, B  *Pars sinistra.*
C, C,   C  *Portio cerebri sinistra, quæ sectionis serie à reliquo cerebro ablata, hic resupina iacet.*
D, D,   D  *Lineæ partim cerebri anfractus, et partim uariũ cerebri substãtiæ colorẽ cõmonstrantes. quicquid enim extra lineas consistit, quasi luteũ & subcinericiũ magis est: quicquid intra, ad a missim album uistur. quemadmodum E & F in dextra & sinistra cerebri parte luteum est: G*
E. F.
G, H.   *uerò & H album prorsus, & interdum rubris punctis interstinctum.*
I, I   *Callosum corpus utrinᵹ à cerebri substantia, cui alioqui continuatur, liberum.*
K, K   *Callosi corporis portiuncula, adhuc sinistræ cerebri parti quæ adempta est, continua.*
L, L   *Dexter cerebri uentriculus.*        M, M  *Sinister cerebri uentriculus.*
N, N   *Sinistri uentriculi superioris sedi portio.*
O, O   *Plexus cerebri ab imagine quã cum extimo fœtus inuolucro similem exigit, χοειοἰδὴς nuncupatus.*
P, P   *Aranearum modo graciles uenæ dextri & sinistri uentriculi substãtiæ hoc in loco connatæ, ac ab illis diductæ uasis, quæ nuper commemoratũ, & secundis nõ absimilem plexum extruunt.*
Q   *Venulæ à nuper quoᵹ cõmemoratis uasis in tenuẽ cerebri membranã sub callosi corporis ante riori sede huc excurrentes, & incerta serie (quemadmodum & P notatæ) inter resecandum se offerentes.*

QVINTA SEPTIMI LIBRI FIGVRA.

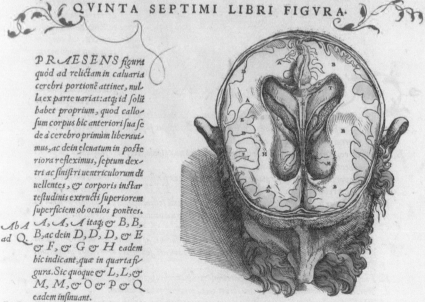

PRÆSENS *figura quòd ad relictam in caluaria cerebri portionẽ attinet, nul la ex parte uariat: atᵹ id solũ habet proprium, quod callo sum corpus hic anteriori sua se de à cerebro primùm liberaui mus, ac dein eleuatum in poste riora refleximus, septum dex tri ac sinistri uentriculorum dĩ uellentes, & corporis instar testudinis extructi superiorem superficiem ob oculos ponĕtes.*

Ab A   A, A, A *itaᵹ & B, B,*
ad Q.  *B, ac dein D, D, D, & E & F, & G & H eadem hic indicant, quæ in quarta fi gura. Sic quoque & L, L, & M, M, & O & P & Q eadem insinuant.*

R, R,   R  *Notatur inferior callosi corporis superficies. est enim id à sua sede motum, atque in poste riora reflexum.*

S, T, V  Supe-

# THE INNER SELF

Sheri A. Butler, MD

I'd like to see your amygdalae.
But, why should you show them to me?
You've been nearly denuded of everything human,
Uncapped, skinned and gory.
You have no reason to trust my gentle hands.
Transference, my eye!  Unlike you,
I still have both of mine working.
My mind's eye can picture my own retina,
Even though they say the eye sees not itself.
But you don't stand a chance.
What holds you in,
What fills your empty spaces,
Your curlicues of glorious gyri?
Why would someone look at you this way?
Are they looking for your body ego,
Digging for your id?
I could have told them
There are easier ways to find them,
To locate what is human in you.
Someone dealt you a blow,
Cut you off
Why should you uncover and show me your inner world?
I suspect thoughts have formed in there that
You'd prefer to show to no one, ever!
And there you are, no way to stop my stares.
You don't know how I love
The velvet ventricular linings.
The fluid dance of sparking neurons
In their cozy dendritic tangles.
They make the nest for the grim superego.
The warm elbow of the temporal lobe
The criss-cross of the chiasm,
The racing striatum
That speeds motion on and on.

You could say, I like what I see
In you, deep within.
Should you spill some CSF on my couch,
Like transparent feelings
Vulnerable and a little leaky
Always, always messy
In their gray and pink coatings
Sulking sulci, avoiding the speech center's
Clever wording…
Oh, what a headache!
Rest it, here,
With nothing to cover it up,
Nothing to hide behind.
You can let it all out now,
There is finally the space,
Finally the peace.

# Guardian Angel

Jack Coulehan

The hole at the center of my brain
looks like angel's wings. My guardian
is lying on his belly looking down
through an open window at the base
of my skull. I imagine he keeps
a checklist. Heart. Pancreas. Lungs.
And so forth. When I was a child, he sat
on my shoulder and whispered advice
about resisting temptation. He was weak,
though, and soft-spoken. Much of the time
I didn't pay attention to his prodding,
so he faded like a watercolor scene
in bright sun. Flew home to a Renaissance
altarpiece, where less was expected
of angels, and I was left to defend
my own virtue. It seems he is back now,
lying prone at the center of my brain.

I might be making too much of the gap
in the image. It's a wing-shaped sac
of fluid, my book says, positioned
to refresh the cells and drain their bilge,
a system of plumbing. The sac's shape
is coincidence. But I'm remembering
my guardian angel, and it looks like him
peering down, a cat on a windowsill
recording what's going on – Oxytocin,
dopamine, testosterone. And saying
nothing. In a sense it was comforting
to be part of a scheme, with an angel
assigned to my shoulder, inept though he was,
to whisper advice. Anonymous now,
he listens, observes, and is eerily
detached. He could be anyone's angel.

## VESALIUS VIEWS THE VENTRICLES

Mel Konner

Hippocrates, that man of many oaths
And immortal teacher of physicians,
Said it first and best:

> *"Men ought to know that*
> *From nothing else come joys, delights, laughter*
> *And sport, sorrows, griefs, despondency, and*
> *Lamentations. By it, we acquire*
> *Wisdom and knowledge; we see and hear, we*
> *Sleep or lie awake, we know what is foul*
> *And what is fair, what is bad and what good,*
> *What is sweet, and what unsavory. And,*
> *By the same organ we become mad or*
> *Delirious, fears and terrors assail*
> *Us. All this we endure from the brain, when*
> *It is not in health. In these ways I hold*
> *That the brain exerts the greatest power*
> *In us. It is our best interpreter*
> *Of every thing that emanates from air."*

Not the liver, with its sloshing humors
Purportedly pulsing us into moods
And temperaments – fury, melancholy,
Sluggishness, hope – not even the vital
Heart, thumping life itself through the tightly
Woven hollow threads of the whole fabric,
But the jelled ugly blob of curvatures
And wrinkles squat in the skull's bowl: the brain.
And so it would be down through centuries.

Galen made a fresh pledge insistently
To probe the flesh of animals in hopes
Of finding out what makes us humans tick.
Forbidden from dissecting cadavers,

He vivisected apes and oxen,
Sucking *pneuma* out of the ventricles,
Making beasts moribund because bereft
Of animal spirits. Aristotle
Likewise proved cause and effect, or so he
Hoped. For more than a millennium
Galen reigned and yet Aristotle waned,
At least his method did, and Galen's own
Experimental bent was shadowed by
His dicta, committed to memory
Generation after generation.
Thus bookishness displaced observation
And doctors' minds were dominated
By authority, until Vesalius.

This Dutch boy, descended from physicians,
Put his finger in the dyke against floods
Of willful ignorance masquerading
As received, indelible wisdom. He
Studied Galen, but he examined
Excavated bones in the charnel house
Of the Cemetery of the Innocents,
In Paris. Driven out of there by war,
He ended up in Padova, and on
The day he took his medical degree,
The chair of surgery and anatomy
Was offered him. He sat. *Explicator
Chirurgiae.* "Explainer of Galen"
It might have been, but Vesalius thought
Not. Trashing tradition, he made human
Dissection his first and overriding
Law. He looked. He cut. He saw. He pulled
Apart. And he drew. Tirelessly, he drew.

But more even than the meticulous,
Exquisite drawings, we recollect
What Vesalius taught from the pit of that
Stunning, vertiginous anatomical

Theater in Padova — and theater
It was — glinting almost vertically
Up and up with the eyes of doctors and
Students from throughout the world, the master's
Hands in the cadaver, the onlookers
Leaning acrophobically to not miss
One movement of his fingers or his probe,
Craning necks, cocking ears to hear him say
What Galen himself surely would have said
If he had catapulted forward fourteen
Centuries to Padova: When Galen
And your own eyes differ, believe your eyes.

Now we see and probe the brain electric,
Questioning its charges and tingling them
A bit our way, watching dials as currents
Ebb and flow in mysterious warm springs,
That feed streams of ions' spiraling rush.
We penetrate the skull with carpenters'
Hardware if need be to slice and suck at
Troubles of the mind. We draw its tissues
With massive, near-magical machines that
See detail and clarity no ancient
Ever dreamed of, and without harming one
Of its treasured skill-bearing, memory-keeping,
Love-evoking cells.

                          But mostly, if we
Can, we manipulate its molecules
With potent potions taking shape in pills,
To lift spirits, assuage inchoate fear,
Banish the maddest thoughts of persecution
Or conspiracy, quell plans that drive us
Into the wildest peril, sometimes up
To the taking of our own lonesome lives.
We even help fidgety, drifting children
To focus on texts, diagrams, and drawings
That may blaze their path to their best lives —

One day perhaps to know Vesalius
And thank him for unfolding to our eyes
Not only the fabric of the body,
Intricate and beautiful to be sure,
But the finer, softer, infinitely
Variable fabric of the human soul.

# INVITATION TO EKPHRASIS

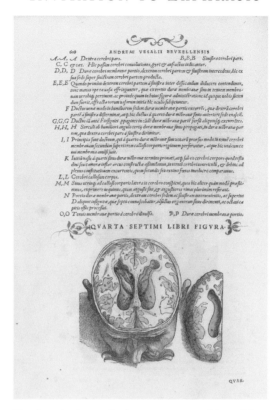

Vesalius, Andreas. *De humani corporis fabrica libri septem.*
(Basel: Johannes Oporinus, 1543), page 608.

# Concluding Poetical Postscript

L *Hæc protuberans sedes, cordis gratia hic in sinistrum adeo prominet. id namq; una cum ipsius in uolucro inter membranas thoracem diuidentes comprehensum, in sinistrum longe magis quàm in dextrum porrigitur. atque huius potissimum tuberis occasione præsentem figuram ex sinistro po tius, quàm dextro latere expressimus.*

M *Vena sinistro pectoris ossis lateri exporrecta, & sinistræ thoracem interdiuidenti membranæ uarios surculos offerens.*

N *Arteria sinistro pectoris ossis lateri exporrecta, & similiter ac uena M insignita ramulos si nistræ thoracem intersepienti membranæ exhibens.*

O,O *Ramuli à uena ac arteria deducti, quæ secundum pectoris ossis sinistrum latus à iugulo ad abdo minis regionem pertingunt.*

P,P *Neruus septi transuersi sinister, hic conspicuæ thoracem intersepientis membranæ superficiei in progressu adnatus.*

Q *Vena in hominibus potissimum à iugulo una cum septi transuersi neruo deorsum excurrens, & membranæ thoracem intersepienti ramulos deriuans.*

R,S,T, V *Pulmonis pars sinistram thoracis cauitatē occupans. ac R & S huius partis sedem notant, quæ costis, seu ipsas succingenti mēbranæ proxima est, gibbá ue cernitur. T uero & V eius par tis sedem indicant, quæ priusquam collaberetur, exteriori superficiei membranæ thoracem inter diuidentis committebatur. Rursus R & T partis huius pulmonis superiorem insinuant fibram, seu lobum. S autem & V inferiorem.*

## SECVNDA SEXTI LIBRI
### FIGVRA.

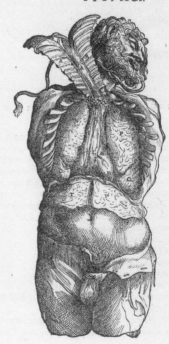

SECVN-

Vesalius, Andreas. *De humani corporis fabrica libri septem.* (Basel: Johannes Oporinus, 1543), page 560. Courtesy of Universitätsbibliothek Basel

# ON THE DIFFICULTY OF ARTICULATING THE BODY

Fady Joudah

1.

A skull on its head.
A spine for a seahorse.
A sacrum for an armadillo.
A diaphragm for a sting ray.

And the ribcage a flower, a brain
combed and braided, cocoon for breath.

You wanted precision better than this,
dove into concinnity's lacuna, the marbles
of hand and foot, the oedipal skeleton

on a cane solving a riddle of flesh.
Ahead of your time, you didn't turn
your subjects into Greek beauties but rather
into bodybuilders of a Mr. World contest.

Were those farmer or soldier muscles? Who
back then possessed a body this magnificent
to willingly give it up to you?

Along with Titian's pupil, you'd have been
hired on the set of *Aliens*, won an Oscar
for special effects. As if the corpses

were ancestral spirits for Goya's
black paintings. In your text

you speak with ease of lynching cadavers.
Oh, zygomaticus and sternocleidomastoid,

is this what homeless men and felons lived for?
The skull sits itself down to look at itself:

a migraine into baobab veins.
And the filamentous, fibrillar trees,
dendritic and fluid, to where

do they take us but underground?
The viscera an Athena
disemboweled or the archaic bust of Apollo
spilling its guts and sex. And the heart,

like the moon, unbeautiful when up close
or did you know of papaya then,
of avocado, of large-seeded fruits
for cerebrum and cerebellum?

How difficult it was to acquire
a woman's body, display dimorphism
when man was mostly the dissectible storm.
(Children have always been off limits.)

Andreas, our muscles have softened,
our lactiferous ducts have atrophied,
but the body remains more than history

and less than origin: a maker
made in the Anthropocene.


2.


On May 12, 1543, my dear Vesalius, a bigamous man
in Basel lost his head, killed his first wife,
was executed, and his corpse gifted to you,

to us. Through your articulation,
his skeleton is immortal in a museum, his bones

bending with time. Was he beheaded?

Beheading would've offended
your scientific temperament as would have
any disruption of the gross architecture

of beauty. You did with what you had.
I hear there was execution
by drowning in your day, Andreas,

we call it waterboarding now,
and that's the rumor I prefer
to spread: for any cadaver properly hung

can be drained of water. Though we've
mostly shifted our anatomical theatre
to harvesting cells and cloning clones.

As with innocent Henrietta Lacks,
that bigamous murderous man had a name:
Jakob Gebweiler. That Weiler translates

as *Hamlet* amuses me. Did the authorities
discuss with you their method
of eye-for-an-eye prior to the donation?
Did Jakob know

he'd end up under your knife and saw?
How grateful were you
for his crime? We used to call

upon mystics to guide us through
serendipity, upon psychiatrists
for synchronicity, statisticians for the inexplicable
as purpose-filled, stochastic

full of sting you'd appreciate, or mere spandrel:
like the sounds heart valves snap

for systole, diastole, those aren't

what the valves were put on this earth for.
What did Jakob look like?

And what about his murdered wife,
shouldn't her name be archived as well?
Behind a great man, a butchered woman.

Did Jakob have a beard? Was he that man
in chapter six, the one and only clear exhibit

of a full face in your bestseller book?
Or is that your face
imagined when prematurely dead

after a pilgrimage to the Holy Land?
Later you make it clear to us
that you had more than one head

available to you as you dissected the brain
of shaven and unshaven men.
But that fellow in chapter six,

with his pants and scrotal sac,
whose arms you lopped off
or tied behind his back for his thorax

to open in yoga breath, that man
whose heart and lungs, that man
with noose around his neck

tilting his extinguished gaze to the left,
whose sternum you excised

into costal wings, a caterpillar's
metamorphosis complete.

Like Odysseus tied to his mast
against the Sirens.
Like Saint Sebastian tied to a tree.

What kind of tree was it?
And if to a stake in a meadow,
what wild bloom in the field?

Marble bust of Andreas Vesalius unveiled in 1965 in Zakynthos, Fotis Ladikos Square (formerly Vesal Square). Note that today we believe Vesalius was born on the last day of December 1514. Photographs by Guy Cobolet for Himetop – The History of Medicine Topographical Database (himetop.net)

# VESALIUS IN ZANTE.

## (1564)

### BY EDITH WHARTON.

SET wide the window.  Let me drink the day.
I loved light ever, light in eye and brain—
No tapers mirrored in long palace floors,
Nor dedicated depths of silent aisles,
But just the common dusty wind-blown day
That roofs earth's millions.
           O, too long I walked
In that thrice-sifted air that princes breathe,
Nor felt the heaven-wide jostling of the winds
And all the ancient outlawry of earth!
Now let me breathe and see.
           This pilgrimage
They call a penance—let them call it that!
I set my face to the East to shrive my soul
Of mortal sin?  So be it.  If my blade
Once questioned living flesh, if once I tore
The pages of the Book in opening it,
See what the torn page yielded ere the light
Had paled its buried characters—and judge!

The girl they brought me, pinioned hand and foot
In catalepsy—say I should have known
That trance had not yet darkened into death,
'And held my scalpel.  Well, suppose I *knew?*
Sum up the facts—her life against her death.
Her life?  The scum upon the pools of pleasure
Breeds such by thousands.  And her death?  Perchance

The obolus to appease the ferrying Shade,
And waft her into immortality.
Think what she purchased with that one heart-flutter
That whispered its deep secret to my blade!
For, just because her bosom fluttered still,
It told me more than many rifled graves;
Because I spoke too soon, she answered me,
Her vain life ripened to this bud of death
As the whole plant is forced into one flower,
All her blank past a scroll on which God wrote
His word of healing—so that the poor flesh,
Which spread death living, died to purchase life!

Ah, no! The sin I sinned was mine, not theirs.
Not *that* they sent me forth to wash away—
None of their tariffed frailties, but a deed
So far beyond their grasp of good or ill
That, set to weigh it in the Church's balance,
Scarce would they know which scale to cast it in.
But I, I know. I sinned against my will,
Myself, my soul—the God within the breast:
Can any penance wash such sacrilege?

When I was young in Venice, years ago,
I walked the hospice with a Spanish monk,
A solitary cloistered in high thoughts,
The great Loyola, whom I reckoned then
A mere refurbisher of faded creeds,
Expert to edge anew the arms of faith,
As who should say, a Galenist, resolved
To hold the walls of dogma against fact,
Experience, insight, his own self, if need be!
Ah, how I pitied him, mine own eyes set
Straight in the level beams of Truth, who groped
In error's old deserted catacombs
And lit his tapers upon empty graves!
Ay, but he held his own, the monk—more man
Than any laurelled cripple of the wars,
Charles's spent shafts; for what he willed he willed,
As those do that forerun the wheels of fate,

Not take their dust—that force the virgin hours,
Hew life into the likeness of themselves
And wrest the stars from their concurrences.
So firm his mould; but mine the ductile soul
That wears the livery of circumstance
And hangs obsequious on its suzerain's eye.
For who rules now? The twilight-flitting monk,
Or I, that took the morning like an Alp?
He held his own, I let mine slip from me,
The birthright that no sovereign can restore;
And so ironic Time beholds us now
Master and slave—he lord of half the earth,
I ousted from my narrow heritage.

For there's the sting! My kingdom knows me not.
Reach me that folio—my usurper's title!
Fallopius reigning, *vice*—nay, not so:
Successor, not usurper. I am dead.
My throne stood empty; he was heir to it.
Ay, but who hewed his kingdom from the waste,
Cleared, inch by inch, the acres for his sowing,
Won back for man that ancient fief o' the Church,
His body? Who flung Galen from his seat,
And founded the great dynasty of truth
In error's central kingdom?
                                        Ask men that,
And see their answer: just a wondering stare,
To learn things were not always as they are—
The very fight forgotten with the fighter;
Already grows the moss upon my grave!
Ay, and so meet—hold fast to that, Vesalius.
They only, who re-conquer day by day
The inch of ground they camped on over-night,
Have right of foothold on this crowded earth.
I left mine own; he seized it; with it went
My name, my fame, my very self, it seems,
Till I am but the symbol of a man,
The sign-board creaking o'er an empty inn.
He names me—true! *"Oh, give the door its due*
*I entered by. Only, my masters, note,*

*Had door been none, a shoulder-thrust of mine*
*Had breached the crazy wall*"—he seems to say.
So meet—and yet a word of thanks, of praise,
Of recognition that the clue was found,
Seized, followed, clung to, by some hand now dust—
Had this obscured his quartering of my shield?

How the one weakness stirs again! I thought
I had done with that old thirst for gratitude
That lured me to the desert years ago.
I did my work—and was not that enough?
No; but because the idlers sneered and shrugged,
The envious whispered, the traducers lied,
And friendship doubted where it should have cheered,
I flung aside the unfinished task, sought praise
Outside my soul's esteem, and learned too late
That victory, like God's kingdom, is within.
(Nay, let the folio rest upon my knee.
I do not feel its weight.)  Ingratitude?
The hurrying traveller does not ask the name
Of him who points him on his way; and this
Fallopius sits in the mid-heart of me,
Because he keeps his eye upon the goal,
Cuts a straight furrow to the end in view,
Cares not who oped the fountain by the way,
But drinks to draw fresh courage for his journey.
That was the lesson that Ignatius taught—
The one I might have learned from him, but would not—
That we are but stray atoms on the wind,
A dancing transiency of summer eves,
Till we become one with our purpose, merged
In that vast effort of the race which makes
Mortality immortal.
                    "*He that loseth*
*His life shall find it*": so the Scripture runs.
But I so hugged the fleeting self in me,
So loved the lovely perishable hours,
So kissed myself to death upon their lips,
That on one pyre we perished in the end—
A grimmer bonfire than the Church e'er lit!

Yet all was well—or seemed so—till I heard
That younger voice, an echo of my own,
And, like a wanderer turning to his home,
Who finds another on the hearth, and learns,
Half-dazed, that other is his actual self
In name and claim, as the whole parish swears,
So strangely, suddenly, stood dispossessed
Of that same self I had sold all to keep,
A baffled ghost that none would see or hear!
*"Vesalius? Who's Vesalius? This Fallopius*
*It is who dragged the Galen-idol down,*
*Who rent the veil of flesh and forced a way*
*Into the secret fortalice of life"*—
Yet it was I that bore the brunt of it!

Well, better so! Better awake and live
My last brief moment, as the man I was,
Than lapse from life's long lethargy to death
Without one conscious interval. At least
I repossess my past, am once again
No courtier med'cining the whims of kings
In muffled palace-chambers, but the free
Friendless Vesalius, with his back to the wall
And all the world against him. O, for that
Best gift of all, Fallopius, take my thanks—
That, and much more. At first, when Padua wrote:
"Master, Fallopius dead, resume again
The chair even he could not completely fill,
And see what usury age shall take of youth
In honors forfeited"—why, just at first,
I was quite simply credulously glad
To think the old life stood ajar for me,
Like a fond woman's unforgetting heart.
But now that death waylays me—now I know
This isle is the circumference of my days,
And I shall die here in a little while—
So also best, Fallopius!
                    For I see
The gods may give anew, but not restore;
And though I think that, in my chair again,

I might have argued my supplanters wrong
In this or that—this Cesalpinus, say,
With all his hot-foot blundering in the dark,
Fabricius, with his over-cautious clutch
On Galen (systole and diastole
Of Truth's mysterious heart!)—yet, other ways,
It may be that this dying serves the cause.
For Truth stays not to build her monument
For this or that co-operating hand,
But props it with her servants' failures—nay,
Cements its courses with their blood and brains,
A living substance that shall clinch her walls
Against the assaults of time.   Already, see,
Her scaffold rises on my hidden toil,
I but the accepted premiss whence must spring
The airy structure of her argument;
Nor could the bricks it rests on serve to build
The crowning finials.   I abide her law:
A different substance for a different end—
Content to know I hold the building up;
Though men, agape at dome and pinnacles,
Guess not, the whole must crumble like a dream
But for that buried labor underneath.
Yet, Padua, I had still my word to say!
*Let others say it!*—Ah, but will they guess
Just the one word—?   Nay, Truth is many-tongued.
What one man failed to speak, another finds
Another word for.   May not all converge
In some vast utterance, of which you and I,
Fallopius, were but halting syllables?
So knowledge come, no matter how it comes!
No matter whence the light falls, so it fall!
Truth's way, not mine—that I, whose service failed
In action, yet may make amends in praise.
Fabricius, Cesalpinus, say your word,
Not yours, or mine, but Truth's, as you receive it!
You miss a point I saw?   See others, then!
Misread my meaning?   Yet expound your own!
Obscure one space I cleared?   The sky is wide,
And you may yet uncover other stars.

For thus I read the meaning of this end:
There are two ways of spreading light; to be
The candle or the mirror that reflects it.
I let my wick burn out—there yet remains
To spread an answering surface to the flame
That others kindle.

Turn me in my bed.
The window darkens as the hours swing round;
But yonder, look, the other casement glows!
Let me face westward as my sun goes down.

EDITH WHARTON.

*Note.*—Vesalius, the great anatomist, studied at Louvain and Paris, and was called by Venice to the chair of surgery in the University of Padua. He was one of the first physiologists to dissect the human body, and his great work "The Structure of the Human Body" was an open attack on the physiology of Galen. The book excited such violent opposition, not only in the Church, but in the University, that in a fit of discouragement he burned his remaining manuscripts and accepted the post of physician at the Court of Charles V., and afterward of his son, Philip II. of Spain. This closed his life of free enquiry, for the Inquisition forbade all scientific research, and the dissection of corpses was prohibited in Spain. Vesalius sank into the rich and successful court physician, but regrets for his past life were never wholly extinguished, and in 1561 they were roused afresh by the reading of an anatomical treatise by Gabriel Fallopius, his successor in the chair at Padua. From that moment life in Spain became intolerable to Vesalius, and in 1563 he set out for the East. Tradition reports that this journey was a penance to which the Church condemned him for having opened the body of a woman before she was actually dead; but more probably Vesalius, sick of his long servitude, made the pilgrimage a pretext to escape from Spain.

Fallopius had meanwhile died, and the Venetian Senate is said to have offered Vesalius his old chair; but on the way home from Jerusalem he was seized with illness, and died at Zante in 1564.]

# TRANSLATIONS

## INTRODUCTION TO THE TRANSLATIONS

Richard M. Ratzan

This translation section contains poems written about Vesalius and his Fabrica. They are remarkable for several reasons. First they reflect an almost instant and universal appreciation, in real time, of his magnificent accomplishment, both in medicine and in art, by writers from Spain to Hungary, in an age of no mass transportation or communication and still the early days of the printing press. It is not a co-incidence that so many of these poets use the word "ars, artis" to indicate not just Vesalius's art/skill but also the striking graphic art in the *Fabrica*, woodcuts commonly felt to have originated in Titan's studio. Despite the widespread criticism of the *Fabrica* from Galenists, most humanists and physicians realized, and quickly, what had just happened in the history of anatomy and who had effected it – an unknown 28 year old from Brussels. His contemporaries like Sambucus and Eber and Melanchthon not only appreciated his work but incorporated it into their world views. Incredible, to me at least, is the fact that these poems circulated widely, most likely in printed format, most often in books, probably, in 16th Century Europe. Not surprisingly, this circulation and copying by hand lead to spelling errors, as in Melanchthon's fly-leaf poem with *fluentes* for the original *ruentes*, metrical equivalents.

Secondly, it is perhaps a consequence of this realization – that Vesalius had uncovered uniquely human anatomy, unlike Galen's often animal-derived observations – that these poets used similar metaphors and similes, like Montano and Sambucus (see later in this book), both using the Latin verb *lateo*, "to be concealed."

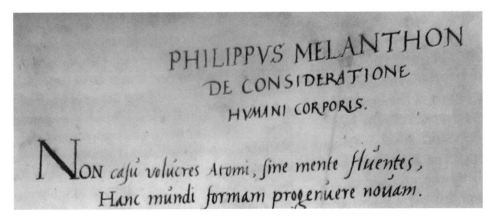

Replacement of original "ruentes" with "fluentes" by book owner. Note variant spelling of "Melanchthon". Courtesy of Univesity of Pécs, Klimó Library

Two poems (by Montano and Sambucus [I.S.]) handwritten under portrait of Vesalius. Library Company of Philadelphia. Pg A6v from De humani corporis fabrica // *Six Vesa Log 30.F

Thirdly, it is not surprising, given the thoroughly Christian milieu in which these 16th and, in the case of Jakob Balde, 17th Century writers saw Vesalius's achievement that they viewed the revelations of human anatomy in the Fabrica as but the working of a Christian God (be it the God of a Jesuit poet like Balde or the God of a Lutheran poet like Melanchthon) to reveal His universal design on the microcosmic scale of the human body. This argument from design is present in many of the poems, which were all written, save for the sonnet by Varchi, in Neo-Latin, despite the poets having first languages from Spanish to German to Hungarian, a phenomenon that deserves a few words of explanation.

Neo-Latin, a term first used self-consciously in the late 1700's, was the Latin used by the educated and scholars from roughly 1400 to 1900 in Europe, and is also called "Renaissance Latin" and "Early Modern Latin." After Rome fell, Latin survived, mostly due to Christianity which used it as a lingua franca in Europe. As Sidwell writes in *The Oxford Handbook of Neo-Latin*, "Christianity is the great and encompassing fact that explains the longevity of CL [Classical Latin] and its transmutation into ML [Medieval Latin]." (Oxford page 16) Medieval Latin survived, in part due to its preservation in written rather than spoken form. As IJsewijn put it

> … while Latin was dying on the people's lips. it started a new life among the
> learned classes, and thus resulted in a period of an amazing development and
> a new flourishing which lasted for about ten centuries. During this period,
> which we call the Middle Ages, the impact of the ancient heritage was always
> present, but adherence to its principles, models and examples often varied
> substantially. (IJsewijn, page 3)

Neo-Latin was the continuation of Medieval Latin, albeit with grammatical and orthographic alterations along the way, but now – unlike the written Latin of the Middle Ages – with a conscious effort that IJsewijn traces to Italian Humanism to return to a more educated, purer form of literary Latin – the Latin of Cicero – especially Cicero – Caesar, Catullus and Livy. As such it became – for hundreds of years, until governments encouraged and sometimes compelled usage of the vernacular of national languages – the language of literary discourse, from poetry to religious tracts to philosophical papers to the text of Vesalius. As Nichols comments, much of the poetry in Neo-Latin is fine, especially the shorter forms, like odes and epodes and elegies, and most especially when they are addressing pastoral topics. (Nichols pages 1-84) The Neo-Latin poets did not find the epic a form in which they were likely to excel. They were fine epigrammatists, as poets like Montano and Sambucus demonstrate. Save for Jakob Balde, who also wrote shorter poems, the following poems are evidence of the facility of Neo-Latin poets to capture, as I discuss in the introduction to Montano, the essence of Vesalius and the revolutionary contributions of his *Fabrica*.

# Philip Melanchthon (1497 - 1560)

De consideratione humani corporis

*With a learned hand Durer could paint the face of a living Philip, not his mind*

Woodcut of Philip Melanchthon by Albrecht Dürer. Courtesy of National
Gallery of Art

Born Philipp Schwarzerdt in 1497 in Bretten, Germany, a town near the French border, Philip Melanchthon (fn1), like many Medieval European humanist scholars and academicians, adopted a Latinate version of his name. Since "Schwarzerdt" means, in German, "black" ("Schwarz") "earth" ("erdt"), Melanchthon translated "black earth" into Greek, or "Μέλαν" "black" and "χθών" "earth," further transliterating the Greek into the Roman alphabet, or "Melanchthon." Early in his life, Melanchthon was exposed to and taught Greek, Latin and the Classics, including Aristotle. Indeed, his first academic post was as an instructor of Greek at the University of Wittenberg, his residence for many years. Soon after arriving in Wittenberg he changed his focus to theology, maintaining his background in Greek, Latin and other humanistic studies.

Melanchthon was a very important 16th Century educator, theologian, poet and promoter of Lutheranism, the new reading of the Scriptures and view of Christianity enunciated by his good friend, Martin Luther. Indeed, Melanchthon was such a dedicated teacher − not just of Lutheranism − that he was known as the "Praeceptor Germaniae," or "Teacher of Germany." Luther and Melanchthon, very close friends, are credited with helping initiate the Reformation. Melanchthon was such an ardent apologist for his friend's reformulation of Christianity that, as Erasmus summarized it, "est ipse, pene ut ita dixerim, ipso Luthero lutheranior," or "Melanchthon is more Lutheran than Luther." (Kusukawa page 4 bottom) Melanchthon's advocacy, however, was less passionate, more cautious and scholarly than Luther's. Together with Luther and Justus Jonas, Melanchthon helped write the influential and foundational Augsberg Confession in 1530 at the Diet of Augsberg. One of the earliest written declarations of Lutheranism, The Augsberg Confession established one of its essential tenets, justification by faith alone ("*sola fide*"), i.e., man's salvation is through faith in Jesus and His Gospel alone, not through his abilities or her works.

As part of his humanistic interest in apparently non-religious knowledge, Melanchthon was eager to embrace new discoveries in mathematics and science, especially astrology, astronomy and anatomy. Melanchthon was, according to Fleisher, at the epicenter of Reformation Humanism which, in addition to using drama and poetry "in the service of the Lutheran cause," [Fleischer], extolled in poetry the wonders of science, mathematics and anatomy − as in this poem − and, thereby, God's Providential design. As Kusukawa (Transformation of Natural Philosophy) and Nutton (Wittenberg

Anatomy) elucidate, although Melanchthon welcomed the anatomical discoveries of Vesalius, and their corrections of Galenic anatomy, they were utilized in a particularly Lutheran way, that is, to demonstrate the presence of God in anatomy and his salvific role in human life. Melanchthon found no conflict or contradiction, unlike 20$^{th}$ Century creationists, between the Christian Bible's story of creation and the study of anatomy with man as its subject. As the poem in question illustrates, the study of anatomy of mankind is but the unveiling of the presence, for those instructed how to see and with the faith to recognize it, of God as a wise, beneficial shaper of atoms – but *not* in an Epicurean fashion! – into a being that will in turn worship God, his creator. This view was not strictly Lutheran, however. As Kusukawa reminds us, quoting Singer, Vesalius shared this theocentric notion of anatomy:

> For He who is True Wisdom will teach us, not as beings formed of this substance which comes into being and passes away, but [as beings formed] of a spiritual substance which resembles His own. But since up to now we are that which frail Reason declares us to be, we shall explore the ingenuity of the Artificer of the Universe, as shown in the remaining parts of the brain, according to our powers as men. (Kusukawa Transformation, page 119, Singer 1952, page 40)

The significance and Lutheran meaning of Melanchthon's poem are clear. The circumstances surrounding the genesis of this poem, however, are less clear. What we do know is that the poem exists in an autograph form, most likely in Melanchton's hand, in a copy of the *Fabrica* in the National Library of Medicine. It also exists as exemplars in other copies of the *Fabrica* in a printed format, and that Melanchthon wrote it on January 25, 1552, since he dated the poem at the bottom as written on the Day of Conversion of St Paul, 1552. However, we do not know for certain that this copy of the *Fabrica* originally belonged to Melanchthon. We also do not know if there was a personal meeting of Melanchthon and Vesalius or, if so, where or when although most scholars would suggest Augsberg or Wittenberg in the early 1550's. Nor do we know why or how the exemplars, some with typographical errors, came into existence or when.

The poem is 28 lines long composed in Neo-Latin in elegaic couplets, a verse form so called since Roman poets like Catullus, Ovid, Propertius and Tibullus often used it to write elegies in Latin. Elegaic verse consists of recurring couplets of two lines, first a line in dactylic hexameter followed by a line in dactylic pentameter. Although there are other conventions there is no defined length and most elegaic poems are short. I feel that this poem, which is 28 lines long, with a clear break at line 15, represents a conscious decision by Melanchthon to write a double sonnet. This idea is not as unreasonable as it sounds since Melanchthon was a poet who helped foster the humanistic studies, including poetry, in 16th Century Germany, writing, in a letter, "In die Herzen der Dichter hat Gott eine starke Empfindung gelegt," or "God has instilled strong feelings in the hearts of poets." (Hartfelder, 320) There is, however, no strong tradition of sonnets in Germany at this time, much less double sonnets. The form of this poem, as I elucidate below, is suggestive.

Mine is not the first translation of this poem. The classicist Dorothy Schullian translated it beautifully in a 1954 paper. (Schullian) While hers is a literary interpretation, I have tried to capture the many internal echoes within each sonnet and between the sonnets. The first 14 lines set up the apparent chaos of the universe as a foil for the second fourteen lines, the apparent chaos of a human body. The first sonnet dispels the appearance of random atoms as prime movers (a clear refutation of Epicureanism) in favor of mere materials shaped by a wise God who is the same God who carefully designs and plans not only the universe of the first sonnet but the purposeful human body of the second sonnet.

1. Melanchthon's name is spelled many different ways in pre-modern publications: Philip, Philipp, Phillip and even, occasionally. Melanthon. In this book we shall use only "Philip Melanchthon."

philippus Melanchthon
de consideratione
humani corporis.

Non casu volucres Atomi, sine mente ruentes,
    Hanc mundi formā progenuere nouā
Formauere sed mens sapiens ac optima, mundi est.
    Consilio seruans condita cuncta suo.
Quae clara impressit passim vestigia rebus,
    Conditor agnosci possit ut inde Deus.
Nosse vias numerosa ac ordinis, atq; tenore
    Immotū recti iudicia atq, mali
Non haec ex coecis Atomis sapientia venit,
    Verū est naturae prospicientis opus.
Sic etiam posimus coeli terraq; perennes,
    Quodq; vrahut certa sidera cuncta vices,
Testantur vere numen sapiensq; bonūq.
    Esse quod has leges condidit atq, regit.
Sic non humano cocreta in corpore mebra,
    Sponte sua, et casū nata sine arte putes.
Singula consulto certos distinxit ad usus,
    Cū templū vellet nos Deus esse sibi.

Poem by Philip Melanchthon about Vesalius and his Fabrica and the meaning of human anatomy in God's Universe. Handwritten, probably by Melanchthon himself, first page of two, in a copy of the Fabrica belonging to the National Library of Medicine. Courtesy of the National Library of Medicine

I have tried in the following translation to preserve the correspondences, the echoes as it were, between lines 1–14, what I call the first sonnet, and lines 15–28, the second sonnet. Whereas the first sonnet describes the Providential nature of God as (Lutheran) planner of the universe, the second draws the comparison to His workings in the world of man, specifically, the man of

Diuina in cerebro radios sapientia spargit
  Cum verbo mentes, luce suaq, regit.
At cor Iustitiae domus est, sentitq dolores,
  cum punit sontes vindicis ira Dei.
Adflatuq, dei purgatu gaudia sentit
  Et vita fruitur non pereunte Dei.
Formatu ad tantos compos cu videris usus
  Factore agnoscas & reuerere Deum.
Ipsius & templu non labes ulla prophanet,
  pollutu abyciat, ne grauis ira Dei.

Noribergae Die
  Conuersionis Pauli
    1550.

Vesalian anatomy. By syntax, diction and punctuation I have therefore essayed to keep the translation as close to Melanchthon's original, tightly constructed (as tightly constructed as the body he praises God for making!) and ordered poem while making it as poetic as such confines permit. The schematic below will demonstrate these echoes and my argument.

Of note is Melanchthon's preference for "vindicis ira Dei", "the wrath of a vengeful God" (line 22). This seems to have been a phrase that appealed to him since he uses it three times in one volume of his poetry and criticism - twice in poems and once in an interpretive and poetic translation of Sophocles's "Ajax", lines 1081 - 1083. (Bretschneider, Corpus Reformatorum, Vol. X)

## Philip Melanchthon de consideratione humani corporis

1 Non casu volucres atomi, sine mente ruentes,
    Hanc mundi formam progenuere novam.
  Formatrix sed mens sapiens ac optima mundi est,
    Consilio servans condita cuncta suo.
5 Quae clara impressit passim vestigia rebus,
    Conditor agnosci possit ut inde Deus.
  Nosse vias numerorum ac ordinis, atque tenere
    Immotum recti iudicium atque mali.
  Non haec ex caecis atomis sapientia venit,
10 Verum es naturae prospicientis opus.
  Sic etiam positus coeli terraeque perennes,
    Quodque trahunt certae sidera cuncta vices,
  Testantur vere numen sapiensque bonumque
    Esse, quod has leges condidit atque regit.
15 Sic non humano concreta in corpore membra
    Sponte sua, et casu nata sine arte putes.
  Singula consulto certos distinxit ad usus,
    Cum templum vellet nos Deus esse sibi.
  Divina in cerebro radios sapientia spargit,
20 Cum verbo mentes luce suaque regit.
  At cor iustitiae domus est, sentitque dolores,
    Cum punit sontes vindicis ira Dei.
  Adflatuque Dei purgatum, gaudia sentit
    Et vita fruitur non pereunte Dei.
25 Formatum ad tantos corpus cum videris usus,
    Factorem agnoscas et venerere Deum.
  Ipsius et templum non labes ulla prophanet,
    Pollutum abiiciat ne gravis ira Dei.

## Concerning the human body

1   Not by mindless chance did atoms fleet
    Engender this new shape to our world.
    Rather, its Shaper was the wisest mind in our world
    Preserving the whole he had planned, then made,
5   He left his imprint everywhere to gleam
    That all might thereby recognize its Maker as God
    And know the vectors of numbers, both ordinal and
       cardinal,
    And possess an unshakable judgment of right and
       wrong.
    Not in atoms blind did this wisdom originate,
10  Rather it is the work of a Providential nature.
    So too do the eternal co-ordinates of heaven and earth
    And the fixed orbits steering all the stars
    Truly bear witness to a spirit, both wise and good,
    A spirit that made the rule of law.
15  Likewise, not by artless chance – lest you think it –
    Did the body's members coalesce of their own will.
    With careful planning did God apportion to each its
       own fixed purpose
    Since God wished us to be his temple.
    His divine wisdom radiates throughout our brains,
20  With his word and light he rules our minds.
    Whereas it is the heart that is the home of justice, and feels grief
    When God in vengeful wrath punishes sinners.
    Once cleansed by the breath of God, it rejoices
    And God's eternal life enjoys.
25  When you contemplate a body shaped to so many
       purposes
    It is God, its Creator, you should recognize and venerate.
    And let no stain profane His temple
    Lest God in his severe wrath raze it in its
       desecration.

## Philip Melanchthon de consideratione
## humani corporis

1    Non casu volucres atomi, sine mente ruentes,
        Hanc mundi formam progenuere novam.
     Formatrix sed mens sapiens ac optima mundi est,
        Consilio servans condita cuncta suo.
5    Quae clara impressit passim vestigia rebus,
        Conditor agnosci possit ut inde Deus.
     Nosse vias numerorum ac ordinis, atque tenere
        Immotum recti iudicium atque mali.
     Non haec ex caecis atomis sapientia venit,
10       Verum es naturae prospicientis opus.
     Sic etiam positus coeli terraeque perennes,
        Quodque trahunt certae sidera cuncta vices,
     Testantur vere numen sapiens que bonumque
        Esse, quod has leges condidit atque regit.
15   Sic  non humano concreta in corpore membra
        Sponte sua, et casu nata sine arte putes.
     Singula consulto certos distinxit ad usus,
        Cum templum vellet nos Deus esse sibi.
     Divina in cerebro radios sapientia spargit,
20       Cum verbo mentes luce suaque regit.
     At cor iustitiae domus est, sentitque dolores,
        Cum punit sontes vindicis ira Dei.
     Adflatuque Dei purgatum, gaudia sentit
        Et vita fruitur non pereunte Dei.
25   Formatum ad tantos corpus cum videris usus,
        Factorem agnoscas et venerere Deum.
     Ipsius et templum non labes ulla prophanet,
        Pollutum abiiciat ne gravis ira Dei.

## Concerning the human body

1      Not by mindless chance did atoms fleet

        Engender this new shape to our world.

        Rather, its Shaper was the wisest mind in our world

        Preserving the whole he had planned, then made,

5      He left his imprint everywhere to gleam

        That all might thereby recognize its Maker as God

        And know the vectors of numbers, both ordinal and

            cardinal

        And possess an unshakable judgment of right and

            wrong.

        Not in atoms blind did this wisdom originate,

10    Rather it is the work of a Providential nature.

        So too do the eternal co-ordinates of heaven and earth

        And the fixed orbits steering all the stars

        Truly bear witness to a spirit, both wise and good,

        A spirit that made the rule of law.

15    Likewise, not by artless chance – lest you think it –

        Did the body's members coalesce of their own will.

        With careful planning did God apportion to each its

            own fixed purpose

        Since God wished us to be his temple.

        His divine wisdom radiates throughout our brains,

20    With his word and light he rules our minds.

        Whereas it is the heart that is the home of justice, and feels grief

        When God in vengeful wrath punishes sinners.

        Once cleansed by the breath of God, it rejoices

        And God's eternal life enjoys.

25    When you contemplate a body shaped to so many

            purposes

        It is God, its Creator, you should recognize and venerate.

        And let no stain profane His temple

        Lest God in his severe wrath raze it in its

            desecration.

## Benedetto Varchi (1502 - 1565)

Vesalio mio – A Sonnet to Andreas Vesalius
Translated from the Italian by Dario Del Puppo

Cover of Varchi's Book of Sonnets, 1555.
Courtesy of Google Books

Benedetto Varchi (1503-1565) was a Florentine humanist, historian, and poet who is remembered for his sixteen-volume Storia Fiorentina written between 1527 and 1538, but unpublished until 1721 because of its frank and truthful narrative of political history. Varchi was also the author of philosophical and linguistic works. His treatise in the form of a dialogue, *Ercolano* (1570), is an ardent defense of spoken Florentine with respect to the literary and classicizing Tuscan promoted by Pietro Bembo (1470-1547). Although a proponent of the Florentine republic, Varchi became a member of Duke Cosimo I de' Medici's court and joined the Accademia Fiorentina in the early 1540's. In Florence, he gave public lectures on different topics, including the philosophy and poetry in several canti of Dante's *Divina Commedia*. A prolific poet, Varchi was also deeply interested in the physical sciences, especially in human physiology. His friendship with Andreas Vesalius is well-documented and dates to Varchi's sojourn in Padova (1540) and precedes Vesalius's arrival in Pisa in 1544 (Carlino 2016 pp. 123-4; Corsini 1918 pp. 508-510). In Pisa, Varchi attended dissections of humans conducted by Vesalius. Their correspondence has been preserved (Ciliberto), and we also know that Varchi owned a first edition of Vesalius's text. The Florentine humanist expressed his admiration for the great scientist in the sonnet below. As the poem suggests, Varchi was the intermediary between Vesalius and Cosimo who had hoped to attract the anatomist to the university in Pisa, but Vesalius was lured by a more prestigious post at the court of Emperor Charles V to whom he dedicated his *De humani corporis fabrica* (1543).

Varchi was a Renaissance man with varied and wide-ranging interests. So, his appreciation of Vesalius's scientific achievement should come as no surprise. He attempted to link Vesalius's discoveries to ongoing debates about philosophy and theology and also to those about the relationship between philosophy and poetry. For Varchi, Dante's *Commedia* and Lucretius's *De rerum natura* (the most controversial of ancient poems) transcended distinctions between science or natural philosophy, theology, and poetry. For the Florentine humanist, these epic poems were more than great theological or philosophical works dressed up in beautiful verse. Varchi, undoubtedly, also saw poetic genius in Vesalius's science, and he perhaps also viewed the anatomist as making a contribution to Renaissance debates about the nature of soul and, hence, about the role of reason and imagination in human creativity. Florence had long been a center of Neo-Platonic thought. Varchi's interpretation of Aristotelianism, informed by scientific innovations, such as those of Vesalius, therefore critiqued the prevailing view in Florence. From recent scholarship on his thought (in particular, Andreoni and Sgarbi) moreover, we sense that for the Florentine humanist there is poetry in science and science in poetry. Besides being a gracious invitation to a friend and a genius, the sonnet to Vesalius implies a belief in the 'integralness" of science, philosophy, and art as expressions for Varchi of the indivisible and immortal soul.

*VESSALIO mio,che cosi conto,e chiaro*
  *Il picciol mondo,e le sue parti hauete,*
  *Come hà'l maggior colui,che'l fece,e sete*
  *Solo senza simil,non dico paro:*
*Al Toscan Duce non di uoi men raro,*
  *Intendendo da me come sarete*
  *Sopra Arno in breue alle Pisane mete,*
  *Fu dolce piu,ch'io non so dire,e caro:*
*E ch'io di nuouo caldamente a uoi*
  *Riscriuessi m'impose,e quanto all'opra*
  *Facesse di mestier,tutto fornissi:*
*Mouete dunque,e col fauor di sopra*
  *Venite à lui far lieto,e tragger noi*
  *Col lume nostro di si scuri abissi.*

My Vesalius, so precise and clear
  have you the little world and all its parts,
  like He who made the greater world, and you are
  alone, without peer, not to say without equal.
To the Tuscan lord, no less one of a kind as you,
  hearing from me, that you will soon be
  upon the Arno headed toward Pisa,
  was news more sweet and dear than I can say;
And to you again I warmly write,
  he urged, and whatever you might require
  for your work I should provide:
Make haste, therefore, with the above favor,
  come make him glad and lead us
  with your light from the dark abyss.

V. 1. "so precise and clear" refers to Vesalius' profound and extensive knowledge of the human body, the microcosm of the world. The English translation published by L.R.C. Agnew reads "for I count you as mine." *Conto* in ancient Italian also meant 'famous' or 'measured', hence, 'precise'. In the encounter with Farinata in Inferno X, Virgil admonishes Dante, the pilgrim, to mind his words, "le parole tue sien conte," and Varchi was a brilliant dantista.

V. 2. "have you ... parts": 'knowledge' is implied, but not necessary because Vesalius's knowledge of the 'little world' (the human body) is so complete that he is its master, as God is the master of the universe.

V. 5. The Tuscan lord is Cosimo I de' Medici (1519-1574), the second Duke of Florence from 1537-1569.

V. 7. upon the Arno ... Pisa: A reference to Vesalius's imminent arrival to the studio in Pisa in 1544.

## PAUL EBER (1511 - 1569)

Poem to Vesalius in Melanchthon's **Liber de anima, recognitus ab autore**, 1552

Translated from the Latin
by Richard M. Ratzan

"Weinberg des Herrn" ("Vineyard of the Lord") Epitaph for Paul Eber's grave in the Stadtkirche der Lutherstadt Wittenberg, (1569) from Wikimedia, https://commons.wikimedia.org/wiki/File:Weinberg-WB-1569.jpg
{{PD-Art}} since its author/creator of work died in 1586.

A fellow Lutheran, Paul Eber (1511 - 1569) was one of the inner circle of friends of Melanchthon and Luther. He was a particularly close friend of the former. Lucas Cranach the Younger (1511 - 1586), born in Wittenberg, the epicenter of Lutheranism, not only painted a portrait of Melanchthon for one of his books as well as the funeral Epitaph for Paul Eber's grave above; he also painted an altarpiece in the same church, Stadt- und Pfarrkirche St. Marien zu Wittenberg (Town and Parish Church of St. Mary's in Wittenberg), the leftmost panel of which depicts Melanchthon baptising a baby:

"Melanchton tauft" ("Melanchton baptises") from Wikimedia:
https://commons.wikimedia.org/wiki/File:Melanchthon-tauft.jpg

Born in Kitzingen in Franconia in 1511, Eber, like his older friend Melanchthon, became an ardent Christian scholar early in life. As professor of Latin grammar in Wittenberg, Melanchthon's academic home as well, Eber revised the Latin translation of the Old Testament. In addition he was Professor of Hebrew. He is best remembered these days, however, as an hymnist. His two best known hymns are "*Wenn wir in höchsten Nöten sein*" ("When we are in utmost need") and "*Herr Jesu Christ, wahr Mensch und Gott*" ("Lord Jesus Christ, true man and God").

The brief poem below first appeared in Melanchthon's *Liber de anima recognitus ab autore*, 1553. It occurs near the end of a letter Melanchthon wrote to Hieronymous Baumgartner, accompanying a copy of the book. In the letter Melanchthon explains his current thoughts on the soul and why he undertook this revision ("recognitus" in the title), i.e., in part because of new knowledge about the body, especially in Vesalius's *Fabrica*. When he mentions Vesalius in the letter, he quotes his good friend Paul Eber's characterization of him in the poem, which Melanchthon incorporates into the letter.

### EPISTOLA

*& Peucerum generum meum. Sed quia nec vacuo animo huic vni operi intentus fui, & peregrinationes nostræ sæpè hanc telam, quam contexere malebam, interruperunt, alicubi desiderari diligentia poterit. Oro igitur eos, qui alijs hæc initia enarrabunt, vt errata candidè emendent, præsertim cum extent iam picturæ Vesalij, & luculentæ descriptiones, de quibus sic inquit Paulus Eberus:*

*Quantum noctu alias stellas cum lumine fratris*
  *Orbem compleuit, vincere Luna solet:*
*Vesalij tantum reliquis liber anteit vnus,*
  *Corpora qua qua sint condita ab arte, docet.*

*Quanquam autem patris tui Hieronyme, iudicio permitto, an hunc meum librum, aut alios tibi proponi velit, tamen de re ipsa scio iudicium eius cum meo congruere. Scit verissimum esse, quod scripsit sapiens historicus Thucydides, κρἁτιʃόν εἰνσἱ ἐν ἁναγκαιοτἁτοις παιδεύεσθ, hoc est, discenda esse maximè necessaria, vt in tota vita præcipua est sapientia, necessaria facere: ita vt in studijs prima sit cura, vt necessaria discantur. Ac verè statuit pater tuus, necessariam esse homini cognitionem doctrinæ, quam Deus illustribus testimonijs Ecclesiæ tradidit. Et ad hanc iudicat has descriptiones potentiarum animæ, præparationem quandam esse. Affert hæc doctrina lucem & legibus, quib. mores hominum regendi sunt. Ostendit enim,*
                                                    *qua*

*Quantum nocte alias stellas cum lumine fratris*
*Orbem complevit, vincere Luna solet:*
*Vesalij tantum reliquis liber anteit vnus,*
*Corpora qui qua sint condita ab arte, docet.*

Quantum nocte alias stellas cum lumine fratris
Orbem complevit, vincere Luna solet:
Vesalii tantum reliquis liber anteit unus,
Corpora qui qua sint condita ab arte, docet.

However much the Moon is wont, when it fills
The earth with its brother's light, to outshine all the other stars,
Just so, surpassing all the rest is this one book of Vesalius,
Who teaches us with his art how bodies are constructed.

Note:
Fascinatingly, two versions of this poem exist, one from the original book,
with *docet* in the last line, the other in an edited volume of Melanchthon's
works from 1840, with *docent* in the last line. (Even more interestingly there
exists a handwritten version of the second *docent* version in an owner's copy,
as reproduced in the book by Márgocsy et al., page 113, in the library in the
University of Pécs.) My feeling is that only *docet* can be correct (besides its
being the earliest printed version) since "qui," which can be singular or plural,
must be masculine. For it to be the relative pronoun as the subject of *docent*
it would have to be the plural neuter *quae* to agree in case and number with
*corpora docent*.

Of further interest, "*qui*," a relative pronoun, if taken as nominative masculine
singular to be subject of "*docet*," could refer to Vesalius or "liber" (book). Since
the book in question is Vesalius's *Fabrica*, this would seem to be a metonymic
distinction without a semantic difference.

Opposite page: Passage from printed letter from Phlip Melanchthon to Hieronymus
Baumgartner, in Melanchthon's Liber De Anima Recognitus, 1580?, 8th page of book, in
which Melanchthon quotes Paul Eber's poem about Vesalius and his Fabrica. Courtesy of
Google Books. Top of page: Enlargement of quoted poem.

# GASPAR BRUSCH (1518 - 1559)

"De poculo Caesareo"

Translated from the Latin by
David M. Ratzan
Richard M. Ratzan

Kaspar (or Gaspar) Brusch. Courtesy of Wikipedia

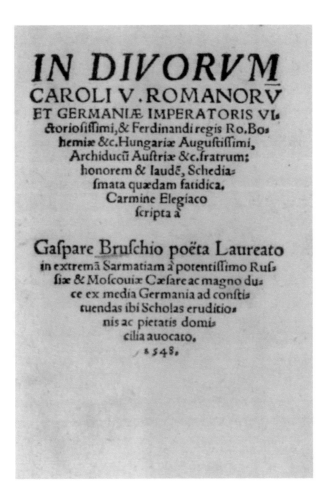

Title page of Gaspar Brucsh's 1548 (first edition) book of
poems containing his poem about the goblet Vesalius gave
him. Courtesy of Google Books

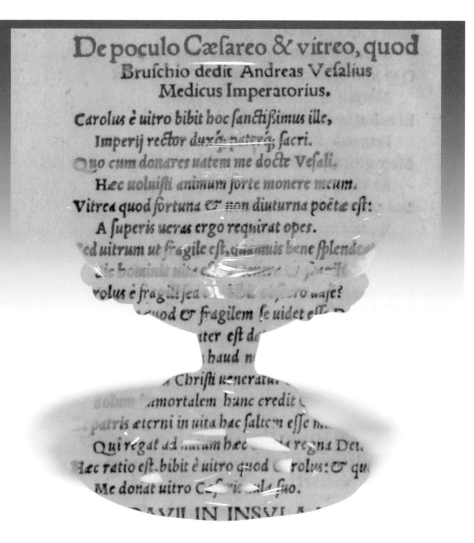

## De poculo Cæsareo & vitreo, quod
### Bruschio dedit Andreas Vesalius
### Medicus Imperatorius.

Carolus è uitro bibit hoc sanctißimus ille,
  Imperij rector duxá̃ patréq́, sacri.
Quo cum donares uatem me docte Vesali,
  Hæc uoluisti animum forte monere meum.
Vitrea quod fortuna & non diuturna poëtæ est:
  A superis ueras ergo requirat opes.
Sed uitrum ut fragile est, quamuis bene splende̅
  ...ic hominis ...
rolus è fragili sed ... uase?
  ...uod & fragilem se uidet e...
  ...ter est d...
  ...haud n...
  ...Christi ueneratu...
  solum ...amortalem hunc credit ...
  ...patris æterni in uita hac saltem esse n...
  Qui regat ad ...um hæc ... regna Dei.
Hæc ratio est, bibit è uitro quod Carolus: & qu...
Me donat uitro C... ... fuo.
  ...VII IN INSVL...

Composite image of period goblet and title page of Brusch's "De Poculo Cæsareo" by editor.

# INTRODUCTION

Gaspar (also written "Caspar" and "Kaspar") Brusch was born in Schlackenwald in Bohemia 1518, the son of a shoemaker, bookseller and merchant. He attended the Latin school in Eger, then attended the University of Tübingen briefly, after which he began traveling widely through Germany, Switzerland, Italy and Austria, collecting material for his writing, which was often scholarly. It is of no little interest that the web of associations in the 16th century around Vesalius includes Brusch's studying with Melanchthon (who also wrote a poem to Vesalius included in this volume) in Wittenberg in 1542. He seems to have earned some of his income from his poetic encomia of nobility and the wealthy, in addition to a salary as a schoolteacher. At the young age of 23, he came to the attention of the Emperor Charles V, who crowned him "Poeta Laureatus" in 1541 at the Imperial Diet at Regensburg.[1]

Brusch published prolifically, both as a poet and a historian. His major historical accomplishments were his *Monasteriorum Germaniae* (1551) and *Magni operis de omnibus Germaniae episcopatibus epitomes* (1549). Additionally, his description of the Fichtelgebirge is still valued by German historians. He became a pastor in Potendorf near Regensburg around 1555 and soon thereafter, in 1559, was murdered in a forest – Horawitz, his biographer, says he was shot through the back of the head – but not robbed, leading the authorities to believe the killer was someone offended by something Brusch had written.

It is unclear how and when Brusch met Vesalius, but in a letter he wrote to Joachim Camerarius in 1546 he recommends a former student of Vesalius. We also know that both he and Vesalius were in Augsburg at the same time in 1551. Known conventionally by the first two words of its title, the poem "De poculo," ("On the cup") was first published in 1548, and seemingly written while Brusch taught Roman writers like Vergil, Terence and Cicero in Lindau on the Bodensee (Lake Constance), which is to say sometime in 1546 or 1547.[2] The poem commemorates Vesalius's presentation to Brusch of a glass cup that had once belonged to Charles V and serves as the coda to a slim volume of "inspired improvisations" dedicated to emperor and his brother Ferdinand I: *In divorum Caroli V. Romanoru(m) et Germaniae Imperatoris victoriosissimi et Ferdinandi regis Ro. Bohemiae etc. Hungariae Augustissimi, Archiducu(m) Austriae etc. fratrum: honorem et laude(m), Schediasmata quaedam fatidica. Carmine Elegiaco scripta à Gaspare Bruschio poeta Laureato ...,* (printed in Augsburg; Munich BSB: Res/Asc. 802).[3] Horawitz hands down a particularly mordant verdict on Brusch's attempt to curry imperial favor with this work: "Das Büchlein ist eines der wenigst erfreulichen aus Brusch's Feder, keines riecht so sehr nach Stellenjägerei, in keinem ist der Syrup und Zucker der Schmeichelei so widerwärtig stark vertreten" ("This little book is one of the least pleasant from Brusch's quill: no other reeks so much of job-hunting, in none is the syrup and sugar of bootlicking laid on so sickeningly thick.")[4] Brusch nevertheless thought these encomia good enough to republish in a second and enlarged edition in 1550, adding two poems immediately preceding "De poculo" and a dedicatory poem to Georg Geinger, the former vice chancellor and current advisor of Ferdinand I, whom he calls his "Maecenas" (a political advisor to the Roman emperor Augustus and famously the patron of Virgil and Horace).

O'Malley in his biography of Vesalius (1964: 213) proposed that Charles V might have given the cup to Vesalius sometime in 1546 in gratitude for his treatment of the Venetian ambassador Bernardo Navagero, and that sometime thereafter Vesalius gave the cup to Brusch. He appears to be in some doubt about when this act of regifting might have taken place, suggesting that it could have even happened as late as 1550 or 1551 (1964: 454, n. 136). It seems, however, that O'Malley was unaware of the first edition of this poem in 1548. It stands to reason that the poem commemorates a gift Vesalius made before 1548, since Brusch had already left Lindau in late 1547. Interestingly, Brusch also touched up "De poculo" for republication, revising the first line.[5] We have printed the text of the first edition, but comment on his revisions in the notes.

Meter and Style

As one might hope of a school master and poet laureate, Brusch was a competent Latin versifier, if not a brilliant one. Elegiac couplets, or a dactylic hexameter followed by a dactylic pentameter, were one of the most popular Latin verse forms in the Renaissance, and Brusch had certainly learned the rules well, which had begun to be rearticulated on the basis of poets like Virgil and Ovid by the likes of Jan de Spauter and those who followed him at the turn of the 16ᵗʰ century.[6] Thus he shows no false quantities (i.e., vowel or syllable lengths) in this poem, gives no prosodic value to *h*, and uses elision freely (unlike medieval Latin poets). In his hexameters Brusch also evinces a stylistically correct preference for third-foot masculine caesurae (line 5 is a conspicuously disastrous exception), dactyls in the fifth foot (the one exception is line 13), and trisyllabic and disyllabic line endings. With respect to the pentameter, he successfully avoids spondees in the second hemiepes (the pentameter was divided into two "half lines," or hemiepes) and ends all but one of his verses with the preferred disyllable (the exception is line 8, which ends in a deprecated trisyllable). Finally, he obeys the general rule that the unit of sense is the couplet.

Though technically correct, his versification (at least in this poem) is decidedly pedestrian. Brusch thus finds himself leaning too ponderously on spondees, particularly in the first foot (e.g., lines 3, 13-15), and making recourse to elision (newly readmitted by Humanist prosody) far more frequently than his classical models, or even some of his contemporaries, recommended (e.g., lines 5, 7-8, 14-15; in all, a total of 13 elisions in just 18 lines), with five lines having two or even three elisions.[7] He also has a tendency to elide monosyllables other than *est*, a practice which was increasingly considered poor form (e.g., lines 7, 14-16). His vocabulary and word placement is repetitious: at certain points this serves his theme (see the notes), but overall it suggests that his powers of expression were somewhat constrained and limited by metrical necessity. This is not to say that Brusch was utterly incapable of turning out a nice line. Indeed, his pentameters are often quite pleasing and well constructed (e.g., lines 2, 4, 6, 10 and 18); and, as some of the notes below show, he is at times able to use rhetorical devices such as word order, variation, and repetition to good effect.

Themes

As noted above, the occasion for this poem was Vesalius's gift of a glass drinking vessel, which, Brusch tells us, had been used by Charles V himself. When refracted through his poetic lens, this glass is translated into a symbol or, perhaps more accurately, its materiality becomes a touchstone for a web of symbolic meaning that he proceeds to weave.

Brusch first asks what it means that Vesalius, a learned doctor, has presented him, a *vates* or an inspired poet, with this fragile gift. (See note to line 3 of translation, below.) He concludes that it is to be understood as a warning for him as a poet not to trust to fickle fortune, but to seek a truer foundation from the powers above. It is difficult here not to hear an echo of Horace's programmatic claims to poetic fame in *Odes* Bks. 1-3, where in the first poem he vows that he will strike his head against the stars, if he be granted the status of *vates* (*Odes* 1.1.35-36: *Quod si me lyricis vatibus inseres, / sublimi feriam sidera vertice*), while at the end of the collection he declares that he has succeeded in erecting a poetic "monument more lasting than bronze" (*Odes* 3.30.1: *Exegi monumentum aere perennius*).[8]

This meditation on the fragility of fortune (an important theme for early modern thinkers, such as Machiavelli, e.g., chapter 25 of *The Prince*) leads Brusch to see human existence as essentially glassy: shining and splendid, but also delicate and easily shattered. If so, why would Charles, the invincible ruler of the Holy Roman Empire (*invictissimus* was a standard epithet, and indeed written into the first line of the second edition), use such a symbol? Brusch answers his own question at the center of his poem, where he reaches his prophetic apogee: it is because Charles understands that he is a "fragile god" (line 10: *fragilem … Deum*). It is an arresting image, to be sure; and one that Bruschius immediately proceeds to deconstruct over the next few couplets. Although the entire world is given over to Charles, he nevertheless piously recognizes his own mortality, and is thereby transformed back into a man, with the line ending of 12 echoing 10, as *esse Deum* becomes *esse virum*. This recognition entails the further acknowledgement of the immortality and spiritual sovereignty of the true God in Jesus Christ, confirmed in the final repetition of *esse Deum* in line 14. The proper world-order has now been restored, as Charles is once again God's temporal servant, dutifully ruling His empire as a holy viceroy.

The cup is thus imagined as a double, nested symbol: first for Charles, as a reminder of his splendid, divinely sanctioned, but ultimately limited power on earth; and then for Brusch, as a warning of the fragility of his own fortunes. This lading of so much meaning onto a simple gift may well strike us as overwrought (as it did Horawitz), but gifting, particularly of high value art objects, was a well-established part of Early Modern society, particularly at court.[9] Indeed, Brusch was not the only poet to write about court gifts: Ferdinand I, one of the dedicatees of the volume, had some years earlier commissioned Wilhelm Shurf to write a poem about a unicorn horn that had been a gift of the Polish King Sigismund (1506-1548).[10] In all this Vesalius is represented as nothing but a conduit, bestowing not so much an object as a symbolic talisman of the court on Brusch. In fact, his agency is completely elided in the final couplet as he is made to stand in for the court itself (18: *Me donat vitro Caesaris aula suo*). Significantly, the poem does not establish that Charles marked out this gift especially for Brusch, much less instructed Vesalius to give it to him, although this may have been the case. It seems much more likely, as O'Malley imagined, that the gift was between Vesalius and Brusch (1964: 213). In any event, we see Brusch here inserting himself into the gift exchange economy of the Habsburg court and its trade in symbols.

Notes to Introduction

1   The bibliography on Brusch was most recently collected by J. Flood (2011), *Poets Laureate in the Holy Roman Empire: A Bio-bibliographical Handbook* (Berlin, De Gruyter), pp. 249-256. A. Horawitz's biography remains fundamental: *Caspar Bruschius. Ein Beitrag zur Geschichte des Humanismus und der Reformation*, Prague and Vienna, 1874.

2   Horawitz 1874: 109-116.

3   A digital copy of the book  is now available online via the Bayerische StaatsBibliothek: https://opacplus.bsb-muenchen.de/title/BV001379272.

4   1874: 115.

5   Cf. Horawitz 1874: 125, who notes the new dedication, changes to the title page, and the addition of new poems, but not the re-editing of this or any of the other poems in the first edition. This book is now scanned and online, courtesy of the Bayerische StaatsBibliothek: https://opacplus.bsb-muenchen.de/title/BV009009404

6   Ford, Philip J., "Neo-Latin Prosody and Versification", in: Brill's *Encyclopaedia of the Neo-Latin World*, General Editor Craig Kallendorf. Consulted online on 21 February 2020 <http://dx.doi.org/10.1163/9789004271296_enlo_B9789004271012_0005>. See also J. IJsewijn and D. Sacré (1998). *Companion to Neo-Latin studies, Part II: Literary, linguistic, philological and editorial questions.* Leuven, Belgium: Leuven Univ. Press. Pp. 423-33.

7   Ovid, the master and exemplar in the Early Modern period of the elegiac couplet, admits approximately one elision every four lines. See Kent, R. G. "Likes and Dislikes in Elision," *Transactions of the American Philological Association* 54 (1923),

86-97.

8    On the early modern knowledge and reception of Horace, see Carlsmith, C.
     (2013). "A Roman Poet in the Venetian Republic: The Reception of Horace in
     Sixteenth-Century Bergamo." *Sixteenth Century Journal*, 44(4) 963 - 984.

9    See H. Watanabe-O'Kelly (2002), *Court Culture in Dresden: From Renaissance
     to Baroque*. New York, Palgrave and the dissertation of I. Horacek (2015),
     "Alchemy of the gift : things and material transformations at the court of Rudolf
     II," unpublished dissertation, University of British Columbia. http://hdl.handle.
     net/2429/52830.

10   Horacek, "Alchemy" (2015): 145-146.

## Text of the 1548 original publication

*De poculo Caesareo & vitreo, quod Bruschio dedit Andreas Vesalius Medicus
Imperatorius.*

> *Carolus è vitro bibit hoc sanctissimus ille*
> > *Imperii rector duxq(ue) paterq(ue) sacri.*
> *Quo cum donares vatem me docte Vesali,*
> > *Haec voluisti animum forte monere meum.*
> 5 *Vitrea quod fortuna & non diuturna poëtae est:*
> > *A superis veras ergo requirat opes.*
> *Sed vitrum ut fragile est, quamvis bene splendeat, ipsa*
> > *Sic hominis vita est & tenera & fragilis.*
> *Carolus è fragili sed cur bibit obsecro vase?*
> 10 *Nempe quod & fragilem se videt esse Deum.*
> *Ille quidem terris pater est datus omnibus, at se*
> > *Mortalem tamen haud nescit is esse virum,*
> *Idcirco patrem Christi veneratur Iesu,*
> > *Solum immortalem hunc credit & esse Deum*
> 15 *Se patris aeterni in vita hac saltem esse ministrum,*
> > *Qui regat ad nutum haec omnia regna Dei.*
> *Haec ratio est, bibit è vitro quod Carolus: & quod*
> > *Me donat vitro Caesaris aula suo.*

Translation

On the imperial crystal goblet, which Andreas Vesalius, Imperial Physician, gave to Bruschius

> The most holy Charles himself drank from this glass,
>> Ruler, leader, father of a holy empire.
> And when you, learned Vesalius, bestowed this on me as a poet,
>> You perhaps wanted to warn my soul of the following:
> 5    For the poet, fortune is glassy and ephemeral:
>> From the gods, therefore, let him seek true wealth.
> Yet just as glass is fragile, however much it may gleam,
>> So is human life itself delicate and fragile.
> But why, pray, did Charles drink from a fragile vessel?
> 10    Surely because he sees that he is a fragile God.
> He is indeed a father given to all the lands, but he
>> Well knows that he is himself a mortal man;
> Therefore he worships the father of Jesus Christ
>> And believes that He alone is Immortal and God,
> 15    While he himself is but the servant of the eternal father in this life,
>> Who is to rule all these kingdoms by the will of God.
> This is the reason why Charles drank from a glass, and why
>> The court of Caesar presents me with his own glass.

Notes to translation

1.  In the second edition of 1550 the first line was amended to read: *Carolus è vitro bibit invictissimus isto.* "Charles the invincible drank from this very glass." *Invictissimus* was a standard epithet in Charles' imperial titulature. The reasons for the change may have been political, since the substitution destroys the echo of *sanctissimus* in line 2 (see next note), but it is also not without its stylistical advantages, as B. revises a clunky chiastic order (i.e., A - B - b - a - a: **Carolus è** *vitro bibit* _hoc_ **sanctissimus ille**) with a more balanced imbricated line (i.e., A - B - a - b: **Carolus è** *vitro* bibit **invictissimus** _isto_).

2.  A very nice line: *sacri* at the end of the pentameter modifies *imperii* in hyperbaton, with the order echoing that of the hexameter: *Carolus* (i.e., the *imperator*)… *sanctissimus ~ imperii … sacri.*

3.  B. relates himself to Vesalius syntactically with parallel and interlocking predicative phrases, contrasting his role as an inspired *vates* with Vesalius's as a learned scientist, i.e., **vatem** _me_ **docte** _Vesali_ (A - a - B -b), thematizing a commonplace divide, if not antagonism, between philosophy and poetry. The juxtaposition thus calls attention to an important difference in vocation, signaled in the title of this collection: *schediasmata quaedam fatidica.* Sir Philip Sidney in his *Defense of Poesy* (written in the late 1570s, but published posthumously in 1595) has much to say on the relationship between philosophy and poetry, and says this of the figure of the *vates*: "Among the Romans a poet was called *vates*, which is as much as a diviner, foreseer, or prophet, as by his conjoined words, *vaticinium* and *vaticinari*, is manifest; so heavenly a title did that excellent people bestow upon this heart-ravishing knowledge." (Sidney, P. *The Defence of Poesy*. Cambridge, MA; Hilliard and Brown, 1831: page 9)

4.  One desired quality of a pentameter was to coordinate the words in hyperbaton at the end of each hemiepes or half-line. Thus *animum* is modified by *meum*, each standing at the end of its respective half-line. Over time, there was a recognition of a classical preference for having the adjective precede the noun, as we see in line 6 (*veras … opes*; cf. lines 9 (a hexameter), 10, and 18); but this convention was perhaps not yet well established in the mid-16th century. The other main rhetorical figure was to have the related pair bookend the verse, as we see in lines 2 (see note above) and 12.

5.  There may be an element of Humanist practice that escaped us, but if not, this line is perhaps the most incompetent in the poem. The elision of *fortuna* and *et* at the third foot means that there is no caesura at all. Worse still from a rhythmical

perspective, this leaves a diaeresis at the end of the third foot, dissolving the line neatly in half, leaving it broken-backed. Finally, in order to arrive at this unhappy result, B. must employ not one, but two elisions.

6. The final *o* of *ergo* usually scans as long, but in this period final *o* was often seen as a *syllaba communis*, or a vowel whose quantity could be treated as long or short according to the poet's need. *Requirat* is either jussive or potential subjunctive.

9. For the hyperbaton connecting *fragili* (placed right before the caesura) and *vase* at the end of the line, see the note to line 4 above.

10. B. accentuates the shocking image of a fragile God by delaying the word *Deum* until the end, putting the stylistic preference for coordination at the end of the hemiepes (see note to line 4 above) to good rhetorical effect. This might seem close to blasphemy or idolatry, but it is not only the capitalization that suggests that it is indeed God (as opposed to some "deity") to which B. is assimilating Charles: in the immediately preceding poem B. also declaims that Charles is the very image of God, the face of piety itself (*De imagine divi Caroli V. Schediasma à Bruschio eiaculatum, cum videret comedentem Caesarem*, "An inspirational utterance of Bruschius when he saw the emperor eating"). See the note to line 12.

11. The punctuation of the 1548 edition mistakenly placed a comma after *at*, which was corrected in the second edition. It was permissible to end a hexameter with two monosyllables, cf. line 17. We are using here the punctuation of the second edition.

12. The hyperbaton of *mortalem … virum* (cf. notes to lines 2 and 4) parallels that of line 10 as B. begins to resolve the oxymoronic figure of the *fragilem … Deum*. B. here demonstrates command of a particular stylistic refinement of the pentameter (on display elsewhere in his work), which allowed a monosyllable that was not *est* to stand before the caesura only if preceded by another monosyllable or a pyrrhic ( ˘ ˘ ), like *tamen*. This achievement, however, is somewhat vitiated by his recourse to the colorless and grammatically redundant pronoun *is*.

13. A heavily spondaic line, with the rhythm making no apparent contribution to the meaning. *Iesu* is the regular genitive form.

14. Another heavily spondaic line with two somewhat clumsy elisions in the first hemiepes. Here the echo of line 10 (*esse Deum*) is surely intentional, replacing the image of Charles as a fragile temporal God with that of the one true immortal God the Father, the spiritual King of Kings. The syntactical connection of lines

13-15 is somewhat loose. In these three lines there are two independent clauses, i.e., those dependent on *veneratur* (12-13) and *credit* (14), and two dependent clauses in *oratio obliqua* set off by *credit*, i.e., *hunc ... esse Deum* (14) and *se ... esse ministrum* (15). There is, however, only one possible conjunction: *et* in line 14. Whether this is postponed and should be taken to connect *veneratur* (12-13) and *credit*, or if instead it should be taken to connect *immortalem* and *Deum* as predicates in line 14, is difficult to decide. The fact that there is certainly no connection between the two dependent clauses, i.e., *et* in line 14 cannot be taken as connecting the two infinitives in indirect statement, weighs in favor of the latter interpretation, since this would mean that there would be parallel asyndeta between the independent and dependent clauses. In all events, we have added conjunctions not in the Latin in order to make clear what we read as the intended meaning.

15.  Yet another spondaic line with three elisions, two of which are monosyllables. Charles finally assumes his rightful role as God's chosen temporal authority on earth, having moved through a series of predicates from *Deus fragilis* (10) to *vir mortalis* (12) to *minister patris aeterni*.

16.  For this use of the subjunctive, see Gildersleeve's *Latin grammar* (1895 reprint in 2003 by Bolchazy-Carducci), §630.

18.  *Aula* here, as in English, is used metonymically to mean the court, i.e., courtiers. *Suus* is normally reflexive, and so should properly refer to the grammatical subject, i.e., the *aula*. However, it is commonly used as a purely possessive adjective (instead of the regular genitive of the pronoun *is*, i.e., *eius*) when the speaker or author is emphasizing the possession of the logical subject, as in this case, where B. is saying that he received Charles' *own* cup. Cf. Kuehner-Stegmann, *Ausfuehrliche Grammatik der lateinischen Sprache* (4th ed., 1962), 1.1 (Satzlehre: Erster Teil), §117, A.4 (pp. 603-606).

# BENITO ARIAS MONTANO (1527 - 1598)
from Virorum doctorum de disciplinis benemerentium effigies XLIIII

Translated from the Latin by
Richard M. Ratzan

BENEDICTVS ARIAS MONTANVS
*Hispalim illustras patriam* MONTANE, *secunda*
*Doctrina fama & fertilis eloquy.*
*Surgit sublimæ per te noua gloria linguæ,*
*Vatibus & sacris lux rediuiua datur:*
*Macte bonis animi vir magne & postera sæcla*
*Munere victuro demerare Pater.*

B i

Benito Aris Montano. Courtesy of Google Books

An able humanist, linguist, extremely knowledgeable (and thrifty) book collector for his master, Philip II of Spain, Benito Arias Montano was, most famously, the editor of the renowned polyglot Bible of Antwerp in 1572 printed by the same Christopher Plantin (1520 - 1589), in Antwerp, who worked with Sambucus (see later in this book). Born in 1527 in Fregenal de la Sierra, in Extremadura in the southwestern Kingdom of Spain, near its border with the Kingdom of Portugal, Montano began his studies early in Seville at the age of 19. He studied Hebrew and the Bible in Alcalá, where he also distinguished himself not only in poetry and in Hebrew but also in Chaldean and Syriac, earning the epithet, "The Spanish Jerome." He later studied medicine and botany and was admitted in 1560 to the Order of Santiago, entering the Monastery of San Marcos de León.

Having come to the attention of Philip II, the latter entrusted Montano with the printing of the Polyglot Bible in five languages, a project involving many transactions, both public and secret, and affairs political and religious, that lasted four years. Although the Bible was well received by some, all was not always smooth sailing for Montano, however.

A colleague, León de Castro, whose translation of the Vulgate Bible (i.e., in Latin) Arias had opposed in favor of the Hebrew, arguing that the latter was a more accurate source of information about Jesus, accused Montano of heresy, as Castro also did the famous writer, Fray Luis de León, a fellow congregant. Although Luis de León spent 4 years in prison suffering ill health, fortunately powerful allies supported Montano, who never went to prison.

Along with the Polyglot Bible, Montano and Plantin published Montano's *Monumenta humanae salutis*, a book of 72 Latin odes on religious subjects. In addition to his poetry, Montano published many well received commentaries, in Latin, on books of the Bible. He was finally able to retire to Extremadura where he died in 1589. Montano seems to have been a gentle, kind, learned and forgiving man who even felt Castro, his accuser, had been incited by the devil rather than more harsh human motives. As a biographer wrote:

> Small of stature and certainly not robust, witty and charming in conversation, he combined the directness of the scholar with a singular gentleness and attraction. The Duke of Alba, twenty years his senior, Pope Gregory XIII, the young King Sebastian [ of Portugal], Philip II himself, all evidently fell under the spell. (Bell, page 54)

In 1572, Montano wrote the poems – quatrains – for a publication in Antwerp by Philips Galle entitled *Virorum Doctorum de Disciplinis Benemerentium Effigies XLIIII* (Forty-four Images of Learned Men Distinguished in their Disciplines). In an elegant 2005 reproduction of the 1572 original, Canseco and Antolín make several important points about this collaboration. As they stress, the choice of the men for these likenesses was guided by a threefold agenda: first, the utility of the professional work of these men for the rest of mankind; second, the amplification of the notion of humanistic disciplines as they had been redefined by new sciences, mathematics and technologies during the Renaissance; and lastly, to stretch the boundaries of orthodoxy in reaction to the straitened guidelines of the Council of Trent. (Canseco and Antolín, page 41)

As these authors also point out, in an essay entitled, "Rhetoric and Ekphrasis in the Effigies XLIIII," Montano modeled his quatrains after the epigrams of Martial, attempting not so much to present a four line biography as to capture the essence of the man and his signal contributions:

> Las *Effigies* fueron concebidas de forma emblemática, esto es como la suma de palabra e imagen. La imagen la puso el buril de Philips Galle; la palabra, la pluma de Arias Montano. Y Montano concibió el texto a modo de epigrama; por eso redactó sus versos con el metro propio del género epigrámatico, el dístico elegíaco, y se atuvo a los rasgos esenciales del epigrama: la *brevitas*, cifrada en los dos dísticos elegíacos de cada elogio, y la *venustas*, la gracia basada en la sutileza. El texto, pues, no pretendía ser un biografía de retratado, ni extensa ni sumaria, sino tan sólo aprehender y transmitir, con elegancia o con agudeza, un rasgo de su alma y de su ingenio. Tampoco son epigramas satíricos, ni amorosos, ni epitafios, sino precisos epigramas laudatorios, y por ello Montano usó de los recursos retóricos y estilísticos del encomio poético y lo hizo con la variedad que caracteriza toda la colección. (Canseco and Antolín, page 56)

> The Effigies were conceived with an emblematic form, that is to say, as the sum of word and image. Philips Galle's burin applied the image, Arias Montano's pen, the word. And Montano conceived the text in the fashion of the epigram; therefore he composed his verses with the meter appropriate to the dramatic genre of epigram, the elegiac distich, and maintained the essential traits of the epigram: *brevitas*, encapsulated in the two elegiac distichs of each elegy, and *venustas*, grace grounded in subtlety. The text, then, did not pretend to be a biography of the portraited, either extensive or summary, but only to apprehend and transmit, with elegance or acuity, a trait of his soul and his genius. Neither were they satirical or amorous epigrams, or burial, but epigrams of praise and precision, and therefore Montano employed the rhetorical and stylistic means of the poetic encomium and did so with the variation that characterizes the entire collection. (translated by RMR)

Two poems (by Montano and Sambucus [I.S.]) handwritten under portrait of Vesalius. Courtesy of the Library Company of Philadelphia. Pg A6v from *De humani corporis fabrica //* *Six Vesa Log 30.F

A N D R E A S  V E S A L I U S  B R U X E L L E S I S
A N A T O M I C O R U M  F A C I L E  P R I N C E P S

ANDREAS VESALIVS,
BRVXELLENSIS.

*Corporis humani qui membra minuta fecaret*
*Vefalio nullus doctior extiterat.*
*Hic Medicis auxit Pictoribus auxit & artem,*
*Dum fubit internas quæ latuëre vias.*

C 3

Portrait of Andreas Vesalius from *Virorum Doctorum de Disciplinis Benemerentium Effigies XLIIII*, 1572. Courtesy of Google Books

## ANDREAS VESALIUS OF BRUSSELS
## ADEPT PRINCE OF ANATOMICIANS

Of those who would dissect the minute parts of the human body
There was no one more learned to surpass Vesalius.
He furthered their art for physicians, furthered their art for painters,
While exploring those inner passages that had remained hidden.

# JOHANNES SAMBUCUS (JÁNOS ZSÁMBOKY) (1531 - 1584)
Quis sine te felix Medicus

Translated from the Latin by Richard M. Ratzan

Johannes Sambucus. Courtesy of Wikipedia

Born János Zsámboky (or Zsámboki) in Nagyszombat (now Trnava, Slovakia, but then part of the Kingdom of Hungary not far from its Western border with Austria), Iohannes Sambucus, the Latinate name he assumed, was a fascinating humanist. Like so many physicians (Anton Chekhov, Walker Percy, William Carlos Williams, Richard Selzer), he often felt more comfortable in the world of the humanities, especially literature, than medicine. As Visser notes, translating a passage from his 1555 Poemata:

*Phoebo me, ac medicis dedi colendum,*
*Donec quid magis accidit venustum*
*Et meo placet simul palato.*
*Consultum hoc studio tamen propinquis*
*Et meae cuperem bonae saluti*
(Sambucus, 1555, Poemata, page 31.)

I have devoted myself to Phoebus Apollo and
medicine, until something more elegant
comes along, which also pleases my taste.
By this study, however, I wish to help my dear
ones and my own good health. (Visser)

Sambucus was most famous as a book collector, the owner of a vast and
widely coveted library, and author of several influential works, especially
his 1564 *Emblemata cum aliquot nummis antiqui operis*, a book of emblems
(published by Plantin, the same printer who published the work for which
Benito Arias Montano — see earlier in this book — wrote his descriptive poetic
quatrains). He was also quite interested in Cicero.

The quatrain in this volume accompanied a woodcut of Vesalius, one of 59,
including an ironic one to himself as the final image, in his 1574 book *Icones
Veterum Aliquot, Ac Recentium Medicorum, Philosophorumque Elogiolis Suis
Editae, Opera.*

DE D. IOAN. SAMBVCO. I. L. 67.

Te, qui præclaros Medicos depingis, & ornas,
 Quid fugit? es pectus, bibliotheca, labor.
Facta Ducum texis, scriptores vndique clausos
 Exquiris, studio Græcia, Roma pater.
Vulgò grassantes morbos, Anazarbea purgas:
 Dij tribuant vitæ tempora longa tuæ.
Dij ciues, vrbem, qui te genuere parentes,
 Pannoniam & foueant, nil minuantque dies.

Portrait of Sambucus in
his own *Veterum aliquot
ac Recentium Medicorum
Philosophorumque Icones*,
1574. Courtesy of Google
Books

VESALIVS. 32.

Quis fine te felix Medicus, promptúsque Cherurgus?
Ni artis fubiectum, membra, fitúmque fciat?
Sæcula tot pars hæc latuit, porcum atque catellos,
Non homines prifci diffecuére Sophi.

Portrait of Andreas Vesalius in the *Veterum aliquot ac Recentium Medicorum*
*Philosophorumque Icones* by Sambucus, 1574. Courtesy of Google Books

What physician would be successful without you, or surgeon ready?

    If he did not know the subject of his art, the limbs and their anatomy?

For so many centuries did this region remain obscured, pig and puppies –

    Not men – did earlier Experts dissect.

# Jakob Balde (1604 - 1668)
Satura XII

Translated from the Latin by Anthony Macro and Richard M. Ratzan

Portrait of Jakob Balde.
Courtesy of Google Books.

Bust of Jakob Balde in the
Ruhmeshalle, Munich. Courtesy of
Wikimedia

Within the world of Neo-Latin writers and poets, there is a microcosm, albeit not a small microcosm, of Jesuit Neo-Latin writers, especially poets. Foremost among these, in the minds of many Neo-Latinist scholars, is Jakob Balde (1604–1668). Born in Ensisheim in Alsace, in 1604, while studying law at the University of Ingolstadt, he famously heard Jesuits chanting prayers in a nearby monastery while unsuccessfully serenading a young woman and then and there transferred his energy and affections from women to Jesus, more especially the Society of, or the Jesuits. He was ordained Priest in 1633 in the midst of a devastating Thirty Years War (1618–1648). He became the tutor of the sons of Duke Albert of Bavaria and then his friend, advisor and priest to Count Palatine Philipp Wilhelm, dying in 1668.

# SATYRA XII.

*Vesalii anatomici præstantissimi laus. Contra Atheos*

Sit Fabius faba ventosa,& caput artis inane.
  Plena tamen bulga est,& avito turgidula asse.
Ampla domus,multi tituli Salamantica parvum
Nutrijt.ulterius raptum per castra,per urbes,
Compostellanis trivit Callæcia clivis.
Hinc trahit ingenij famam.vix credere possis,
Ornatis quantas promittat porticibus spes.
Tecta subi,& prope barbaricum mirabere luxum.
    Ante fores ludit Siren;& limine in ipso
Dispositi occurrunt Centauri;aliæque Chimæræ
Mille locis pendent medioque umbone locantur,
Quacunque aspicias,& *Mira & Bella* videbis.
Hinc stat rhinoceros,vel coruu rhinocerotis:
Inde colorati squamato ventre dracones.
Vnus ei similis,quem pubes Dardana quondam
Tibridis excelsas Epidauro traxit in arceis.
Quid memorem conchas Tyrrheno ex æquore lectas,
Lucenteis vario picturatóque recessu?
Vipera viva natat vitreo conclusa cutullo:
Et potum illæso despumat gurgulioni.
Ales Mygdonius vituli pede continet ovum,
Aut soleam ferri sonipes quam Martis in Hæmo
Perdidit,excussam rapido per inhospita cursu.

Composite image of beginning of Balde's Satura XII, "Sit Fabius faba ventosa" by editor.
Courtesy of Google Books

Balde was nothing if not prolific, writing in a variety of genres on religious subjects, especially the Virgin Mary, but also Horatian odes and epodes, becoming known as "The Horace of Germany." Although Balde was widely known and respected during his lifetime, his reputation suffered a decline after his death with a brief resurgence 100 years later when Johann Gottfried Herder, the great German poet, discovered him and brought him to the attention of many, including Goethe, highly praising his poetic skills. Herder published an appreciation of Balde in the late 1790's with many translations (not, however, any of his satires) in a three-volume work entitled *Terpsichore*, calling Balde the German Horace and writing:

ein Dichter Deutschlands für alle Zeiten : manche seiner
Oden sind von so frischer Farbe, als wären sie in den
neuesten Jahren geschrieben. (Herder, 1881)

a poet of Germany for all time: some of his Odes are of
such a fresh color that they might have been written just
yesterday. [transl RMR]

Unfortunately, essentially all of Balde's verse is in Neo-Latin, severely
restricting its appeal and availability to a wider reading audience.

Too, the Horatian moments are surrounded by condensed, compact
syntax. His poetry is also frequently overburdened with many classical
allusions, sometimes to the bewilderment of a reader who understands
them but not their importance in the context. As Nichols writes, "Even
Balde's Latin is Baroque in the ways it twists and distorts classical usage and
meanings." (Nichols, page 81)

This Satire is one of many in a book of medical satires. It uses Vesalius, as
does Melanchthon, as a starting point to expound on the universe and man in
particular as proof of an intelligent, all encompassing God, whose works far
surpass any of man and whose design of man demonstrates, compared to the
workings of, say, an elephant, his superior nature, albeit as still a small part of
God's greater creation. Indeed, the resonances between Melanchthon's poem,
"De consideratione humani corporis," see above, and Balde's are interesting as
shown below:

Compare Melanchthon, lines 9-14

Non haec ex caecis atomis sapientia venit,
Verum es naturae prospicientis opus.
Sic etiam positus coeli terraeque perennes,
Quodque trahunt certae sidera cuncta vices,
Testantur vere numen sapiensque bonumque
Esse, quod has leges condidit atque regit.

to Balde lines 71-75:

Astra vides oculis: illum, qui condidit astra,
Mente videre nequis? certis, en, legibus æther
Vertitur: & credis nullo rectore moveri?
Teque tuasque manus, atque ipsos consule sensus:
Omnia testantur Numen justumque piumque.

Too, both emphasize the verbs *condere* (fashion) and the noun *lex* (law) with respect to God's fashioning and governing universe and man. There is no evidence that we could find that Balde knew of Melanchthon's poem or was influenced by it.

## SATYRA XII

Vesalii anatomici præstantissimi laus. Contra Atheos

| | |
|---|---|
| 1 | Sit Fabius faba ventosa, & caput artis inane. |
| 2 | Plena tamen bulga est, & avito turgidula asse. |
| 3 | Ampla domus, multi tituli. Salamantica parvum |
| 4 | Nutriit. ulterius raptum per castra, per urbes, |
| 5 | Compostellanis trivit Callæcia clivis. |
| 6 | Hinc trahit ingenii famam. vix credere possis, |
| 7 | Ornatis quantas promittat porticibus spes. |
| 8 | Tecta subi, & prope barbaricum mirabere luxum |
| 9 | Ante fores ludit Siren; & limine in ipso |
| 10 | Dispositi occurrunt Centauri: aliæque Chimæræ |
| 11 | Mille locis pendent, medioque umbone locantur. |
| 12 | Quacunque aspicias, & *Mira* & *Bella* videbis. |
| 13 | Hinc stat rhinoceros, vel cornu rhinocerotis: |
| 14 | Inde colorati squamato ventre dracones. |
| 15 | Vnus ei similis, quem pubes Dardana quondam |
| 16 | Tibridis excelsas Epidauro traxit in arceis. |
| 17 | Quid memorem conchas Tyrrheno ex æquore lectas, |
| 18 | Lucenteis vario picturatoque recessu? |
| 19 | Vipera viva natat vitreo conclusa culullo: |
| 20 | Et potum illæso despumat gurgulioni. |
| 21 | Ales Mygdonius vituli pede continet ovum, |
| 22 | Aut soleam ferri: sonipes quam Martis in Hæmo |
| 23 | Perdidit, excussam rapido per inhospita cursu. |
| 24 | Haut indigna quidem visu. sed si nihil ultra est. |
| 25 | Perdidimus tempus. Fernelius interea me |

Satyra XII

In Praise of the eminent Anatomician, Vesalius. Against atheists

| | |
|---|---|
| 1 | Fabius may be a windy bean and a fellow void of skill. |
| 2 | His purse, nonetheless, is bulging and swollen with the coin of his grandfather. |
| 3 | A house in Salamanca, replete with family title, nourished him as a child; |
| 4 | Thereafter, carried off through the fortresses and towns of Galicia, |
| 5 | The precipitous pilgrims' road to Compostela wore him down. |
| 6 | Hence he earned his reputation as a man of character. |
| 7 | You could scarcely believe how great was the promise he offered from within his ornate gates. |
| 8 | Go inside, and you'll be amazed at the outlandish extravagance: |
| 9 | Before the doorway, a siren sings, and on the very threshold, |
| 10 | Centaurs, stationed here and there, saunter up; and assorted Chimaeras, |
| 11 | Positioned center-stage, are variously poised. |
| 12 | Wherever you look, you'll see wondrous and pretty things. |
| 13 | Here stands a rhinoceros – or the horn of a rhinoceros, |
| 14 | There tinted serpents with scaly bellies. |
| 15 | One is similar to the one the young Romans |
| 16 | Once brought from Epidaurus into the lofty citadels on the Tiber. |
| 17 | What should I say of the shells plucked from the Tyrrhenian sea, |
| 18 | Each shining in its variegated, painted recess? |
| 19 | A live viper swims enclosed in a glass goblet, |
| 20 | And digests a draught with gullet unharmed. |
| 21 | A Mygdonian bird  is guarding her egg with a calf's foot, |
| 22 | Or the spent iron-shoe of a war-horse, cast off |
| 23 | In a rapid charge in the desolate terrain of Thrace. |
| 24 | But even if there's nothing more, these are not unworthy sights to behold. |
| 25 | Fernelius and I were spending time together, |

26   Vesaliusque aliquis privam duxisset in Aulam:
27   In qua spectandum per singula membra cadaver
28   Distinctosque tomos, avolsa carne, dedisset.
29   Vt caput & collum, costæque & venter, & ossa,
30   Articulique pedum, & varia internodia crurum
31   Nexibus inter se miris aptata cohærent:
32   Emicat in parvo divina potentia Mundo.
33   Ardua cernenti metricus miracula truncus
34   Exhibet, & summi Figuli commendat honorem.
35   Relligione [sic] tremo: sacer horror concutit artus.
36   Formidata eadem placet irritatque voluptas.
37   Quid mihi Circensem jactas Romana libido?
38   Curve cruentandas populi crudelis arenas?
39   Stent licet Augusti Traianorumque columnæ:
40   Et sixti medias obeliscus dividat auras:
41   Omnia Vesalii statuæ spectacula vincunt.
42   In quibus utilitas an delectatio major?
43   Heic contemplari generis primordia nostri
44   Ac finem liceat. Quod eris, quod es, atque fuisti.
45   Hinc discas nam non homo monstrat, homucio quid sit.
46   Istae sunt latebræ, quas spes, dolor, ira, timores,
47   Et cum tristitiis habitarunt gaudia. Vultus
48   Hic potuit lenæ placuisse. foramina bini
49   Sunt oculi: per quæ, nondum nudata, Cupido
50   Intendens arcus, plumbum trajecit & aurum.

26    Meanwhile, Vesalius himself, had he been there, would have taken us into the private hall,
27    To offer for view the individual limbs
28    And dissected parts of a corpse, with flesh removed,
29    Showing how the head, neck, ribs, belly, and bones,
30    And the joints of the feet and the various articulations of the legs
31    Are united, fitted together by wondrous connections.
32    There gleams, in this small world, Divine Power.
33    The measured torso presents lofty miracles for the beholder,
34    And commands the respect of the distinguished Supreme Potter.
35    I tremble in awe; a holy frisson makes my limbs quake;
36    An alarming desire simultaneously pleases and disturbs.
37    Why does my passion for all things Roman throw the Circus in my face,
38    Or the people's Colosseum, the sand of which is waiting to be stained with gore?
39    Although the columns of Augustus and the Trajani may stand tall
40    And Sixtus' obelisk may divide the breezes,
41    Vesalius's statues surpass every popular show.
42    In which of them does the greater utility or pleasure lie?
43    Here one may learn to contemplate the origin and end of humankind –
44    What you'll be, what you are, and what you have been.
45    For hence you may learn it's not mankind that reveals what a man becomes in life.
46    Those hiding places where your hope, grief, anger, fear –
47    In company with unhappiness – have made their home.
48    A procuress could be satisfied with this look: both eyes of ours are slits,
49    As yet unopened, through which Cupid,
50    Taking aim with his bow, has shot both lead and gold.

51    Hæc fodit stimulis; hæc vertebra torsit amanteis:
52    Quis credat veteri, subducta pelle, decori?
53    Heu! breve ver, longæque hyemes! mutatio quanta?
54    Quæ nunc forma viri? speculo juveniliter usus
55    Nunc ipse est speculum, speciemque ostendit inanem,
56    Nimirum domus est Animæ pulcerrima, Corpus.
57    Donec eam spirans impleverit incola vita;
58    Fabra manet, lætumque nitens & commoda sedes.
59    Post mortem, simul emigrat dulcissimus hospes,
60    Mandra sit, egelidis Vmbrarum pervia flabris.
61    Procidui remanent muri: pictura recessit.
62    Qualia Vandalicis a flammis rudera restant.
63    His ego quem moneo? tecum est mihi sermo, Cipere:
64    sæpe audite Deum, maneisque negare profundos,
65    Ac Superos. quasi cuncta vagis erroribus orta
66    Pervadant temere, collisaque casibus, Orbem.
67    Non dubitas, quin sit Mens parva in corpore parvo;
68    Et dubitas, an sit Mens magna in corpore magno:
69    Naturæ cui tota patent sacraria, nescis
70    Naturæ Auctorem, miro glaucomate captus?
71    Astra vides oculis: illum, qui condidit astra,
72    Mente videre nequis? certis, en, legibus æther
73    Vertitur: & credis nullo rectore moveri?
74    Teque tuasque manus, atque ipsos consule sensus:
75    Omnia testantur Numen justumque piumque.
76    Ædificatus homo est. ædilem habuisse negabis?
77    Ergo opifex operis nullus fuit hujus? Epeus
78    Troiani tamen auctor Equi memoratur. Homone
79    solus fortuito compagem crevit in unam

51  These lovers he hollows out with his arrowheads; these lovers' limbs
    he racks:

52  Who would credit the body's former beauty, once the flesh had
    been peeled away?

53  Alas, Spring is short, Winters long! How great the change!

54  What is a man's physical shape today? From having used the mirror
    in his youth,

55  He himself is now his own mirror, and reflects a hollow image.

56  The Soul's loveliest home is surely the body,

57  As long as life within breathes and fills it.

58  It remains a well-wrought object, glistening and glad, a comfortable
    abode.

59  Yet after death, as soon as the sweetest of guests departs,

60  It becomes a stable, open to the icy transit of the Shades;

61  The mind's image recedes, while the tumbled walls remain,

62  Like residual rubble from the Vandals' flames.

63  Who is my audience for this advice? I'm talking to you, Ciperus.

64  Listen [my readers] to God frequently, and deny the spirits of the
    dead below,

65  And those above, as if all things, risen from random error

66  And chance collision, blindly traverse the world.

67  You do not doubt whether a small Mind exists in a small body,

68  Yet you doubt whether a great Mind exists in a great body.

69  You for whom the sacraments of nature are revealed, don't you

70  Recognise Nature's Author, blinded as you are by a wondrous
    glaucoma?

71  You see the stars with your eyes; cannot you see with your mind's eye

72  Him who has made the stars? Lo, the heaven revolves according to
    fixed laws;

73  And yet you believe that it is moved without a governor.

74  Consider yourself and your own hands and your very own senses:

75  Everything bears witness to a divine power, dutiful and fair.

76  Mankind is a building. Are you going to say that he didn't have a
    building inspector?

77  That there was no craftsman in charge, no one such as Epeus,

78  The acclaimed builder of the Trojan horse? Did mankind alone

79  Come to be, by some fortuitous flux, in a single construction,

80   Affluxu, vitale Chaos? sed gratia formæ,
81   Porrectæ sed frontis honor, sed candida cervix,
82   Cunctaque concentum formantia membra reclamant.
83   Corporibus nudis & inermes nascimur, inquis.
84   Quid tum? rostra, ungues, squamae, juba, cornua, dentes;
85   Quæ diversa feris, homini manus unica præstat.
86   An vero infantem telis onerare decebat?
87   Et rupta armatum vitulis concurrere fronte?
88   Tota mole premit terram, qui maximus inter
89   Quadrupedes elephas & prudentissimus audit.
90   Parte solum nostri minima contingimus: & cum
91   Aurea suspenso metimur sidera vultu;
92   Per tenues rimas mox scintillantia blandis
93   Connivent oculis, atque invitare videntur.
94   Quanta seges rerum? totam tamen unica messem
95   Tot spectabilium collectam pupula claudit.
96   Ianitor Auditus, quoties modulamina pulsant.
97   Dulces aure sonos, portis admittit apertis.
98   Sed nihil ac Mens est æque mirabile. Vestæ
99   Detrectat soror hæc aut Terrae filia dici.
100   Ex summo regale genus deducit Olympo.
101   Portio cælestis, divinæ particula auræ.
102   Immensi sine fine capax, impervia Leto.
103   Languida membra jacent stratis; tamen illa vagatur.
104   In somnis. Montes, saltus, mare, flumina, silvas,
105   Lustra petit, tortaque volat pernicius hasta.
106   Dumque volat, venti & cæli secura quiescit.
107   Totum agitat corpus. tota est in corpore toto.

80    As a living Chaos? Yet man's grace of form,

81    The dignity of his extended brow, his gleaming white neck,

82    And every moulded limb of his body, protest that he was blended
      in harmony.

83    We are born defenseless, with bodies naked, you say.

84    So what? Beaks, claws, scales, manes, horns and teeth

85    Present so much variation in beasts, while the hand uniquely
      distinguishes man.

86    Was it really fitting that a baby be burdened with weapons of war?

87    Or that a huntsman with a brow broken with horns challenge a heifer?

88    The elephant, largest and cleverest of quadrupeds, presses down on
      the ground

89    With his entire mass, and listens most attentively,

90    While we touch the ground with our smallest part.

91    And as we survey the gleaming stars in heaven with uplifted gaze

92    They soon begin to sparkle through slender slots in the sky,

93    Causing us to blink as though inviting us to gaze with gentle eyes.

94    However great the number of stalks of grain in the field may be,

95    Yet one eye alone can take in the whole of a harvested crop.

96    As often as harmonies drive their sweet sounds through the air, so
      our Gatekeeper,

97    Our sense of hearing, admits them through the open portal of
      our ears.

98    Yet nothing is quite as marvellous as the Mind,

99    Whether she refuses to be recognised as Vesta's sister or mother
      Earth's daughter.

100   From the heights of Olympus, she brought down a regal race.

101   A celestial portion, an atom of the divine breeze,

102   Infinite, vast in scope, impervious to death.

103   While we lay our weary limbs down on the bed, she however is on
      the move:

104   In our sleep, she explores mountains, woodland, sea, rivers, forests, and

105   Moors, and takes wing swifter than a flying spear.

106   As she flies, she's in repose, untroubled by wind and sky.

107   She stimulates the whole body, and she is wholly present in the
      whole body.

108     Atque suos instar Citharœdi temperat artus.

109     Hos immota movet. præsentem agnoveris esse:

110     Quomodo sit, nescis. cupies numerare, sed una est.

111     Observas unam? triplici se munere prodit.

112     *Unde autem hoc monstrum*, quærit doctissimus Afer.

113     Imperat, & nutum sequitur manus, accelerat pes;

114     Vix ut ab imperio facti properatio distet.

115     Ipsa sibi mandat, sua nec mandata capessit.

116     *Unde istud monstrum*, & sceptri vis grata rebellis?

117     Scilicet exsilium caussa [sic] est certaminis hujus.

118     Dum petit exsolvi, patriosque inquirit in axes;

119     Luctantis retinent captivam vincula Carnis.

120     Hinc consanguineus dolor, & pudor, iraque. Miles

121     Sola facit geminas acies sibi: sola minatur

122     Exceptura minas, suaque est Pharsalia: Cæsar

123     Pompeiusque suus. contorquet pila retorquens,

124     Hostis amica simul. dubitando vulnere victrix

125     Vincitur: & secum pugnat, secumque triumphat.

126     Spiritus est, in quem nil horrida juris habet mors;

127     Materiæ crassa quia non educitur alvo.

128     Perpetuis vicibus putres variante figuras:

129     Corrumpi, vertique nequit virtute Dei stans.

130     Vtque olim rupta Gedeonis flamma Iagena

131     Clarius elucens Madianica  castra fugavit:

108    She pictures herself as a citharist controlling her limbs.

109    Unmoving in herself, she moves them; you'll have recognised her presence,

110    But as to how it happens, you have no idea; you'll want to count, yet there is only one of her.

111    Are you aware of her singularity? She presents herself in triplicate.

112    *What is the origin of this prodigy*, inquires that most learned Afer fellow.

113    She gives the command; the hand obeys the authorizing nod, and the foot quickly follows,

114    So slight is the movement removed from the command.

115    She commands herself, yet does not carry out her own instructions.

116    *What is the source of that prodigy of yours?* And whence the pleasing force of the rebellious sceptre?

117    Of course, exile is the cause of this tension.

118    While she seeks release [from the body's prison], she consults her forefathers' celestial axes.

119    The bonds of flesh hold her fast in captivity as she struggles against them.

120    Hence kindred grief, and shame, and anger. A lone soldier,

121    Solitary she wages twin battle-lines for herself. Threatening, she solely

122    Receives her own threats and she is her own Pharsalia, Caesar and Pompey.

123    Reversing their flight, she returns javelins whirling back at their throwers:

124    She is friend and foe at the same time. Victor and victim of a questionable wound,

125    She fights against herself, and triumphs over herself.

126    She is the spirit over which grim death has no jurisdiction:

127    She is not delivered from a gravid womb of bodily substance,

128    Amidst perpetual change, involving shifting, diseased features;

129    Depending on the grace of God, she cannot be damaged or changed.

130    As when Iagena was destroyed, Gedeon's flame,

131    Shining yet brighter, put to flight the army of the Medianites,

132   Sic Animus, fracto mortali carcere, purus
133   Emicat, & supra nubes ac sidera fertur,
134   More globi, rídetque suae ludibria testæ.
135   Vt posita larva, se, siparioque remoto,
136   Comicus ostendit Ludis popularibus Actor.
137   Et tu semifero Chironi æquande Cipere,
138   Talis Pæonia tantusque Magister in arte.
139   Esse Animam credis tantummodo sanguine mistam
140   Temperiem humorum, ventorum more meantem
141   In venis: fato solvendam rursus in auras
142   Communeis: unde & ventis sua constet origo?
143   Hæc illum, qui consilio non futilis auctor
144   Omnibus ambitur votis? qui cernit acutum
145   In morbis, quantum non lynx, præpesque, Tonantis
146   Lictor, anhelantem cervum speculatus ab æthra,
147   Tiresias idem cæcus, sed dispare forma,
148   Numinis ad radios & clarum noctua Solem.
149   Huic mediam clava sit fas pertundere venam.
150   Indignum certe vitáque animaque stolonem,
151   Claudite Orestæa vesanum compede cives.
152   Nam quæ alia est, si non hæc est manifesta phrenesis?
153   Hoc etiam vere demens, quod amabilis error
154   Nutriat, & sese dementem nesciat esse.
155   Quæ nota Stultorum propria est, ex traduce ducta
156   Regis, apud Montem Tmolum: quo judice Lydus
157   Accepit merito longas, licet inscius, aures.

132    So the Soul, once its bodily prison has been broken,

133    Flashes forth in its purity and is borne above the clouds and stars

134    Like a heavenly sphere, and laughs at the absurdity of her confinement to a earthly vessel.

135    As when the comic actor reveals himself at the Popular Games,

136    Once he's removed his mask and the curtain is drawn back.

137    You too, Ciperus, the accomplished and famous Master of Paeonian Arts,

138    The very equal of the half-wild Centaur, Chiron,

139    Believe that the breath of Life, only just mixed with blood,

140    Is a blend of fluids, coursing through the veins like wind,

141    To be released again by fate into the air we all breathe,

142    Whence even its own origin in the winds may be composed.

143    Does this sound like the thinking of one who is confident in his judgement,

144    Who is solicited in every prayer? One who diagnoses the danger in diseases,

145    Not like the lynx and the Thunderer's attendant eagle,

146    As he keeps watch from the sky for a panting deer,

147    But like the blind Teiresias, though in different shape –

148    A night-owl, in the presence of the bright sun and rays of light emanating from a divine presence?

149    For him it is right and fitting to operate on the central vein with a wooden drill,

150    To remove a sucker unworthy of life and growth.

151    Citizens, lock up the frenzied one with Orestes' fetters.

152    For what is this, other than a case of manifest madness?

153    There's real madness here, too, which a charming error nourishes,

154    And fails to recognise the madness in itself.

155    This is a characteristic of fools proper, derived from a scion

156    Of a King's vine on Mt. Tmolus, where the Lydian [Midas],

157    Acting as a judge, deservedly, though unaware, acquired long ears.

Notes to Jakob Balde's Satyra XII
"In Praise of the eminent Anatomician, Vesalius. Against atheists"

1. As Kivstö notes in her Medical Analogy in Latin Satire (see Bibliography at end of this book), "He [Pythagoras] would not take so much as a bite of an animal, but followed a simple diet of lentils (lens), beans (faba) and peas (pisum); as Balde punned, Pythagoras was a triplex senator and esteemed over such noble Romans as Lentulus, Fabius or Piso (poem 5) [in Torvitas]." Kivstö, page 156.

4. The reference is to the Camino de Santiago, the mediaeval pilgrims' way that leads across the mountains of Northern Spain (Galicia) to the tomb of St. Iago (St. James) in the Cathedral of Santiago de Compostela.

10: Centaur: mythological male monster, half-human, half-beast: head, arms, trunk of a man; lower body and legs of a horse. Chimaera: female fire-breathing monster, 'lion in front, snake behind, she-goat in middle' (Hom. Iliad, 6, 181).

15-16. *pubes Dardana…Epidauro*: Epidaurus, a city in the Argolid, on the S shore of the Saronic Gulf, was the site of the sanctuary of Asclepius, the god of healing, son of Apollo. Following the advice of the Sibylline Books, the Romans in 291 BC brought the snake of the healing god Asclepius (or the god himself) from his sanctuary in Epidaurus to Rome to contain a pestilence, and established a healing cult on the island in the Tiber. (Livy 10, 47, 7; Val. Max. 1, 8, 2; Ovid Met. 15, 622-745.)
Dardanus, the founder of the dynasty of Trojan Kings, stands as metonym for Trojan, which in turn is a metonym for Roman, as Aeneas, a Trojan Prince, was the founder of Rome (via Latium). Thus: Dardanus>Troianus>[Aeneas>] Romanus.

21. *ales Mygdonius*: (a) *ales*: 'a large bird, fowl, bird of prey' (OLD s.v. *ales* 2 1.) (b) the Mygdones were a Macedonian tribe, a part of which emigrated and settled in Asia Minor (Pliny Nat. 4, 35; 5, 126); hence Mygdonius = "Phrygian" (e.g., Hor. Carm. 2, 12, 22.). Ovid (Trist. 5, 1, 11) refers to

Caystrius ales, i.e., a swan, that haunted the banks of the river Cayster that empties into the Aegean at Ephesus. Hence the bird to which Balde is alluding here may be a swan. This line is, as are so many in this poem, difficult – not to translate but to decipher. Two possibilities are: (1) "A Mygdonian bird with a calf's foot is guarding her egg" and (2) "A Mygdonian bird is guarding her egg from a calf's foot." In favor of the former is the mention in line 9 above of Chimaeras; against is the nonsensical meaning. In favor of the latter is the superior logic to the former translation. If one imagines the reader traversing a hall of wonders, one can imagine a Mygdonian bird guarding its egg from the adjacently positioned calf in the hall. (At least, one can imagine that as easily as one can imagine a bird with a calf's foot.) Against it is the tortured construction of "continet pede" to mean "guard/surround/limit" with "with" understood and the ablative. We have chosen the more logical, less grammatically likely, alternative.

For Mygdonius, see also line 156 below, when Lydus is the legendary king Midas, described by Hyginus (Fab. 191,1) as rex Mygdonius.

26. The sudden and unexplained introduction of the two pluperfect subjunctive verbs *duxisset* (line 26) and *dedisset* (line 28) gives the reader pause. We have elected to construe them as contrary-to-fact despite there being no identifiable protasis and, indeed, translate them as what Vesalius would have done had he been there. Taking them as indicative is equivalent to understanding that Vesalius is in fact doing the guiding and explaining, meaning that this poem takes place in Padua which is an unlikely scenario.

34. P. Nigidius Figulus (c. 98-45 BC): learned savant; friend of Cicero; the cognomen means "potter".

37-38. Circus Maximus: the prime arena in Rome for chariot racing, though it could be adapted for athletic games, wild-beast fights, and, by flooding the inner surface, mock sea-battles. Colosseum, whose amphitheatre could also be flooded, was the stage of the popular gladiatorial combats, where prisoners of war, criminals, and slaves fought to the death.

39. *Augusti Traianorumque columnae*: in the Roman Forum: (a) the two columns standing at the entrance to the remains of the northern of the twin

basilicas that once stood either side of the temple of Mars Ultor, in the Forum Augusti, dedicated by Augustus in 2 BC; (b) Trajan's column, dedicated in AD 113 as part of the Forum Troiani by Hadrian in memory of his adoptive father's conquest of the Dacians.

44. "*Ac finem liceat. Quod eris, quod es, atque fuisti.*" Balde liked these parallel verbal clauses. Cf.: Carmina Lyrica Book 2, Ode XXXIII, line 35: "*Quod nunc es, fuimus. Quod sumus, hoc eris.*"

49. Cupid, son of the goddess of love, Venus.

60. Neubig proposes a corruption/typographical error of the original text here and instead of the *egelidis* in the 1651 edtion has emended it to *et gelidis*. His arguments are convincing.

62. Vandala: Germanic people who 'wandered' into western Europe in the fourth and fifth centuries AD, and sacked Rome in AD 455.

63. It is unclear who "Ciperus" is. The 1651 edition has "*Cipere*", but Neubig reads "Cypere" (vocative of Cyperus), translating it to "Binse", which means "bulrush" in German. Both Hippocrates (κύπειρον, galingale, Diseases of Women) and Pliny the Elder (*cyperus*, Natural History 12.26) mention the use of cyperus, a genus of sedges, as a pharmaceutical.

64. We feel there is a typographical error in this line and that it should be the plural imperative *negate*, correlative with *audite*, not the dangling infinitive *negare*.

70. It is unclear what *glaucoma* means here. In Greek, γλαυκός means "gleaming" but can mean "bluish green" or "grey". A 1743 text by Rüdiger is entitled *Abhandlung von dem grauen Stahr und dem Glaucoma oder grünen Stahr* (Treatise on the gray Star and the Glaucoma or the green Star). Neubig's note, reflecting the thinking of the day, reads: "glaucoma (γλαύκωμα glaucedo), der grüne Staar, eine meergrüne Verdunkelung der Hornhaut, wobei man vor den Augen alles blau und grau zu sehen glaubt." (In English: "glaucoma [γλαύκωμα glaucedo], the green star, a sea-green darkening of the cornea, a condition in

which one thinks one is seeing everything in front of him as blue and gray," translation by RMR.) In fact, a present day Swiss site about glaucoma still calls it "green star". (https://augenzentrum-dietikon.ch/en/green-star-glaucoma/). *Glaucedo*, in Neubig's note above, refers to bloom or a whitish powdery, waxy covering of a plant.

71-2. This conjunction of eyes, vision and the realization that God and his providential nature are behind astronomy (our seeing the stars and the heavens) recalls Melanchthon's exhortation, in a letter to Grynaeus, of Plato's argument that our eyes were given to us for the sake of seeing the stars. Melanchthon furthers this argument by contrasting the belief in a providential God that the study of astronomy engenders with that of atheists, which meant, as Kusukawa reminds us, unbelievers in the true religion rather than an affirmed disbelief in any God. One must also remember the subtitle of this poem, which is "Against Atheists." (in: Kusukawa, Transformation, page 2)

76. "*Ædificatus homo est. ædilem habuisse negabis?*" Although we translated *aedilem* as "building inspector", it is clearly analogous to the sentiment Melanchthon expresses in his De Anima: "*Nunc inchoata hac consideratione Deum architectum agnoscamus, et illius perfectae sapientiae desiderio accendamur.*" (Melanchthon Corpus Reformatorum, 13, De Anima, page 57), Given this incomplete consideration, let us now recognize God as Architect, and let us burn with a desire for that perfect wisdom." (translation, RMR) Compare also Vesalius's calling God the "Artificer of the Universe," in Introduction to Melanchthon's *De Consideratione Humani Corporis*, in this book.

77. Epeus: builder of the "Trojan Horse" (Hom., Odyssey 8, 493).

92. We have chosen to take *rimas* as the slits in the sky and not metaphorically as slits (pupils or nearly closed eyelids) of the eye. Neubig enlists support for this reading with a similar use of *rima* in Balde's Carmen 4.41.25

100. Olympus: highest mountain in Greece, home of Zeus and the family of gods.

112. *Afer*: (a) as substantive or adjective: = "(an) African"; (b) a Roman

cognomen, whose significance is unknown here.

118. *axes*: the axis is the line through the center of the Earth and other celestial bodies around which they revolve.

122-125. the district around the Thessalian town of Pharsalus, where, in 48 BC, the revolutionary and charismatic Julius Caesar defeated the Roman senatorial army led by Pompey the Great. Lucan devotes Book 7 of his epic poem, the Pharsalia, written in AD 42, to an extended description of the battle. In Pompey's ranks was the republican Stoic, M. Porcius Cato, whose memory Lucan celebrates in the epigrammatic line:
*victrix causa deis placuit, sed victa Catoni* (Luc.1, 128) which Balde has in mind here.

130-131. cf. OT, Judges, 6-8: Gedion (Gidion) put the Medianites to flight by a concerted attack by his soldiers of noise (from smashing pots), fire (from lighting torches), and the sound of trumpets.

137. Chiron: the most humane of the Centaurs, wise in the practice of natural medicine (cf. Hom. Iliad, 4, 219; 11, 831).

138. …Paeonia…: referring to Paean, in origin a Greek god of healing, identified with Apollo and Asclepius.

143. The accusative *illum* suddenly appears with no associated verb. Neubig translates as "Ziemt solche Denkart einem Manne, der" or, "Such thinking is appropriate for a man who" (RMR translation). We have adopted a similar approach to this not uncommon type of ellipsis in Balde.

145. …*Tonantis*: "Thunderer" = Jupiter/Zeus.

147. Teiresias: the blind seer of Thebes, who plays a prominent part in various ancient Greek myths and Tragedies.

151. …*Orestaea*…: Orestes, the son of Agamemnon and Clytemnestra, who in the myth, as developed by the Athenian 5th-cent. tragedians, avenged his

father's murder by his mother and her lover by killing them both. For the act of matricide, he was pursued and driven mad by the Erinyes (Furies), until brought to trial before the court of the Areopagus, in Athens, where he was acquitted by Athena's deciding vote. Aeschylus' trilogy, the Oresteia, provides a complete account of his career.

155-157. *Regis* et cet. (156) = Phanaeus, a King in Chios, whose wines were outstanding, as were those of Mt. Tmolus in Lydia: Virgil, Georgics 2, 97-98, where qualities of wine are compared.

*Tradux* refers to a "side-branch of a vine trained across the space between trees in a vineyard" (OLD).

Lydus: refers to legendary Phrygian king Midas.

The Myth of Midas:

Pan challenged Apollo to a flute-playing contest on Mt. Tmolus, in Lydia, with the personified Tmolus serving as judge. Tmolus decided in favor of Apollo, and King Midas, who was present, dissented. Angered at this, Apollo turned Midas's ears into those of an ass. (Ovid, Met. 11, 146ff.) Another version, where the contest was between Apollo and the satyr, Marsyas, has Midas serving as judge (Hyginus, Fab. 191, as here).

## NOTES TO EKPHRASTIC WORKS

Listed by page on which the Vesalian image for the following ekphrastic work(s) occurs in the book.

80:    "Vesalius at the Gibbet of Montfaucon" by Clare Rossini

For the Vesalian image, see this website on the historiated capitals of Vesalius's *Fabrica*:

http://www.vesaliusfabrica.com/en/original-fabrica/the-art-of-thh2m1963e-fabrica/historiated-capitals.html

See also the section in the bibliography on the historiated capitals in the *Fabrica*.

The historical account of Vesalius taking a corpse from Montfaucon, the famous gibbet in Paris, is not only accurate; it comes from Vesalius's own pen, although O'Malley places the scene in Louvain, not Paris, about 1536, when he obtained a cadaver from a gibbet with the help of a friend, Gemma Frisius:

uideram. Coctionis autem ratione, emolliẽdi in medicina uis docuerat. Lutetia nanꝗ ob belli tumultus Louaniū reuerſus, atꝗ unà cum GEMMA PHRYSIO, æquè celebri Medico ac pauciſſimis conferendo Mathematico, oſſium uidendorū nomine ad eum locū quo magna ſtudioſorum cõmoditate omnes ultimo affecti ſupplicio in publica uia ruſticis proponi ſolent, obambulãs, in eiuſmodi incidi aſſiccatū cadauer, quale latronis erat, quod Galenus ſe ſpectaſſe commemorat. Vti enim hoc aues carne liberarãt, ita ſanè illud quoꝗ ipſas emundaſſe conijcio, quia homo ille ante annū ſtramine duntaxat obuſtus, & quaſi toſtus, paloꝗ alligatus, ita ſuauẽ eſcam auibus exhibuerat, ut nuda undiꝗ eſſent oſſa, eaꝗ ſolis ligamentis hæreret, muſculorum exortibus & inſertionibus duntaxat aſſeruatis. quod in ſuſpenſis nunquam uſu uenit, quum præter oculos (& ſi uulgus aliter arbitretur) uolucres nihil ob cutis craſſitiem dilaniẽt. ac pro-inde integra in his cute, oſſa intus carie afficiuntur, prorſusꝗ ad diſciplinam ſunt inutilia. Aſſic catum itaꝗ & nulla ex parte humidum ſordidum'ue corpus intuens, haudquaꝗ inſperatam ac ſubinde expetitã mihi occaſionẽ prætermiſi. quinimò Gemmæ beneficio palum cõſcendens,

Passage in the Fabrica in which Vesalius describes obtaining a corpse from the gallows. Vesalius, Andreas. *De humani corporis fabrica libri septem.* (Basel: Johannes Oporinus, 1543), page 161. Courtesy of Universitätsbibliothek Basel

Or, quoting O'Malley's translation:

Because of the outbreak of war I returned from Paris to Louvain where, while out walking with that celebrated physician and mathematician Gemma Frisius and looking for bones where the executed criminals are usually placed along the country roads - to the advantage of the students - I came upon a dried cadaver similar to that of the robber Galen mentions having seen. As I suspect the birds had freed that one of flesh, so they had cleansed this one, which had been partially burned and roasted over a fire of straw and then bound to a stake. Consequently the bones were entirely bare and held together only by the ligaments so that merely the origins and insertions of the muscles had been preserved. ... Observing the body to be dry and nowhere moist or rotten, I took advantage of this unexpected but welcome opportunity and, with the help of Gemma, I climbed the stake and pulled the femur away from the hipbone. Upon my tugging, the scapulae with the arms and hands also came away, although the fingers of one hand and both patellae as well as one foot were missing. After I had surreptitiously brought the legs and arms home in successive trips - leaving the head and trunk behind - I allowed myself to be shut out of the city in the evening so that I might obtain the thorax, which was held securely by a chain. So great was my desire to possess those bones that in the middle of the night, alone and in the midst of all those corpses, I climbed the stake with considerable effort and did not hesitate to snatch away that which I so desired. When I had pulled down the bones I carried them some distance away and concealed them until the following day when I was able to fetch them home bit by bit through another gate of the city. (O'Malley 64)

This scene has been captured by an unknown lithographer and first appeared in a Belgian publication, *Les Belges Illustres*:

Vésale et son ami Gemma à Montfaucon.

90:    "Man with a Shovel" by Cortney Davis

From the poet:

"Although all of Vesalius' images are compelling, this one, the man with the shovel, haunted me.  It was the look of anguish on his face, his mouth open in a cry of pain, a yowl that seemed at odds with the almost casual way he uses the shovel as a crutch, his open hand.  As a nurse, I recognized this contradiction − the agony of suffering juxtaposed with the acceptance, almost the invitation, of whatever is to come.

I was intrigued too by the prop Vesalius chose, this odd sort of shovel, sort of spade, a tool seemingly too delicate to do much hard work.  And so the presence of this quirky "shovel" led me to write my response to this image as a "golden shovel" poem, a form invented by poet Terrance Hayes.  Hayes took Gwendolyn Brooks' poem "We Real Cool," in which her "Seven at the Golden Shovel" live large but will "die soon," and ended the last lines of his new poem with the words of Brooks' poem.  Since Hayes' poem appeared in his book, "Lighthead" (2010), many other poets have taken on this form, using not only Brooks' words but words or phrases from other writers, other poems, and other literary sources.  To decipher a Golden Shovel poem, simply read the last word in each line straight down . . . and you will find whatever has been embedded there.  I chose a well-known quote that seemed to fit this man with his shovel, this man who forever cries out, abandoned by Vesalius, his creator."

This image belongs to a rich literary and iconographic tradition involving skeletons and shovels! Most famously, Baudelaire wrote a poem in 1859 entitled "Le Squelette laboureur," included in his popular *Les Fleurs du mal*, a poem which many scholars think was inspired by this image that inspired Cortney. Translated by many poet-translators, from Roy Campbell to Yvor Winters to Seamus Heaney, this poem, even if not an ekphrastic rendering of this particular Vesalian image, certainly adds thoughts one might have while viewing it. Tilby, however, feels that this etiological identification is not so certain since a well-known 1820 painting by Horace Vernet, "Peace and War" in the Wallace Collection, also known as "Le Soldat Laboureur," may have been the fillip for this poem.

Courtesy of Wallace Collection, Creative Commons CC-BY-NC-ND 4.0 (Unported) licence

Saunders and O'Malley (84), as do others, like Ciobanu ("Alas Poor Yorick," see bibliography), place this skeleton in the Danse Macabre tradition. Donnelly feels that Seamus Heaney's version, "The Digging Skeleton After Baudelaire" in his collection, *North*, feels the pain of earlier dispossessed Irishmen and that, in this sense, is true to the Memento Mori spirit of Vesalius's skeleton with a shovel. (See bibliography.)

See, also, a prolonged meditation on this and other images in the osteological and muscleman series by McHugh in this volume.

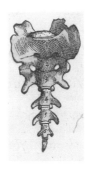

"Jakob Karrer von Gebweiler" by Marc Straus

Jakob Karrer, a bigamist, was executed in 1543 for the murder of his first lawful wife after she exposed him in front of the second wife. Vesalius obtained the newly executed body and reconstructed the skeleton, which is presently in the Basel Vesalianum in the Anatomie der Universitát Basel.

See the following:
O'Malley, pages 137-8

Biesbrouck 2014, "Andreas Vesalius' Corpses"

h0ttps://anatomie.unibas.ch/museum/downloads/Stollberg_uninova114.pdf

for a photograph of this skeleton, see: https://nyamcenterforhistory. org/2016/09/07/vesalius-and-the-beheaded-man/

96
"Artist Statement" by Jenna Le
"St. Thomas at His Desk" by Marilyn McEntyre

As one might imagine, this image has been the fountain of much scholarly ink. Saunders and O'Malley write, "The skeletal Hamlet soliloquizing beside the tomb upon some poor Yorick is perhaps the most greatly admired figure of the osteologic series." (page 86) Pesta analyzes this image vis-à-vis revenge tragedy and the anatomical theater of dissection.

108
St. Bartholomew by Margaret Lloyd

Flaying, the skinning of an animal or human, occurs frequently in this volume.
As a gruesome punishment of humans, it is unfortunately all too often recorded
in myth, historical accounts, literature (especially poetry) and graphic arts.
Perhaps the most celebrated account in Western myth involves Marsyas, a
satyr who foolishly, like Ariadne and so many other mortals in Greek and
Roman myth, entered a doomed contest with an immortal. Marsyas challenged
Apollo to a contest with a flute. Apollo won of course and flayed Marsyas
alive. Flaying, mythological or real, like the figures in Vesalius's *Fabrica*, has
provided artists and writers from Rubens to de Ribera to Janssens to today's
Robin Robertson, as well as the gifted poets in this volume, with material for
the contemplation of identity, cruelty and, in Ms Lloyd's vivid poem, ecstasy
in the face of physical and psychological pain and suffering. Margaret's poem
immediately brings to mind, every time I read it, Chilon Chilonides in his final
scene of suffering in Sienkiewicz' *Quo Vadis*.

St. Bartholomew, the Apostle, the subject of her poem, was said to have
been beheaded and flayed and is often depicted as an old man in the process of
being flayed. Indeed, the statue of him in the Duomo di Milan, Italy, is that of
an *écorché*, a flayed man:

St Bartholomew Flayed, by
Marco d'Agrate, 1562
(Duomo di Milano)
Courtesy of Wikipedia, (CC
BY-SA 2.0)

It is worth noting, at this point, that a related image, often mistakenly assumed to be an image from Vesalius's *Fabrica*, is the striking pose of a flayed man in Valverde's anatomy texts (see bibliography) published after Vesalius's *Fabrica*:

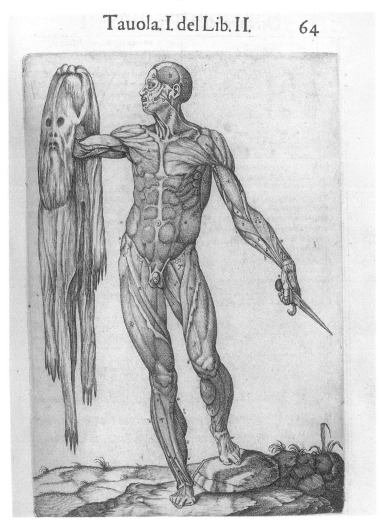

Courtesy of the U.S. National Library of Medicine

See also, with respect to flaying, the following works in this volume: Gonzalez-Crussi, Berlin, Blumenfeld, Kirchwey, Harrison, Campo, Miller ("Marked"), and Depew. Peter Pereira's poem, "Proud Flesh" in this volume, also brings Valverde to mind.

See also the monograph on flaying by Larissa Tracy, in Bibliography.
See also: McHugh in this volume; Ciobanu, "Alas Poor York" and Pesta, "Articulated Skeletons."

114

Note: on the image one of the owners edited the incorrect "Prima" and wrote
the correct "Quarta" since this was the fourth muscle man plate. As Márgocsy
et al. note, this was the most frequent editing encountered during their census.

118:    "The Muscles on the Muscle Man" by Michael Salcman

From the poet:

"Vesalius was not the only anatomist and artist to carry out the dissection of
cadavers hauled up into the upright position by pulley though he may have
been the first to do so in humans. The British artist George Stubbs (1724-
1806), perhaps the finest and most accurate painter of animals in history,
especially famous for his depictions of horses and dogs, used a pulley system to
facilitate the anatomical study of his larger specimens. An imaginary but typical
painting by Stubbs of a horse attacked by a jungle cat created in this manner
was the subject of the poem 'Stubbs Not Seen' collected in my book *The Clock
Made of Confetti* (2007)." (See author's biography at end.)

146

Note an owner, possibly the same owner who corrected plate on page 146 (above) corrected the page number from the incorrect 237 to the correct 235.

172:    "Anatomy Lessons" by David Hellerstein

https://exhibitions.lib.cam.ac.uk/vesalius/artifacts/the-belvedere-torso/

As humanists and artists and printers who would have been familiar with the more famous Greek and Roman sculpture, there is no doubt that Vesalius and whoever the woodblock cutter(s) of the *Fabrica* were and Oporinus, his printer – all would have been familiar with one of the most famous pieces of antiquity – the Belvedere Torso, not known by that name until about the time of the publication of the *Fabrica* when it had been recently moved from Rome to the Cortile del Belvedere – hence its name – in the Vatican where it is today.

The original description by Johann Winckelmann, an 18th Century art historian and archaeologist, is as beautifully apt for this statute as it is for the Vesalian image:

> Like the bare trunk of a grand old oak which has been felled and shorn of its branches and boughs, the statue of the hero sits, mangled and mutilated – head, legs, arms, and the upper part of the breast gone.
>
> The first glance will, perhaps, discover to you nothing more than a misshapen stone; but if you are able to penetrate into the mysteries of art, you will behold one of its miracles, if you contemplate this with a quiet eye. Then will

Hercules appear to you as in the midst of all his labors, and the hero and the god will at once become visible in this stone. (Davidson, 1868)

This exact description, and the generously interpretive gaze of the viewer, is clearly how Rilke viewed the archaic torso of Apollo as he wrote his magnificent poem.

Curiously, given the presence of St. Bartholomew in this volume (see above), it is noteworthy that the depiction of St. Bartholomew – holding his flayed skin – on The Last Judgment by Michelangelo, an avowed admirer of the statue, assumes a Belvederean Torso pose. (See Wikipedia:  https://en.wikipedia. org/wiki/Belvedere_Torso )

The Belvedere Torso. Courtesy of Wikipedia

Vesalius's incorporation – literally – of this image into the Fabrica serves several purposes. As Kusukawa notes in her *Picturing the Book*, it lends "a draftsman's conceit to show off his fashionable antiquarian taste on an occasion when the depiction of a full figure was not required; the Belvedere Torso was, after all, famous for the absence of its head, legs, and arms ..." Additionally, it conveys "some sense of perfection and of canonicity to the anatomical structures [the lower abdomen and renal and seminal veins] revealed." (Kusukawa, *Picturing*, page 215.) Harcourt would extend this conceit to other plates in this series, e.g., 170 and 176 in this volume, which he feels are intentionally statuesque, looking more like "fractured *stone than* [original emphasis] severed flesh." (Harcourt, Andreas Vesalius and the Anatomy of Antique Sculpture')

See also:
https://exhibitions.lib.cam.ac.uk/vesalius/artifacts/the-belvedere-torso/

176:    "Medieval Torso of Peasant Woman, Dissected" by Richard M. Ratzan

With apologies to a much much finer poet with the initials RMR and his stunning "Archaic Torso of Apollo." When I first wrote this, I had just recently read Katharine Park's *Secrets of Women* and Tulloch's life of Lord Acton. I felt his statement about Acton was particularly true of so many people, especially women, not only in the pre-modern era but still today:

"Acton passionately believed that with the disappearance of choice went the possibility of freedom." (Tulloch, p. 97)

See:
Tulloch, Hugh. *Acton*. Weidenfeld and Nicolson, 1988.

## BIBLIOGRAPHY

The bibliography is not meant to be an exhaustive compilation but rather a guide to some of the important resources for the reader who wishes to delve deeper into all things Vesalius. The websites listed are accurate at the time of this writing but, like many websites, may disappear over time.

## VESALIUS

Biography

Burggraeve, A. P. (1841). *Études sur André Vésale.* chez C. Annoot-Braeckman,

Morley, H. (1915). *Anatomy in long clothes: Being an essay on Andreas Vesalius ... As it first appeared in Fraser's magazine.* Chicago: Privately Printed.

O'Malley, C. D. (1964). *Andreas Vesalius of Brussels, 1514-1564.* Berkeley and Los Angeles: University of California Press.

Roth, M. (1892). *Andreas Vesalius Bruxellensis.* Basel: Benno Schwabe. Moritz Roth was a Swiss pathologist and the same physician who described Roth spots in bacterial endocarditis.

Vesalius, A., Garrison, D. H., Hast, M. H. (2014). *De humani corporis fabrica. The fabric of the human body: An annotated translation of the 1543 and 1555 editions of "De humani corporis fabrica libri septem".* Basel: Karger.

*De Humani Corporis Fabrica*

Harcourt, G. (1987). Andreas Vesalius and the anatomy of antique sculpture. *Representations*, 17, 28-61.

Kemp, M. (1970). A drawing for the Fabrica; and some thoughts upon the Vesalius muscle-men. *Medical History.* 14(3), 277-288. Historically important essay, including remarks about Leonardo da Vinci.

Lambert, S., Wiegand, W., Ivins, W. M. (1962). *Three Vesalian essays to accompany the Icones Anatomicae of 1934.* New York, NY: Macmillan. Includes an essay on historiated capitals by Lambert.

Burggraeve, A. P. et al. (1845). *Les Belges illustres.* Bruxelles: Librairie Nationale: Pantheon National.

Margócsy, D. (2019). From Vesalius through Ivins to Latour: Imitation, emulation and exactly repeatable pictorial statements in the *Fabrica. Word & Image*, 35(3), 315-333.

Margócsy, D., Somos M., Joffe S. N. (2018) *The Fabrica of Andreas Vesalius : A worldwide descriptive census, ownership, and annotations of the 1543 and 1555 editions*. Leiden; Boston, MA: Brill.

Osler, William. (1921). *The evolution of modern medicine: A series of six lectures delivered at Yale University on the Silliman Foundation on April 21-28, 1913*. New Haven: Yale University Press.

Saunders, J. B. deC. M., O'Malley, C. D. (1950). T*he illustrations from the works of Andreas Vesalius of Brussels: with annotations and translations, a discussion of the plates and their background, authorship and influence, and a biographical sketch of Vesalius*. Cleveland: World Publishing Co.

Richardson, W. F., Carman, J. B. (1998-2009). *On the Fabric of the Human Body*.  San Francisco: Norman Publishing.
Translation and anatomy: a massive undertaking in seven volumes by a classicist (Richardson) and anatomist (Carman).

Richardson, W. F., Carman, J. B. (1994). On translating Vesalius. *Medical History*, 38, 281-302.

## HISTORIATED CAPITALS

Francis, H. S. (1943). The woodcut initials of the *Fabrica*. *Bulletin of the Medical Library Association*, 31(3), 228-239.

Ollerenshaw, R. (1952). The decorated woodcut initials of Vesalius' "Fabrica". *Medical & Biological Illustration*, 2(3), 160-166.

Rosenkranz, K. (1937). Die initialen in Vesals anatomie: Ein beitrag zur geschichte der anatomischen a¬bbildung. *Sudhoffs Archiv für Geschichte der Medizin und der Naturwissenschaften*, 1(2)(August), 35-46.

Andreas Vesalius: De Humani Corporis Fabrica. Retrieved June 8, 2020, from http://www.dodedans.com/Eholbein-alf-vesalius.htm

Initial Stories: Vivitur ingenio. Retrieved June 8, 2020, from https://exhibitions.lib.cam.ac.uk/vesalius/case/initial-stories/

Lambert S. W. The Initial letters of the Anatomical Treatise, De Humani Corporis Fabrica, of Vesalius. In *Three Vesalian Essays to accompany the Icones anatomicae*.

See full citation above. This is an essay on historiated capitals at Hathi Trust. Retrieved June 8, 2020 from:

https://babel.hathitrust.org/cgi/pt?id=mdp.39015000806144;view=1up;seq=19

## Bibliographies

Opera Litteraeque Andreas Vesalii: Inventory of the Editions of Andreas Vsalius's Works and Letters. Compiled by Manrits Biesbrouck M.D. Roeselare, Belgium. 2019.
Retrieved June 8, 2020, from https://fatherofanatomy.files.wordpress.com/2016/01/2018-12-opera-vesalii-by-maurits-biesbrouck.pdf

Cushing bibliography at Yale. Retrieved June 8, 2020, from http://whitney.med.yale.edu/books/39002086108504/
Harvey Cushing, a famous neurosurgeon, writer (including a massive biography of William Osler) and bibliophile, was an ardent collector of Vesaliana. This bibliography is a listing of his efforts.

Cushing, H., Fulton J. F. (1943). *A bio-bibliography of Andreas Vesalius.* New York: Schuman's.

## Ekphrasis

Hefferan, J. A. W. (2008). *Museum of words: the poetics of ekphrasis from Homer to Ashbery.* Chicago; London: University of Chicago Press.

Hollander, J. (1995). *The gazer's spirit: Poems speaking to silent works of art.* Chicago: University of Chicago Press.

McHugh, H. (2007). The fabric: A poet's Vesalius. *Poetry*, 191(3), 242-261.

Mitchell, W. J. T. (1995) *Picture theory: Essays on verbal and visual representation.* Chicago: University of Chicago Press.

Putnam, M. C. J. (1998). *Virgil's epic designs: Ekphrasis in the Aeneid.* New Haven: Yale University Press.

## ANATOMY AND DISSECTION: HISTORY AND ANALYSIS: MEDIEVAL EUROPE

Barnard, M. E. (2014). *Garcilaso de la Vega and the material culture of Renaissance Europe. Vol. 13.* Toronto: University of Toronto Press.

Biesbrouck, M., Steeno, O. (2012). Leuven: Birthplace of modern skeletology, thanks to Andreas Vesalius, with the help of Gemma Frisius, his friend and fellow-physician. *Acta Chirurgica Belgica*, 112(1), 89-105.

Biesbrouck, M., Steeno, O. (2014). Andreas Vesalius' corpses. *Acta medico-historica Adriatica*, 12(1), 9-26.

Carlino, A. (1999). *Books of the body: Anatomical ritual and renaissance learning.* University of Chicago Press.

Cunningham, A. (2016). *The anatomical renaissance: The resurrection of the anatomical projects of the ancients.* London; New York: Routledge.

Davidson, T. (1868). Winckelmann's description of the torso: Of the Hercules of belvedere in Rome. *The Journal of Speculative Philosophy*, 2(3), 187-189.

Gil, J. (1998). *Metamorphoses of the body.* Minneapolis: University of Minnesota Press.

Nutton, V. (1993). Wittenberg anatomy. In O. P. Grell & A. Cunningham (Eds.), *Medicine and the Reformation* (pp. 11-32). London: Routledge.

Hartnell, J. (2018). *Medieval bodies: Life, death and art in the middle Ages.* New York, NY: W. W. Norton.

Kusukawa, S. (2012). *Picturing the book of nature: Image, text, and argument in sixteenth-century human anatomy and medical botany.* Chicago: University of Chicago Press.

Montross, C. (2007). *Body of work: Meditations on mortality from the human anatomy lab.* New York, NY: Penguin Press.

Park, K. (2006). *Secrets of women: Gender, generation and the origins of human dissection.* New York, NY: Zone Books.

Pesta, D. (2006). Articulating skeletons: *Hamlet, Hoffman,* and the anatomical graveyard. *Cahiers Élisabéthains,* 69(1), 21-39.

Sawday J. (1996). *The Body emblazoned: Dissection and the human body in Renaissance culture.* London: Taylor and Francis.

Tracy, L. (2017). *Flaying in the pre-modern world. Practice and representation.* Woodbridge: Boydell & Brewer.

Valverde, A. J., Tabo, A. A., & Vesalius, A. (1559). *Anatomia del corpo humano composta per M. Giouan Valuerde di Hamuisco: # da luy con molte figure di rame, et eruditi discorsi in luce mandata.* Roma: Per Ant. Salamanca, et Antonio Lafrerj.

Valverde, A. J., Wegener, H., Routh, W., Aslabie, W., & York Medical Society. (1572). *Vivæ imagines partivm corporis hvmani æreis formis expressæ.* Antverpiæ: Ex officina Christophori Plantini.

## Digging Skeleton/Standing "Hamlet" Images

Ciobanu, E. A. (2016). "Alas poor Yorick!" Bodies out of joint in Shakespeare, Baudelaire, Seamus Heaney, Andreas Vesalius and Govard Bidloo. *Analele Universității Ovidius din Constanța. Seria Filologie,* 27(1), 129-153.

Donnelly, B. (2009). 'The digging skeleton After Baudelaire', Seamus Heaney. *Irish University Review,* 39(2), 246-254.

Heaney, S. (1975). *North.* London: Faber and Faber.

Pesta, D. (2006). Articulating skeletons: *Hamlet, Hoffman,* and the Anatomical Graveyard. *Cahiers Élisabéthains,* 69(1), 21-39.

Tilby, M. (2012). Poetry, image, and post-Napoleonic politics: Baudelaire's "Le Squelette laboureur". *Studi Francesi. Rivista quadrimestrale fondata da Franco Simone,* 168 (LVI| III), 422-436.

## Neo-Latin

IJsewijn, J., Sacré, D., & American Philological Association. (1990). *Companion to Neo-Latin studies*. Leuven: University Press.

Knight, S., Stefan, T. (2015). *The Oxford handbook of Neo-Latin*. New York, NY: Oxford University Press.

Mertz, J.J., Murphy, J.P., IJsewijn, J. (1989). *Jesuit Latin poets of the 17th and 18th centuries: An anthology of Neo-Latin poetry*. Wauconda, IL: Bolchazy-Carducci Publishers.

Nichols, F. J. (1979). *An anthology of Neo-Latin poetry*. New Haven: Yale University Press.

## Poems To, For And About Vesalius

Balde, Jakob:
Balde, J. (1651). *Medicinæ gloria per satyras XXII asserta*. Sumptibus I. Wagneri: Monachii.

Balde, J., & Neubig, J. (1833). *Jakob Balde's medizinische satyren, urschriftlich, übersetzt und erläutert von Johannes Neubig, Lat. & Ger.* München.

Jakob Balde in Catholic Encyclopedia. Retrieved June 6, 2020, at: http://www. newadvent.org/cathen/02218a.htm

Herder, J. G., Suphan, B. (1881). *Herders sämmtliche Werke*. Berlin: Weidmann.

Kivistö, S. (2009). *Medical analogy in Latin*. London: Palgrave Macmillan.

Müller, B. (1844). *Jacobi Balde carmina lyrica*. Monachi.
Includes Herder's famous essay on Balde.

Nicolaus, M. (1937). Jacob Balde, the "Horace of Germany". *Classical Bulletin*, 13, 22.

Jacob Balde on Karl Maurer's website: Maurer, a classicist at the University of Dallas, loved Balde, as some classicists do, and constructed a website before he died, age 66, in Philadelphia (1948 – 2015).
His website has an appreciation and many bilingual translations of Balde, including his popular Ode 2.33. Retrieved June 6, 2020, at: http://udallasclassics.org/wp-content/uploads/maurer_files/Balde.pdf

Boisseau M. (1993). The Anatomy theater at Padua. *The Southern Review*, 29, 295.

Boruch M. (2014). Human atlas. In: *Cadaver speak*. Port Townsend, WA: Copper Canyon Press.

Brusch K.
Brusch 1548 edition:
Brusch, K. (1548). In divorum Caroli V. Romanorum et Germaniae imperatoris victoriosissimi et Ferdinandi regis Ro. Bohemiae etc. Hungariae Augustissimi, archiducum Austriae etc. fratrum, honorem et laudem schediasmata quaedam fatidica carmine elegiaco scripta. Lindavi in insula lacus Podamici Acroniana.

Available electronically:
Google Books. Retrieved June 8, 2020, from https://books.google.com

At Munchener Digitalisierungs Zentrum Digitale Bibliothek. Retrieved June 8, 2020, from https://daten.digitale-sammlungen.de/~db/ausgaben/zweiseitenansicht. html?fip=193.174.98.30&id=00028349&seite=13

At Württembergische Landesbibliothek Stuttgart. Retrieved June 8, 2020, from http://digital.wlb-stuttgart.de/sammlungen/sammlungsliste/werksansicht/?no_cache=1&tx_dlf%5Bid%5D=5521&tx_dlf%5Bpage%5D=1
OCLC permalink to this ebook with another link. Retrieved June 8, 2020, from http://www.worldcat.org/oclc/894768977

Brusch 1550 edition:
Brusch, K. (1550). In divorum Caroli V. Romanorum et Germaniae imperatoris victoriosissimi et Ferdinandi regis Ro. Bohemiae etc. Hungariae Augustissimi, archiducum Austriae etc. fratrum, honorem et laudem schediasmata quaedam fatidica carmine elegiaco scripta. Augustae in Rhaetis.

OCLC permalink to this book. Retrieved June 8, 2020, from http://www.worldcat. org/oclc/633652393

Available electronically:
Google Books. Retrieved June 8, 2020, from https://books.google.com.

At Bayerische StaatsBibliothek digital. Retrieved June 8, 2020, from https://reader. digitale-sammlungen.de/de/fs1/object/display/bsb10203026_00001.html

Brusch: Biography

Horawitz, A. (1874). *Caspar Bruschius – Ein beitrag zur geschichte des humanismus und der Reformation*. Prag-Wien: Selbstverlag des Vereines.

Kaspar Brusch(ius). Newald, R. Retrieved June 6, 2020, from https://daten.digitale-sammlungen.de/0001/bsb00016318/images/index.html?seite=708

Eber, Paul

Eber, P. In Melanchthon, P. (1558). *Liber de anima recognitus ab auctore Philipppo Melanchthone*. Vitaebergae: Johannes Crato.

Mcainsh, A. (2016). Bibliographical note identification of Paul Eber as an owner and reader of Vesalius's De Humani Corporis Fabrica. *The Library*, 17(4), 446-450.

Paul Eber (Hymn Writer) on Bach Cantatas Website. Retrieved June 7, 2020, from https://www.bach-cantatas.com/Lib/Eber.htm

Paul Eber. In: German Christian Singers in: Christian Classics Ethereal Library. Retrieved June 7, 2020, from https://ccel.org/ccel/winkworth/singers.eber.html

Paul Eber. In: Hymnary.org. Retrieved June 7, 2020, from https://hymnary.org/person/Eber_Paul

Paul Eber's hymns. Retrieved June 7, 2020, from https://www.bach-cantatas.com/Texts/Chorale133-Eng3.htm https://www.bach-cantatas.com/Texts/Chorale431-Eng3.htm

Melanchthon, Philip

Fleischer, M. P. (1989). Melanchthon as praeceptor of late-humanist poetry. *The sixteenth century journal*. 20(4)(Winter), 559-580.

Hartfelder, K. (1889). *Philipp Melanchthon als Praeceptor Germaniae. Vol. 7*. Berlin: Weidmannsche Buchhandlung.

Kusukawa, S. (1995). *The transformation of natural philosophy: The case of Philip Melanchthon*. Cambridge: Cambridge University Press.

Melanchthon, P., Bretschneider, K. G., Bindseil, H. E., & C, A. S. S. (1842). *Corpus Reformatorum: Volumen X*. Halis Saxonum: Schwetschke.

Melanchthon, P., Bretschneider, K. G., Bindseil, H. E., & C, A. S. S. (1846). *Corpus Reformatorum: Volumen XIII*. Halis Saxonum: Schwetschke.

Melanchthon, P, Belt E, Schullian D. M. (1949). *Observations on the human body: A poem written in Latin by Melanchthon on the fly-leaf of a copy of the first edition of Vesalius' De Humani Corporis Fabrica, 1543: In the Army Medical Library*. Cleveland, Ohio.

Melanchthon, P., Kusukawa, S., & Salazar, C. F. (1999). *Melanchthon: Orations on philosophy and education*. Cambridge: Cambridge University Press.

Schullian, D. M. (1945). Old volumes shake their vellum heads. *Bulletin of the Medical Library Association*, 33(4), 413-438.

Singer, C. J. (1952). *Vesalius on the human brain: Introduction, translation of text, translation of descriptions of figures, notes to the translations, figures*. London: Oxford University Press.

Meyer, N. S. (2006). The anatomy theater. In *The anatomy theater: Poems*. New York: Harper Perennial.

Montano, Benito Arias

Montano, B. A., Galle, P. (2005). *Virorum doctorum de disciplinis benemerentium effigies XLIIII. [Cuarenta y cuatro retratos de sabios beneméritos en las artes liberales]*. L. M. G. Canseco, F. N. Antolín (Eds.). Huelva: Universidad de Huelva.
This is a magnificent reproduction of the original with excellent critical essays.

Barea, J. P. (2000). Ecos de las obras de Marcial y de Erasmo en un epigrama de Arias Montano durante sus estudios en Alcalá. *Calamus renascens: Revista de humanismo y tradición clásica*, 1, 259-276.

Bell, A. F. G. (1922). *Benito Arias Montano*. Humphrey Milford: Oxford University Press.

Gijón, M. R. (2013). Los humanistas Alemanes retratados en *Virorum Doctorum de Disciplinis Benemerentium Effigies XLIIII*. de Benito Arias Montano y Philips Galle. *Etiópicas*, 9, 75-103.

Guerra, L. D. (2013). Imagen del humanismo: El retrato de hombres ilustres en Arias Montano. *Erebea*, 3: 329-360.

Montano, Benito Arias in Spanish Wikipedia. Retrieved June 8, 2020, from  https://es.wikipedia.org/wiki/Benito_Arias_Montano

Montano, Benito Arias on EcuRed. Retrieved June 8, 2020, from https://www.ecured.cu/Benito_Arias_Montano

Montano, Benito Arias in Real Academia de la Historia, Retrieved June 8, 2020, from http://dbe.rah.es/biografias/7898/benito-arias-montano

## Oporinus, John
Rollins, C. P. (1943). Celebration of the four hundredth anniversary of the De Humani Corporis Fabrica of Andreas Vesalius: Oporinus and the publication of the fabrica. *The Yale journal of biology and medicine*, 16(2), 129 – 134.

## Plantin, Christopher
Bowen, K. L., & Imhof, D. (2008). *Christopher Plantin and engraved book illustrations in sixteenth-century Europe*. Cambridge: Cambridge University Press.

## Rossini, C.
Rossini, C. (2012). Vesalius at the gibbet of Montfaucon. In 25th anniversary poetry retrospective. *Green Mountains Review*, XXV(1)(Summer)

## Sambucus
Almási, G. (2009). *The uses of humanism: Johannes Sambucus (1531-1584), Andreas Dudith (1533-1589), and the republic of letters in East Central Europe*. Leiden: Brill.

Sambucus, J. (1555). *Poemata quaedam Joannis Sambuci Tirnaviensis, Pannonii, Patavii conscripta*. Patavii: Gatiosus Perchacinus.

Sambucus, J. (1574). *Icones veterum aliquot, ac recentium medicorum, philosophorumque elogiolis [sic] suis editae*. Antverpiae: Plantin.

Sambucus on website French Emblems at Glascow. Retrieved June 8, 2020, from https://www.emblems.arts.gla.ac.uk/french/books.php?id=FSAb

Visser, A. S. Q. (2004). From the republic of letters to the Olympus: The rise and fall of medical humanism in 67 portraits. In van Dijkhuizen, J. F. (Ed.), *Living in posterity: Essays in honour of Bart Westerweel*. (pp. 299 – 313). Hilversum, Netherlands: Veloren Publishers.

Valverde de Amusco, Juan

Markatos, K., Arkoudi K., Androutsos, G. (2017). Juan Valverde de Amusco (1525–1588): An eminent anatomist of the renaissance or a plagiarist of Vesalius? His work and its impact in renaissance anatomy. *Acta Chirurgica Belgica*, 117(6), 407-411.

Valverde, A. J., Colombo, M. (1607). *Anatome corporis humani avctore Joanne Valverdo: Nunc primum a Michaele Colubo Latine reddita, et additis nouis aliquot tabulis exornata.* Venetiis: Studio et industria Ivntarvm.

Varchi, Benedetto

Agnew, L. R. C. (1963). Varchi and Vesalius. *Bulletin of the History of Medicine* 37(6) (November-December), 527-531.

Andreoni, A. (2012). *La via della dottrina. Le lezioni accademiche di Benedetto Varchi.* Pisa: ETS.

Bramanti, V. (2012) *Benedetto Varchi, 1503-1565. Atti del convegno: Firenze, 16-17 dicembre 2003.* Florence.

Carlino A. (2016). Medical Humanism, rhetoric, and anatomy at Padua, circa 1540. In S. Pender & N. S. Struever (Eds.) *Rhetoric and medicine in early modern Europe.* (pp. 121-138). Routledge.
Documents Varchi's friendship with Vesalius.

Ciliberto, M. (1972) I rapporti tra Vesalio e Varchi alla luce di documenti inediti. *Episteme* VI, 30-39.

Cilberto, M. (2016). Corrispondenza e corrispondenti nel secondo libro dei Sonetti di Benedetto Varchi. *Italique*, XIX, 87-112.

Corsini, A. (1915). *Andrea Vesalio nello Studio di Pisa.* Siena: Tipografia S. Bernardino.

Corsini, A. (1918). *Nuovi documenti riguardanti Andrea Vesalio e Realdo Colombo nello Studio Pisano.* Siena: Tipografia S. Bernardino.

Sgarbi, M. (2015). Benedetto Varchi on the Soul: Vernacular Aristotelianism between reason and faith. *Journal of the History of Ideas* 76(1), 1-23.

Tanturli, G. (2004). Una gestazione e un parto gemellare: la prima e la seconda parte dei Sonetti di Benedetto Varchi. *Italique*, VII, 43-87.

Umberto, P. (1971). *Benedetto Varchi e la cultura del suo tempo*. Firenze: Olschki.

Varchi, B. (1555). *De' sonetti di M. Benedetto Varchi, parte prima*. (page 121). Firenze: Lorenzo Torrentino.

Varchi, B. (2008). *Lettere (1535-1565)*. V. Bramanti (Ed). Roma: Edizioni di Storia e Letteratura.

Wharton E.
Wharton, E., Lewis, R. W. B., & Lewis, N. (1988). *The letters of Edith Wharton, 1874-1937*. New York, NY: Scribner.

Wharton, E. (1902). Vesalius in Zante (1564). *The North American Review*, 175, 625-31.

## Biographies of Contributors

Dennis Barone has edited several poetry anthologies including *Garnet Poems: An Anthology of Connecticut Poetry Since 1776*. He is the author most recently of *Beyond Memory: Italian Protestants in Italy and America, Second Thoughts* (prose), and *Frame Narrative* (poetry).

Richard M. Berlin is a physician and poet who received his undergraduate and medical education at Northwestern University. The winner of numerous poetry awards, his first collection of poems, *How JFK Killed My Father,* won the Pearl Poetry Prize and was published by Pearl Editions. His second collection of poetry, *Secret Wounds,* won the 2010 John Ciardi Poetry Prize from the University of Missouri – Kansas City and was published by BkMk Press. *Secret Wounds* was also selected as the best general poetry book of 2011 by USA Book News. He is also the author of two poetry chapbooks, *Code Blue* and *The Prophecy.* Berlin's poetry has appeared in a broad array of anthologies, literary journals, and medical journals including his column "Poetry of the Times," which has been featured for twenty three years in Psychiatric Times. An Instructor in Psychiatry at the University of Massachusetts Medical School, he is the author of more than sixty scientific papers and has edited two books, *Sleep Disorders in Psychiatric Practice,* and *Poets on Prozac: Mental Illness, Treatment, and the Creative Process.* He practices psychiatry in a small town in the Berkshire hills of western Massachusetts.

Hugh Blumenfeld was an English professor and then had a career as a touring singer-songwriter before becoming a family physician. He practices and teaches in Hartford, Connecticut, on the faculty of the University of Connecticut School of Medicine. He still delivers babies and is also the medical director of a community-based hospice program.

Marianne Boruch's ten books of poetry include *The Anti-Grief, Eventually One Dreams the Real Thing* and *Cadaver, Speak* (Copper Canyon, 2019, 2016 and 2012), three essay collections, the most recent being *The Little Death of Self* (Michigan, "Poets on Poetry Series," 2017), and a memoir, *The Glimpse Traveler* (Indiana, 2011). Her work appears in The New York Review of

Books, Poetry, The New Yorker, American Poetry Review, New England Review, and elsewhere. Among her honors are the Kingsley-Tufts Award for *The Book of Hours* (Copper Canyon, 2011), four Pushcart Prizes, plus fellowships/ residencies from the Guggenheim Foundation, the NEA, the Rockefeller Foundation's Bellagio Center, two national parks (Denali and Isle Royale) and two Fulbright Professorships, the University of Edinburgh in 2012, and the University of Canberra, Australia, in 2019, where she observed the astonishing wildlife to write a neo-ancient/medieval bestiary, a book-length sequence. Boruch taught at Purdue University for 31 years, was the founder of the MFA program there, becoming a Professor Emeritus in 2018. She continues to teach in the Program for Writers at Warren Wilson College.

Sheri A. Butler, MD, is a Training and Supervising Analyst in adult and child psychoanalysis, at the Seattle Psychoanalytic Society and Institute, where she is also the Director.  Her background is in adult and child psychiatry.  She has been writing poetry for publication for many years, and was the poetry editor for The American Psychoanalyst for over ten years.

Librettist, essayist, translator, and author of multiple poetry collections, Scott Cairns was Curators' Distinguished Professor of English at University of Missouri, until leaving that position to serve as Director of the Low-Residency MFA Program at Seattle Pacific University. His poems and essays have appeared in Poetry, Image, Paris Review, The Atlantic Monthly, The New Republic, and many other venues, and both have been anthologized in multiple editions of *Best American Spiritual Writing*. He has blogged for the Religion Section of The Huffington Post. His recent books include *Anaphora* (2019), *Slow Pilgrim: The Collected Poems* (2015), *Idiot Psalms* (2014), *Short Trip to the Edge* (spiritual memoir, 2016), *Endless Life* (translations and adaptations of Christian mystics, 2014), and a book-length essay, *The End of Suffering* (2009). He received a Guggenheim Fellowship in 2006, and the Denise Levertov Award in 2014. His current projects include *Descent to the Heart*, verse adaptations of selections from the writings of Saint Isaac of Syria.

Rafael Campo teaches and practices internal medicine at Harvard Medical School.  His work has been widely anthologized, and has appeared recently or is forthcoming in The Kenyon Review, The New Criterion, The Poetry Review (UK), The Threepenny Review, and elsewhere.

His new and selected poems, *Comfort Measure Only*, has been published by Duke University Press in 2018. He is the Poetry editor for JAMA. For more information, please visit www.rafaelcampo.com.

Jack Coulehan is an Emeritus Professor of Medicine and former Director of the Center for Medical Humanities, Compassionate Care, and Bioethics at Stony Brook University. Jack's essays, poems and stories appear frequently in medical journals and literary magazines, and his work is widely anthologized. He is the author of seven collections of poetry, including *The Talking Cure: New and Selected Poems* (Plain View Press, 2020).

Sarah Cross is an obstetrician, with a subspecialty in high risk pregnancies, at The University of Minnesota and believes there is a powerful and important role for the arts in medicine. She has received several accolades for her poetry including first & second place in the William Carlos Williams Poetry Competition, first place in the Legible Script Creative Arts Contest in poetry, and honorable mention in the New Physician's Creative Arts Contest. Her poems have appeared in over a dozen journals and anthologies. As a member of the editorial board, she reviews poetry for the Journal of Medical Humanities. She lives in Minneapolis with her husband and her three children.

Cortney Davis, a nurse practitioner, is the author of four poetry collections, most recently *I Hear Their Voices Singing: Poems New & Selected* (Antrim Books) and *Taking Care of Time*, winner of the Wheelbarrow Poetry Prize from Michigan State University. She is co-editor of three anthologies, *Learning to Heal: Reflections on Nursing School in Poetry and Prose*, *Between the Heartbeats: Poetry and Prose by Nurses*, and *Intensive Care: More Poetry and Prose by Nurses*. Her poems have appeared in journals including Poetry, Hudson Review, Superstition Review, Descant, Sun, Bellevue Literary Review, Crazyhorse, Poetry East, Sentence, Underground Voices, Rattle, The Antigonish Review, and others. Her honors include an NEA Poetry Fellowship, three CT Commission on the Arts Poetry Grants, Two CT Center for the Book Awards, an Independent Publisher's Benjamin Franklin Gold Medal in Non-Fiction, and six Books of the Year awards from the American Journal of Nursing. www.cortneydavis.com

Dario Del Puppo is Professor of Language and Culture Studies in Trinity College, Hartford, Connecticut. His research deals with the manuscripts and early printed books of Medieval and Renaissance Italian literature and, more broadly, with popular and material culture in Italy during the 14th-16th centuries. More recently, he has published on Italian food history and culture. He also has a longstanding research interest in the Romantic poet, Giacomo Leopardi.

Rebekka DePew is a family medicine resident who graduated from Vanderbilt Medical School in 2020. She grew up in Florida but also calls Boise, Boston, and Nashville her homes. She loves people, poetry, and the outdoors. She wants to work in Family Medicine so that she can spend her life listening to stories.

Rosalyn Driscoll is a visual artist whose sculptures, installations, collages and photographs explore the senses, perception and the body. Her work conveys the forces at play in the body and in nature, sometimes integrating video into her sculptures, transforming both sculpture and moving images. Driscoll is a member of Sensory Sites, an international collective of artists based in London that investigates the senses and embodied perception. Her book, *The Sensing Body in the Visual Arts: Making and Experiencing Sculpture,* is forthcoming from Bloomsbury in 2020. Her work has been exhibited in the US, Europe and Asia, and been awarded fellowships from the Massachusetts Cultural Council (twice), New England Foundation for the Arts, Helene Wurlitzer Foundation of New Mexico and Dartington Hall Trust, UK. She lives in Western Massachusetts. www.rosalyndriscoll.com

et.stark is a Michigan-born poet, bee-lover, and artist. She was the Book Arts Fellow at Press 43, in association with the Chapbook/Broadside Collaborative and ExpressNewark while attending Rutgers University MFA for creative writing. *i (don't) have a spare tire on my car* is her first chapbook from Kattywompus Press. She has a forthcoming chapbook from Finishing Line Press, New Women's Voices Series, entitled *city of ladies* and some of her poems can be found in Prelude.

Terry Donsen Feder is an artist who teaches at the Hartford Art School and Central Connecticut State University.

James Finnegan has published poems in Ploughshares, Poetry East, The Southern Review, The Virginia Quarterly Review, as well as in the anthology *Good Poems: American Places*. With Dennis Barone he edited the anthology *Visiting Wallace: Poems Inspired by the Life and Work of Wallace Stevens* (U. of Iowa Press, 2009). He is president of the Friends and Enemies of Wallace Stevens (http://www.stevenspoetry.org) and he serves as poetry editor for The Wallace Stevens Journal. He organizes The Charter Oak Readings in Hartford, and before that he ran the WordForge reading series. From 2011-2013 he served as West Hartford's Poet Laureate. He regularly posts aphoristic ars poetica to a blog called 'ursprache' [http://ursprache.blogspot.com/]. Jim lives in West Hartford, Connecticut, with his wife Susan, an artist, and he works as an insurance underwriter of financial institution risk.

After obtaining his MD degree in the National Autonomous University of Mexico (1961), Dr. Gonzalez-Crussi emigrated to the United States and specialized in pathology, with sub-specialization in pediatric pathology. He initiated his career in academic medicine in Canada (Queen's University), and returned to the United States in 1973, where he became Head of Laboratories in Chicago's major pediatric hospital, and Professor of Pathology at Northwestern University School of Medicine. His writings have been dual, medical and literary. In the medical field, he wrote over 200 articles of his specialty and two books on children's neoplasms. In the literary area he has written 20 books, 11 in the English language, and 9 in his native Spanish. His literary work earned him several awards and distinctions, the latest being the Merck Prize in Rome, Italy (2014) for combining medicine and literature in his book *Carrying the Heart*, (translated into Italian as Organi Vitali). He has been retired since 2001. Further biographical information may be seen on a Wikipedia page: https://en.wikipedia.org/wiki/F._Gonzalez-Crussi.

Jessica Greenbaum is a poet and social worker teaching inside and outside academia in NYC. A recipient of awards from the National Endowment for the Arts and the Poetry Society of America, her third book of poems, *Spilled and Gone,* came out in 2019, and she is the co-editor of a poetry Haggadah from the Central Conference of American Rabbis that will appear in 2021. https://poemsincommunity.org/

Jeffrey Harrison is the author of six full-length books of poetry, including *The Singing Underneath*, selected by James Merrill for the National Poetry Series in 1987; *Incomplete Knowledge*, runner-up for the Poets' Prize in 2008; *Into Daylight*, winner of the Dorset Prize and selected by the Massachusetts Center for the Book as a Must-Read Book for 2015; and, most recently, *Between Lakes*, published by Four Way Books in 2020. He has received fellowships from the Guggenheim Foundation, the NEA, and the Bogliasco Foundation, among other honors, and his poems have appeared widely in magazines and journals, as well as in *Best American Poetry*, *The Pushcart Prize* volumes, *Poets of the New Century*, *The Twentieth Century in Poetry*, and other anthologies, and been featured regularly on *The Writer's Almanac,* Ted Kooser's column "American Life in Poetry", Poetry Daily, and other online or media venues. He lives in Massachusetts and can also be found at jeffreyharrisonpoet.com.

James A. W. Heffernan, Professor of English Emeritus at Dartmouth College, has written extensively on the relations between literature and visual art. His books include *The Re-Creation of Landscape: A Study of Wordsworth, Coleridge, Constable, and Turner* (1985); *Representing the French Revolution: Literature, Historiography, and Art* (1992); *Museum of Words: The Poetics of Ekphrasis from Homer to Ashbery* (1993); and *Cultivating Picturacy: Visual Art and Verbal Interventions* (2006).

David Hellerstein MD is a physician and writer in New York. A Professor of Clinical Psychiatry at Columbia, he does research combining clinical trials with neuroimaging of mood disorders, and more recently on the use of psychedelics in treating psychiatric disorders. His books include *A Family of Doctors*, a history of the five generations of MDs in his family, and *Heal Your Brain*, a nonfiction work integrating neuroscience advances into psychiatric treatment. He has written for the New York Times, Harper's, Esquire, and North American Review, and has received four MacDowell Colony Fellowships and the Pushcart Prize Best Essay Award. For many years he has taught a creative nonfiction writing class to Columbia P&S medical students, who have published their classwork in Lancet and the New England Journal of Medicine. His website is: www.davidhellerstein.com.

Fady Joudah has published four collections of poems, *The Earth in the Attic, Alight, Textu*, a book-long sequence of short poems whose meter is based on cellphone character count; and, most recently, *Footnotes in the Order of Disappearance*. He has translated several collections of poetry from the Arabic. He was a winner of the Yale Series of Younger Poets competition in 2007 and has received a PEN award, a Banipal/Times Literary Supplement prize from the UK, the Griffin Poetry Prize, and a Guggenheim Fellowship. He lives in Houston, with his wife and kids, where he practices internal medicine.

Chuck Joy writes fun poetry, one line at a time. A child psychiatrist, Chuck is co-chair of the American Academy of Child and Adolescent Psychiatry Art Committee and poetry coordinator for the AACAP News. Recent publications include *Percussive* (Turning Point, 2017), a collection of poems with a narrative quality; *Said the Growling Dog* (Nirala Publications, 2015), a collection of poems featuring setting; and *The Opposite of Gifts* (Heyman Productions, 2018), a chapbook. More at chuckjoy.com

Karl Kirchwey is the author of seven books of poems. He has edited two anthologies for the Everyman's Library Pocket Poets series, *Poems of Rome* (2018) and, forthcoming in spring 2021, *Poems of Healing*. He is currently at work on a new book of poems, including poems about medicine and the body, called *Opoponax*. His publication of French poet Paul Verlaine's first book is called *Poems Under Saturn*, and he is translating the work of Italian poet Giovanni Giudici (1924-2011). He is Professor of English and Creative Writing at Boston University, where he serves as Associate Dean of Faculty for the Humanities in the College of Arts and Sciences.

Mel Konner went to Brooklyn College, CUNY; his MD and PhD are from Harvard. He did field research for two years among San (Bushman) hunter-gatherers of Botswana. His books include *The Tangled Wing: Biological Constraints on the Human Spirit, The Jewish Body, The Evolution of Childhood*, and most recently, *Women After All: Sex, Evolution, and the End of Male Supremacy*. He is a Fellow of the American Academy of Arts and Sciences and the American Association for the Advancement of Science and has written for Nature, Science, The New England Journal of Medicine, The New York Review of Books, The New York Times, The Wall

Street Journal, Newsweek, and many other publications. Recently he has been writing plays; one is in development at Theater Emory and another is a semifinalist in the Eugene O'Neill Center's annual playwriting competition. He won first prize in the Oberon Poetry Competition for 2018.

Sachiko Kusukawa, PhD, is Professor of History of Science at the University of Cambridge. She is also Dean and Fellow at Trinity College, Cambridge. Her *Picturing the Book of Nature: Image, Text, and Argument in Sixteenth-Century Human Anatomy and Medical Botany* (Chicago: University of Chicago Press, 2012) won the Pfizer Prize of the History of Science Society (USA). She also curated an on-line exhibition of Vesalius at: https://exhibitions.lib.cam.ac.uk/vesalius/

Jenna Le is a poet and academic musculoskeletal radiologist. Her books of poetry are *Six Rivers* (NYQ Books, 2011) and *A History of the Cetacean American Diaspora* (Indolent Books, 2018; 1st ed. Anchor & Plume Press, 2016), the latter of which won Second Place in the 2017 Elgin Awards. Her poems have also appeared in Denver Quarterly, Los Angeles Review, Massachusetts Review, Michigan Quarterly Review, West Branch, and elsewhere.

Margaret Lloyd was born in Liverpool, England, of Welsh parents and grew up in a Welsh community in central New York State. Fairleigh Dickinson University Press published *William Carlos Williams' Paterson: A Critical Reappraisal*, now considered seminal in the field. Alice James Books brought out her first book of poems, *This Particular Earthly Scene*. Plinth Books published Lloyd's second collection of poems, *A Moment in the Field: Voices from Arthurian Legend*. *Forged Light* was published by Open Field Press in November 2013, and *Travelling on Her Own Errands: Voices of Women from The Mabinogi* was published in 2017 in Wales by Gwasg Carreg Gwalch. Her poetry honors include a National Endowment for the Humanities grant, fellowships to Breadloaf and to Hawthornden Castle in Scotland, and a writing residency at Yaddo. A poet and painter, Lloyd is a Professor Emeritus of English at Springfield College. She lives in Florence, Massachusetts. Website: www.margaretlloyd.net

Marilyn McEntyre has taught American literature and medical humanities for over 30 years, most recently at the UC Berkeley-UCSF Joint Medical Program. She is a writer and fellow in the Program in Medical Humanities at UC Berkeley whose work brings together literature, language, spirituality and medicine. Her books include five volumes of poetry; *Patient Poets: Illness from Inside Out*; and *Caring for Words in a Culture of Lies*. Her two most recent books are *Speaking Peace in a Climate of Conflict* and *Dear Doctor*. With Anne Hunsaker Hawkins she co-edited the MLA volume *Teaching Literature and Medicine*. (See www.marilynmcentyre.com)

Heather McHugh is an emeritus professor from the University of Washington in Seattle. She occasionally still takes literature students at the MFA Program for Writers at Warren Wilson College near Black Mountain NC, as well as privately (https://warpsichord.com). Her latest publications are Feeler (a chapbook from Sarabande) and Muddy Matterhorn (poems 2009-2019), from Copper Canyon Press. McHugh was raised in Virginia where her father directed a marine biology laboratory on the York River. Educated in New England, she spent forty years teaching, writing, translating, and presenting literature to audiences all over North America. She calls the Pacific Northwest home. Her lifetime's work has attracted many awards. In 2009 she was awarded a MacArthur "Genius Grant."

Tony Macro is Professor of Classical Languages, emeritus, at Trinity College, Hartford, CT. He is the co-author of *Proclus: On the Eternity of the World* (de Aeternitate Mundi), 2001, as well as numerous articles and reviews on Asia minor.

Amit Majmudar's newest poetry collection is *What He Did in Solitary* (Knopf, 2020). His verse translation of the Bhagavad-Gita is entitled *Godsong* (Knopf, 2018). He has served as Ohio's first Poet Laureate, and he is also a diagnostic nuclear radiologist and internationally published novelist.

Irène P. Mathieu is a pediatrician, writer, and public health researcher. She is the author of *Grand Marronage* (Switchback Books, 2019), *orogeny* (Trembling Pillow Press, 2017), and *the galaxy of origins* (dancing girl press, 2014). Her honors include Yemassee Journal's Poetry

Prize, the Bob Kaufman Book Prize, and Editor's Choice for the Gatewood Poetry Prize. Her poems have appeared in *American Poetry Review, Narrative Magazine, Boston Review, Southern Humanities Review, Los Angeles Review, Callaloo, TriQuarterly*, and elsewhere. A Fulbright and Callaloo fellow, she holds a BA in International Relations from the College of William & Mary and a MD from Vanderbilt University.

Leslie Adrienne Miller's sixth collection of poems is *Y* from Graywolf Press. Her previous collections include *The Resurrection Trade* and *Eat Quite Everything You See* from Graywolf press, *Yesterday Had a Man In It, Ungodliness* and *Staying Up For Love* from Carnegie Mellon University Press. She has been the recipient of the Loft McKnight Award of Distinction, two Minnesota State Arts Board Fellowships in Poetry, a National Endowment for the Arts Fellowship in Poetry, and the PEN Southwest Discovery Award. Miller's poems have appeared in Poetry, Best American Poetry, American Poetry Review, Antioch Review, Kenyon Review, Harvard Review, Georgia Review, Ploughshares, and Crazyhorse. Professor of English at the University of St. Thomas in St. Paul, Minnesota, since 1991, she holds degrees in creative writing and English from Stephens College, the University of Missouri, the Iowa Writers Workshop, and the University of Houston.

A 2015 Guggenheim Fellow in Nonfiction, Dr. Christine Montross is Associate Professor of Psychiatry and Human Behavior at Brown University. She is the author of *Waiting for an Echo: The Madness of American Incarceration.* Her first book, *Body of Work: Meditations on Mortality from the Human Anatomy Lab*, was recognized as one of the best nonfiction books of 2007 by The Washington Post; and *Falling Into the Fire: A Psychiatrist's Encounters with the Mind in Crisis*, was named a *New Yorker* Book to Watch Out For. Dr. Montross practices inpatient psychiatry in Rhode Island and conducts forensic psychiatric evaluations.

Wynne Morrison is a physician practicing pediatric palliative care and critical care at the Children's Hospital of Philadelphia. She teaches at the Perelman School of Medicine at the University of Pennsylvania. Her academic interests are pediatric ethics and the medical humanities. Writing poetry helps to keep her sane.

Stacy R. Nigliazzo BSN RN CEN is the award-winning author of *Scissored Moon* (Press 53, 2013). Her poems have appeared in numerous journals and anthologies including the American Journal of Nursing, Bellevue Literary Review, Beloit Poetry Journal, Ilanot Review, Thrush, and the Journal of the American Medical Association. She is co-editor of the anthology *Red Sky, Poetry on the Global Epidemic of Violence Against Women* (Sable Books 2016). She lives in Houston, Texas and has worked as an emergency room nurse for the past twelve years.

Danielle Ofri, MD, PhD, is an internist at Bellevue Hospital and NYU School of Medicine, as well as editor-in-chief of the Bellevue Literary Review She writes regularly for the New York Times, Slate Magazine and other publications about medicine and the doctor-patient relationship. Ofri is the author of five books, including *What Patients Say, What Doctors Hear*. (www.danielleofri.com). Her latest book, *When We Do Harm: A Doctor Confronts Medical Error*, was published in 2020.

Peter Pereira is a family physician in Seattle. His poems have appeared in Poetry, Prairie Schooner, New England Review, Virginia Quarterly Review, Journal of the American Medical Association, and have been anthologized in *180 More: Extraordinary Poems for Everyday*, and the 2007 *Best American Poetry*. They have also been featured online at Verse Daily and Poetry Daily, as well as on National Public Radio's The Writer's Almanac. His books include *What's Written on the Body* (Copper Canyon 2007), which was a finalist for the Washington State Book Award, *Saying the World* (Copper Canyon, 2003), which won the 2002 Hayden Carruth Award, and the limited edition chapbook *The Lost Twin* (Grey Spider 2000).

David Ratzan is the Head of the Library of the Institute for the Study of the Ancient World. His publications include two edited volumes, *Growing up Fatherless in Antiquity* (with Sabine Huebner; Cambridge University Press, 2009) and *Law and Transaction Costs in the Ancient Economy* (with Dennis Kehoe and Uri Yiftach-Firanko; University of Michigan Press, 2015). He is also a member of the Ancient Ink Laboratory in the Center for Integrated Science and Engineering at Columbia University, an interdisciplinary working group investigating the chemical composition and history of ancient inks via Raman spectroscopy and participates in several archaeological excavations in Egypt.

Noah Ratzan works in interaction design, crafting ways to make technologies more useful and usable for people's actual needs and abilities. He specializes in voice interaction design and currently works for Nuance, a global firm focused on artificial intelligence and communications technologies. Noah has written poetry since 1998, and his poetry portfolio was awarded McGill University's Chester McNachten prize for creative writing. The son of two physicians, he has long been fascinated by medicine and its role in society, and he is grateful to participate in these poetic reflections on the works of Vesalius.

Richard M. Ratzan is an emergency medicine physician, internist and writer living and working in West Hartford, Connecticut, with his wife, Susan, a pediatric endocrinologist.

Clare Rossini has three published poetry collections, the most recent of which is *Lingo*, published by the University of Akron Press. She is currently co-editing an anthology titled *The Poetry of Capital*, due out from the University of Wisconsin Press in 2021. Her poems and essays have appeared in journals and anthologies such as The Paris Review, The Kenyon Review, The Iowa Review, Ploughshares, Poetry, and the Best American Poetry series. Her poems have been featured on Connecticut Public Radio and the BBC. She has received fellowships from the Connecticut Commission on the Arts, the Minnesota State Arts Board, the Bush Foundation, and The Maxwell Shepherd Foundation. Rossini taught for many years in the Vermont College low-residency MFA Program. She currently serves as Artist-in-Residence in the English Department at Trinity College in Hartford, teaching creative writing courses and directing an outreach program which places Trinity students in inner-city public school art classrooms.

Michael Salcman: poet, physician and art historian, was born in Pilsen Czechoslovakia. He is the author of 200 scientific articles and six medical books. He served as chairman of neurosurgery at the University of Maryland and president of the Contemporary Museum in Baltimore. He lectures widely about art and the brain. Among many other journals, poems appear in Arts & Letters, Harvard Review, Hopkins Review, The Hudson Review, New Letters, Notre Dame Review, Ontario Review, Pangyrus and Solstice. Featured on Poetry Daily, Verse Daily and All Things Considered, his work has received six nominations for a Pushcart Prize. Salcman is the editor of *Poetry in Medicine*, a popular anthology of classic and contemporary poems on doctors, patients, illness & healing, used in courses on Narrative Medicine (Persea Books, 2015). His collections include *The Clock Made of Confetti* (Orchises, 2007), nominated for The Poets' Prize, *The Enemy of Good is Better* (Orchises, 2011) and *A Prague Spring, Before & After* (2016), winner of the 2015 Sinclair Poetry Prize from Evening Street Press. His latest collection, *Shades & Graces* (Spuyten Duyvil, 2020), was the inaugural winner of the Daniel Hoffman Legacy Book Prize. He is Special Lecturer in the Osher Institute at Towson University.

Lawrence J. Schneiderman, MD, was professor emeritus in the Departments of Family Medicine and Public Health, and Medicine at the University of California San Diego School of Medicine. Founding co-chair of the Medical Center Bioethics Committee, he was an invited visiting scholar and visiting professor at institutions in the United States and abroad, and was a recipient of the Pellegrino Medal in medical ethics. He conducted empirical research on end-of-life care, and provided ethics consultations and invited talks for a variety of audiences, including academics and practitioners in medicine, law and philosophy, as well as the lay public. Schneiderman's articles and books, include *The Practice of Preventive Health Care* (Addison Wesley), *Wrong Medicine: Doctors, Patients, and Futile Treatment*, with Nancy S. Jecker, Ph.D. (Johns Hopkins), and, *Embracing Our Mortality: Hard Choices in an Age of Medical Miracles* (Oxford). He has also written a novel, *Sea Nymphs by the Hour* (Bobbs Merrill), short stories (Pushcart Nomination) and plays (DramaLogue Award, Beverly Hills Theatre Guild/Julie Harris Award). Dr. Schneiderman died in 2018.

Nina Siegal is the author of *The Anatomy Lesson*, (Nan A. Talese/Doubleday, 2014, a novel inspired by the true story behind Rembrandt's 1632 masterpiece, "The Anatomy Lesson of Dr. Nicolaes Tulp," which depicts Amsterdam's chief surgeon undertaking a "festive" dissection in the winter of 1631, followed by a banquet and a torchlight parade through town. Siegal conducted extensive research in the Amsterdam city archives to learn about the dead man in the painting, Aris Kindt, and the social, political, and art historical context of the painting. Siegal is also a journalist who writes frequently for The New York Times and other publications about fine art and culture in Europe. She has a MFA in fiction from the Iowa Writers' Workshop and a BA in English from Cornell University. She currently lives in Amsterdam with her family.

Marc Straus began writing poetry seriously in 1991 when he joined a workshop at the 92nd Street Y. Within the next year, his poems were accepted to major literary journals including Field, Ploughshares, Kenyon Review and TriQuarterly. In 1993, he was the recipient of a poetry fellowship at Yaddo. Straus has three collections of poetry published by TriQuarterly Books - Northwestern University Press. His play in verse, *NOT GOD* (2006), was staged Off Broadway. He is the recipient of numerous awards including the Robert Penn Warren Award in the Humanities from Yale School of Medicine. Straus frequently writes about cancer medicine, about the dialogue between patients and health care providers, about ethics, and most importantly, about how information is conveyed and received. He practiced oncology 35 years and currently owns MARC STRAUS, a leading gallery of contemporary art in New York City.

Ian Suk B.Sc., B.M.C., a Professor in the Department of Neurosurgery, with a joint appointment at Art as Applied to Medicine at John Hopkins University, specializes in imaging complex neurological surgeries for various medical journals and textbooks. He also teaches several graduate courses in Medical Illustration at the Department of Art as Applied to Medicine. His didactic and beautiful renderings truly encompass the realms of both art and science. Upon graduation with Honors from the University of Toronto, Department of Biomedical Communications in 1993, he embarked on an illustrious career at M.D. Anderson Cancer Center in Houston, TX. He was recruited to Johns Hopkins in 2002 and to date, his work has been published in 45 medical textbooks, and over 130 peer-reviewed scientific papers, of which more than 50 were featured on the Cover. His work has won numerous awards from the Association of Medical Illustrators. He is the first Medical Illustrator to attain the rank of full professor at Johns Hopkins since the inception of this Specialty in 1911.

Boris Veysman, MD, grew up in Moscow just in time to witness the communist parades and the Cold War, Perestroika and the coup attempt of 1991, with ever-present political change and uncertainty. He immigrated to the US with his parents David and Marina, who left their careers behind to allow a better future and opportunities for their son. Boris was inspired to study medicine by his grandmother, who never lost passion for healing in her 40 year career as a physician. She believed that the essence of doctoring is an honorable constant across time, borders, ideology and culture. Boris graduated from Cornell University and Yale School of Medicine, and completed his residency in Emergency Medicine at New York University and Bellevue Hospital.  After 10 years in the emergency department of a regional trauma center, he now practices urgent and primary care medicine in his hometown in New Jersey. His narratives have been published in the JAMA, British Medical Journal, Annals of Internal Medicine, Annals of Emergency Medicine, the Washington Post, Health Affairs, ACEP News, and the New England Journal of Medicine website, as well as aired on National Public Radio. Medicine remains a passion and a constant of meaningful and satisfying work, while narrative is an opportunity to share this feeling with others.

Pediatrician Kelley Jean White has worked in inner city Philadelphia and rural New Hampshire. Her poems have appeared in Exquisite Corpse, Rattle and JAMA. Her recent books are *Toxic Environment* (Boston Poet Press) and *Two Birds in Flame* (Beech River Books.) She received a 2008 Pennsylvania Council on the Arts grant.

John L. Wright, MD, is a retired endocrinologist who practiced at the Swedish Medical Center in Seattle where he also served as Vice President for medical staff affairs; he is Clinical Professor Emeritus in medicine at the University of Washington. John has been writing and publishing poetry and stories for past thirty years starting in 1988 when he was fifty-eight.

Brian J. Zink is Professor and Senior Associate Chair for Education and Faculty Development in the Department of Emergency Medicine at the University of Michigan Medical School. In his 30 year career in emergency medicine he has been a researcher in alcohol effects in trauma, Associate Dean for Student Programs at the University of Michigan Medical School, and served as the inaugural Chair of Emergency Medicine at the Alpert Medical School of Brown University (2006-2018). Dr. Zink was honored to serve as President of the Society for Academic Emergency Medicine (2000-01) and the Association of Academic Chairs of Emergency Medicine (2012-13). Dr. Zink has had a long interest in creative writing, poetry, and humanities in medicine. Dr. Zink wrote the first comprehensive history of US emergency medicine, *Anyone, Anything, Anytime* (2nd edition) and won the William Carlos Williams Medical Student Poetry Prize in 1983.